COUNSELING TECHNIQUES

Improving Relationships with Others, Ourselves, Our Families, and Our Environment

Rosemary A. Thompson, Ed.D., NCC, LPC

ACCELERATED DEVELOPMENT
A member of the Taylor & Francis Group

USA	Publishing Office:	ACCELERATED DEVELOPMENT
		A member of the Taylor & Francis Group
		1101 Vermont Avenue, NW, Suite 200
		Washington, DC 20005-3521
		Tel: (202) 289-2174
		Fax: (202) 289-3665
	Distribution Center:	ACCELERATED DEVELOPMENT
		A member of the Taylor & Francis Group
		47 Runway Road, Suite G
		Levittown, PA 19057-4700
		Tel: (215) 629-0400
		Fax: (215) 629-0363
UK		Taylor & Francis Ltd.
		1 Gunpowder Square
		London EC4A 3DE UK
		Tel: 0171 583 0490
		Fax: 0171 583 0581

COUNSELING TECHNIQUES: Improving Relationships with Others, Ourselves, Our Families and Our Environment

3 4 5 6 7 8 9 0   BRBR   9 8

This book was set in Times Roman by Monotype Composition, Inc. Edited by Judith L. Aymond. Technical development by Cynthia Long. Cover design by Michelle Fleitz. Printing and binding by Braun-Brumfield, Inc.

A CIP catalog record for this book is available from the British Library.
♾ The paper in this publication meets the requirements of the ANSI Standard Z39.48-1984 (Permanence of Paper)

Library of Congress Cataloging-in-Publication Data

Thompson, Rosemary
    Counseling techniques : improving relationships with others, ourselves, our families, and our environment / Rosemary A. Thompson.
        p.   cm.
    Includes bibliographical references and index.

    1. Psychotherapy.   2. Counseling.   I. Title.
RC480.T449   1996
616.89'14—dc20   96-7064
                                                                              CIP

ISBN 1-56032-488-0 (case)
ISBN 1-56032-397-3 (paper)

DEDICATION

This book is dedicated to Charlie, who at 17 began to nurture, strengthen, and support all our most rewarding relationships as a couple.

TABLE OF CONTENTS

PART B
IMPROVING RELATIONSHIPS IN GROUPS

CHAPTER 5
CLASSIC GESTALT TECHNIQUES   69

CHAPTER 6
NONVERBAL AND METAPHORICAL TECHNIQUES   81

CHAPTER 7
GROUP ENERGIZERS   89

PART C
IMPROVING RELATIONSHIPS
WITH OURSELVES AND OTHERS

PART D
IMPROVING RELATIONSHIPS
WITH OUR ENVIRONMENT

CHAPTER 14
LOSS, GRIEF, AND POSTTRAUMATIC LOSS
DEBRIEFING   **189**

PART E
IMPROVING RELATIONSHIPS WITH OUR FAMILY

CHAPTER 15
ECLECTIC TECHNIQUES FOR USE WITH FAMILIES   **201**

CHAPTER 16
PARADOXICAL STRATEGIES   **219**

PART F
TREATMENT PLANS, CONTRACTUAL FORMS,
AND INVENTORIES

CHAPTER 17
DETAILED SESSION AND TREATMENT PLANS   **233**

CHAPTER 18
SELECTED INVENTORIES, CHECKLISTS, AND
CONTRACTS   275

LIST OF FIGURES

PREFACE

As counseling and psychotherapy evolved, their growth mirrored the zeitgeist of each given time period. The 1960s was touted as the decade of person-centered therapy with an emphasis on feelings, focusing on the congruency between the ideal and real self; the 1970s was the decade of behaviorism and behavior therapy, focusing on measurable and observable data to monitor client change and growth; and the 1980s emerged as the decade of cognition and cognitive therapy, focusing on the client's ability to change perceptions, attitudes, and thinking regarding the human condition. The 1990s rapidly emerge as what some have termed **the age of dysfunction** and the decade of eclecticism. Eclectic therapy approaches are a response to the growing diversity of client needs and expectations.

Diversity is clearly illuminated from a multicultural and socioeconomic perspective. Multicultural counseling practice takes into consideration the specific values, beliefs, and actions that must be considered in light of clients' race, ethnicity, gender, religion, historical experience with the dominant culture, socioeconomic status, political views, lifestyle, and coping skills for acculturation or differentiation. Among the socioeconomically poor, for instance, great diversity is found among the single mother, a skip generation parent, an elderly person on a fixed income, an unskilled laborer, an unemployed individual, a migrant farm worker, an immigrant, a homeless person, and a growing population of children living in poverty.

Essentially, no single theory can account fully for the myriad of phenomenon that characterize the full range and life span of human experiences. Further, adhering to exclusive models in counseling and psychotherapy could be perceived as limiting therapeutic options when working with clients, especially when options are considered within the context of culture, ethnicity, interpersonal resources, and systemic support. thus, any single theory and associated set of techniques is unlikely to be equally or universally effective with the wide range of client characteristics, coping skills, and coping opportunities.

In addition, through research and articulation, we are beginning to recognize and acknowledge the following trends in counseling and psychotherapy:

The field of counseling and psychotherapy is rapidly emerging as an educational-developmental model that is holistic, reflecting an integration of the mind-body split (i.e., the interdependence of physical and psychological well-being) and the realization that both coping skills and coping opportunities occur in systems (i.e., individuals live, grow, or become defeated in family systems, organizational work groups, community, or culture).

Group work to promote functional attitudes and coping skills, as well as continuous feedback to the client and support networks, are becoming more effective.

Homework assignments, treatment planning, and follow-through designed to put increased responsibility on the client are mandated in many public and private settings. Treatment planning that reflects many alternatives and combines methods in a logical and systematic way to maximize a positive therapeutic impact also is occurring.

Collaboration between the client and other therapists with the emphasis on interdisciplinary collaboration is emerging.

Involvement of the family as partners to the therapeutic process is encouraged.

The use of brief therapy, multiple therapies, and eclectic approaches are becoming systematically integrated in treatment planning.

Efforts to promote public confidence and trust, and ethical responsibility in the counseling profession, is an ongoing priority.

The utilization of professional counselors in all aspects of the health care delivery system, addressing the mental health and developmental needs of all people, is being encouraged in the public and private sectors.

Bringing a multicultural awareness to all aspects of the helping profession— with sensitivity to values, beliefs, race, ethnicity, gender, religion, historical experience with the dominant culture, socioeconomic status, political views, and lifestyle—is being integrated into therapeutic practice.

Promoting standards for training, accreditation, licensure, and ongoing professional growth and development is systematically promoted, structured, and monitored.

Greater attention is being given to issues unique to women and to how gender roles shape coping styles and coping opportunities, particularly in the areas of depressions, victimization, poverty, violence, and abuse.

Well-articulated strategic plans for human rights—to address such issues as violence, specific needs of at-risk populations, suicide, gender and sexuality, HIV and AIDS, and people with disabilities—are continually emerging.

Counselors, mental health professionals, and therapists are evolving rapidly as *cybernauts searching cyberspace* for instant access to other counselors around the world as well as to a host of other counseling and mental health resources. Sharing ideas and resources, a dialogue about mental health issues revolving around a host of topics—self-esteem, multicultural issues, restructuring school counseling, career planning, theory into practice, professional development opportunities, assessment, and perspectives from practitioners around the world—is only beginning to emerge as a tremendous opportunity for interaction and shared professional development.

It is clear that the mental health and counseling profession has grown and changed extensively during the past four decades. Inherently, the resourceful, responsive, and responsible therapist of the next millennium should have within his or her therapeutic repertoire a full spectrum of counseling techniques to meet the demands of an increasing diverse and demanding clientele.

A caveat: This book does not assume full coverage of all the practical procedures with which counselors need to be familiar in order to select and assess clients, implement appropriate counseling techniques, and evaluate the therapeutic process. This book neither promotes a generalized application of a particular technique nor is it a comprehensive handbook covering all the strategies that a helping professional might want to assimilate into his or her helping style. Addressing more than 250 systems of counseling and psychotherapy, however, this book is perhaps a beginning.

This book does seek to provide helping professionals with critical skills to assist their clients' interpersonal functioning. The focus is on improving relationships—those with others, ourselves, our families, and our environment. Fundamentally, a counseling technique is viewed here as a strategy. A strategy is a plan. A plan is a counselor's intention. Counseling techniques in this book are intended to be broadly applicable to a wide range of client problems—depression, phobias, addictive disorders, school-related problems, stress, shyness, bereavement, crisis intervention, and family dysfunction, to name a few. Each "technique" provided in this book is followed by a "counseling intention," as outlined in Chapter 2, and a brief "description."

ACKNOWLEDGEMENTS

Throughout my career as educator and counselor, it has become increasingly difficult to know from where much of my knowledge and many of my ideas came. Perhaps they represent metacognitions between the academic experiences, professional development, and the sharing of ideas between practitioners and colleagues. I call them my own from the perspective that I have made them my own, but I am well aware that most were given to me by someone else. As a *literature scavenger,* I merely have organized and reframed information in a more systematic way. In the Bibliography and References, I have listed all the sources consulted when preparing this book.

There are a number of individuals, however, who alerted me to new perspectives and conceptual models, and who provided feedback. Those individuals who guided me through my *academic career* were Fred Adair, Nina Brown, and Kevin Geoffroy. Appreciation also is extended to all graduate students in counseling at Old Dominion University, Norfolk, Virginia, and the New England School Counselors Institute, Lyndonville, Vermont, who provided feedback and suggestions for many of the techniques in this book. A special acknowledgement is extended to Joseph Hollis and his staff for his steadfast support of my *writing career* and his vision for the profession of counseling.

ACKNOWLEDGEMENTS

PART A
COUNSELING
AND
PSYCHOTHERAPY

COUNSELING THEORY, PHILOSOPHY, OR CONCEPTUAL MODEL?

Many researchers and practitioners have taken the arduous task of attempting to define the *theoretical aura* that surrounds counseling practice. The image of a *theoretical aura* is introduced to the reader to reflect the continuum of debate about whether or not counseling and psychotherapy are guided by a theory, a philosophy, or a conceptual model. Caple (1985) stated that a theory is a formally organized collection of facts, definitions, constructs, and testable propositions that are meaningfully related. Ginter (1988) emphatically asserted that, "therapy cannot exist without theory" (p. 3). A theory serves as a conceptual map and the fundamental foundation of counseling practice meaningfully relating therapeutic constructs, counseling intentions, and client outcomes. Within the theory are specific functions. Boy and Pine (1983) outlined six *functions* of theory that make counseling pragmatic. Theory

> helps counselors find unity and relatedness within the diversity of existence;
> compels counselors to examine relationships they would otherwise overlook;
> gives counselors operational guidelines by which to work and helps them in evaluating their development as professionals;
> helps counselors focus on relevant data and tells them what to look for;
> helps counselors assist clients in the effective modification of their behavior; and
> helps counselors evaluate both old and new approaches to the process of counseling. It is the basis from which new counseling approaches are constructed. (p. 251)

To separate theory from the context of the theorist can distort our perception not only of the theory but also of its application to the client and his or her world. Thus, Hansen, Stevic, and Warner (1986) outlined four requirements of an effective *theoretical position*:

> It is clear, easily understood, and communicable. It is coherent and not contradictory.
> It is comprehensive, encompassing explanations for a wide variety of phenomena.
> It is explicit and generates research because of its design.
> It is specific in that it relates methods to outcomes. (p. 356)

Brammer and Shostrom (1977) further stressed the value of a theoretical *framework* for the counselor:

> Theory helps to explain what happens in a counseling relationship
> and assists the counselor in predicting, evaluating, and improving
> results. Theory provides a framework for making scientific observa-
> tions about counseling. Theorizing encourages the coherence of
> ideas about counseling and the production of new ideas. (p. 28)

Here, counseling theory can be very practical by helping to make sense out of the counselor's observations. But is it practical? Does it serve as a formative perspective that is routinely consulted to meet the needs of every new client who is counseled. Kelly (1988) stated "The ultimate criteria for all counseling theories is how well they provide explanations of what occurs in counseling" (pp. 212–213). Theory is, at best, a hypothesis or a speculation about people's behavior, their developmental unfolding, and their capacity for adjustment. Counseling theories are perhaps not facts, but rather beliefs, convictions, or dogma held by the therapist regarding human behavior. This less than desirable perspective will continue to emerge if theory is not linked to practice through outcome accountability.

THE THEORETICAL VOID:
VALIDATING RESEARCH AND PRACTICE

To many, counseling research based on theory has not demonostrated outcome accountability. Falvey (1989) illuminated practitioners' problem by stating that practitioners ignore research findings because those findings do not provide consistent, relevant guidelines for understanding therapeutic change in applied settings. Strupp (1981) and Falvey (1989) stressed the importance of linking research and practice. Strupp and Bergin (1969) stressed that psychotherapy research should be reformulated as a standard scientific question: What specific therapeutic interventions produce what specific changes in specific patients under specific conditions? Patterson (1986) responded to this dilemma in the profession and outlined the specifics for such a proposal. As a frame of reference, counselors or therapists would need

> a taxonomy of client problems or a taxonomy of psychological
> disorders (a reliable, relevant diagnostic system);
> a taxonomy of client personalities;
> a taxonomy of therapeutic techniques or interventions;
> a taxonomy of therapists (therapeutic style);
> a taxonomy of circumstances, conditions, situations, or environ-
> ments in which therapy is provided; and
> a [set of] guiding principles or empirical rules for matching all
> these variables. (p. 146)

At present, skeptics continue to articulate that clinical research in counseling and psychotherapy has had little or no influence on clinical practice. This is particularly distressing to counseling and psychotherapy, as disciplines, where the primary goal has been to produce practitioners who would integrate theory into practice to produce new knowledge and understanding. Linden and Wen (1990) suggested that the limited influence of research on practice stems from its failure to provide conclusive evidence regarding the relative effectiveness of psychotherapeutic interventions with different clients and problems. Furthermore, they observed the following:

> When addressing the reasons for a lack of conclusive evidence, it has been argued that the outcome literature is essentially noncumulative and not informative enough for clinicians, that studies lack the power to detect effects, and that the current review and publication process is more of a hindrance than a help for accumulating a solid data base on therapy outcome. The lack of accumulated knowledge has been attributed to a tendency among researchers to conduct mostly analogue studies and typically small-scale, independently initiated, and uncoordinated studies. (p. 182)

Many counseling theories, however, cannot meet the criteria of outcome accountability and perhaps would more accurately be called *counseling models* (Blocher, 1989; Ginter, 1988, 1989). A model serves to identify treatment goals and procedures that are assessed as appropriate for client concerns. An incessant concern raised among critics, however, is that counseling models often lack the formal theoretical delineation that can be empirically validated (Blocher, 1987). From this perspective, counseling models provide more of a philosophical viewpoint than a theory. Corsini (1989) captured this sentiment and has listed 250 different systems of psychotherapy. Kelly (1991) aptly stated that research is needed to ascertain if theory-based counseling leads to better outcomes. Corsini and Wedding (1989) observed that in counseling or psychotherapy, just as in education or politics, ideological enclaves evolve.

> Some enclaves (models of therapy) consist of people who believe that they have the right, the final, the complete, and the only answer . . . that all other systems are incomplete, tentative, weak, or simply mistaken. People within these enclaves tend to read, write and reinforce one another by recounting their successes proving to one another the superiority of their way of thinking and acting . . . alternative positions tend to develop, schismatic groups begin to form and the new configuration of beliefs or tenets are either expelled from the original enclave or take off on their own. (p. 256)

Kelly (1991) further maintained that existing theories of counseling constitute partial perspectives on the complex labyrinth that is the human world and provided the following analogy:

> Picture the situation of three persons standing outside a labyrinth whose structure is unknown to and hidden from them. Each of these persons is in possession of a map that purports to depict the structure of the labyrinth and to show the way to reach its center. In comparing their maps, the three discover, with some surprise, that the maps bear no resemblance to one another. After a few futile moments spent in attempting to convince one another of the unique value of their own maps, the three decide to enter the labyrinth and to navigate it, each relying on his or her own map. They enter the labyrinth, part company, and, after a period of time, meet again at the center of the labyrinth. In discussing what their experience portends regarding the overall structure of the labyrinth, the three conclude that the structure must somehow involve a composition of the divergent details displayed on their three maps. Moreover, because the labyrinth is nothing if it is not an integrated whole, the three conclude that the overall structure of the labyrinth must involve an integrated composition of these divergent details. (p. 115)

Thus, the debate over whether or not the practice of counseling and psychotherapy is empirically anchored in theory or is merely representing one's philosophy or conceptual model continues to divide practitioners. Kelly (1991) stressed that existing theories of counseling and psychotherapy constitute partial perspectives on the complex labyrinth that is the human world. These partial maps are about equally useful in producing effective treatment; however, a significant fraction of clients may be hindered from changing because of the limited nature of theories that guide their treatment. It also is the counselor's or therapist's responsibility to understand that one model of counseling may be too limited when working with an increasingly diverse population (Allen, 1988).

In the long run, conceptual frameworks are helpful, but individuals are too diverse, too complex, and too nebulous for therapists to expect that the ultimate, most comprehensive theoretical model will be discovered. This assumption is supported by the *theory of chaos*, which maintained that human behavior is so complex that no single traditional scientific discipline will enable us to understand the behavior and the causes. The concept of chaos requires a multidisciplinary approach because "complex behavior implies complex causes" (Gleick, 1988, p. 303).

Fortunately, most contemporary counseling texts leave the reader with personal choice inviting creativity, pragmaticism, adaptability, and a foundation for further study. Perhaps Corey (1986), in *Theory and Practice of Counseling and Psychotherapy,* captured a more flexible theoretical position for counselors who struggle with their own modus operandi. Corey (1986) stated the following:

> My hope is that you will remain open and will seriously consider both the unique contributions and the limitations of each therapeutic system. . . . No single model fully accounts for all the dimensions of the various therapies. The danger of presenting one model that all students are expected to advocate to the exclusion of other fruitful approaches is that the beginning counselor will unduly limit his or her effectiveness with different clients. Valuable dimensions of human behavior can be overlooked if the counselor is restricted to a single theory. (p. 2)

LIMITATIONS OF EMBRACING THE CLASSICS

Like most disciplines, as counseling and psychotherapy evolved, their growth mirrored the zeitgeist of the period. The 1960s was the decade of person-centered therapy with an emphasis on feelings; the 1970s, the decade of behaviorism and behavior therapy with a focus on quantifiable, observable data; and the 1980s, the decade of cognition and cognitive therapy to change the way we think about the blight of the human condition. The 1990s appears to be the decade of eclecticism and eclectic therapy in response to client diversity.

Traditionally, counselors and therapists have been painstakingly trained in classic counseling approaches such as psychodynamic, person-centered, behavior, or cognitive-behavior therapies. As counseling and psychotherapy continue to evolve, proponents such as Freud, Rogers, Perls, and Skinner are perhaps becoming more important as historical referents to counseling and therapy than as absolute frameworks of counseling practice. Each approach and its tenets have survived critical debate. For example, although psychoanalysis accounts for unconscious resistance, defense mechanisms, or early recollections, the lengthy techniques of free association and interpretation do not lend themselves to an efficient or accountable therapeutic relationship between client and therapist. Person-centered research indicates that the "necessary and sufficient" conditions of empathy, congruence, and unconditional positive regard are necessary but not sufficient for change in counseling (Bergin & Lambert, 1978). Yet, in a meta-analysis of 143 studies, Shapiro and Shapiro (1982) found cognitive and behavior treatments have more favorable outcomes. There also is some consensus that changes achieved by clients in rational-emotive therapy (RET) are not adequately explained by rational-emotive theory (Dryden, 1984). The classic debate again emerges with Weinrach (1991) who stated that

> RET is a philosophy and a theory of psychotherapy. As a philosophy, it explains the nature of the human experience. As a theory, it defines emotional disturbance; identifies factors that contribute to it; and offers cognitive, emotive, and behavioral ways to treat it efficiently. (p. 374)

Yet Ziegler (1989) maintained that RET is a personality theory.

Concurrently, adhering to exclusive models in counseling and psychotherapy could be perceived as limiting therapeutic options when working with clients, especially when options are considered in the context of culture, ethnicity, interpersonal resources, coping skills, and systemic support. Okum (1990) related how this has been detrimental to the practice of counseling and psychotherapy:

> Each of the major models of psychotherapy has devotees who believe that *their* view is the only correct view. This type of doctrinairism has probably done more harm to the development and credibility of the psychotherapy field than any other single variable, because it has reinforced turf competition and dichotomous thinking such as right or wrong, science or art, good or bad. Therapists afflicted with this doctrinairism are unlikely to select treatments that can be flexibly and effectively tailored to the needs of clients who are experiencing distress related to today's sociocultural context. (p. 3)

Thus, any single theory, including its associated set of techniques, is unlikely to be equally or universally effective with the wide range of client characteristics or dysfunctions. Nance and Myers (1991) argued that counselors or therapists who work from only one theoretical model may be unable to work with a heterogeneous group of clients because they find themselves unable to adapt to a wide range of presenting problems. This is clearly illuminated from a multicultural perspective. Multicultural counseling practice takes into consideration the specific values, beliefs, and actions considered by clients' race, ethnicity, gender, religion, historical experiences with the dominant culture, socioeconomic status, political views, lifestyle, and geographic region (Wright, Coley, & Corey, 1989). It also is clear from a socioeconomic perspective. For example, diversity among the poor can include single mothers, elderly persons, unskilled laborers, unemployed workers, street people, migrant farm workers, immigrants, and homeless people.

Within this framework, adhering to a single theoretical model clearly would be anachronistic.

THEORETICAL INTEGRATIONISM, PLURALISM, OR SYSTEMATIC ECLECTICISM

With inherent limitations of embracing a single theoretical model, many writers are proposing (a) theoretical integration, (b) pluralistism, or (c) eclecticism as an alternative view to meet the diverse needs of clients. *Theoretical Integrationism*—integrating theoretical conceptions from other theories—is based on the premise that when various theories converge therapeutic procedures will be enhanced. Most recent efforts toward integrating theories focused on efforts to combine psychoanalytic and behavior theories (Goldfriend, 1982; Wachtel, 1977, 1987) with the focus on *behavior* and *insight*. This approach also has its limitations and critics (Lazarus & Mayne, 1990; Messor & Boals, 1981). Other alliances have occurred by merging behavioral and Gestalt therapies (Fodor, 1987); cognitive and interpersonal therapies (Safran, 1990); and general psychotherapy principles with theories of information processing (Mahoney & Gabriel, 1987). The limitations of empirical efficacy and issues of accountability also encumber integrationism.

Okum (1990) proposed the concept of *pluralism* as an alternative to single theory or theoretical integration. The focus provides an opportunity for an open system, multifaceted perspective of current and emerging theoretical models of psychotherapy. Pluralism is emphasized to acknowledge and attend to the different levels and diversity of the human experience and the accompanying systems that operate with the client's worldview. Okum (1990) maintained that

> Pluralism allows for consideration of both mind and body, conscious and unconscious, biology and culture, quantitative and qualitative, subjective and objective, masculine and feminine, insight and behavior, historical and ahistorical, directive and nondirective, autonomy and connectedness, content and process, linear and cybernetic causality, along with the other major polarities associated with the dichotomous thinking of the major models of psychotherapy. Pluralism opens up the possibilities of varying and different levels of human experience as well as possibilities of varying and different levels of therapeutic change. It acknowledges the equal value of the different models, takes personal preference into account, and encourages a careful assessment of what model is best

utilized for what person with what problem in particular circumstances. (p. 407)

A pluralistic approach embraces the notion that many appropriate ways exist to treat a client with several different theoretical perspectives to explain the client's problem(s), and at least several different therapists who could be effective for each client. Fundamentally, a therapeutic pluralistic approach accounts for diversity on the part of the client, the therapist, the treatment, and the theoretical rationale.

Many researchers have identified a major shift toward *eclecticism* in the practice of counseling and psychotherapy (Andrews, 1989; Corsini, 1989; Garfield & Bergin, 1986; Ivey & Simek-Downing, 1980; Kelly, 1988; Nance & Myers, 1991; Norcross & Prochaska, 1983; Simon, 1989; Smith, 1982). Yet, eclecticism was defined as a construct as early as 1958 by English and English:

> Eclecticism. n. theoretical system building, the selection and orderly combination of compatible features from diverse sources, sometimes from incompatible theories and systems; the effort to find valid elements in all doctrines or theories and to combine them into harmonious whole. The resulting system is open to constant revision even in its major outlines. (p.18)

In 1982, Smith conducted a survey of 422 members of the American Psychological Association and 41% identified their orientation as eclectic. In the same year, Norcross and Prochaska found that 30% of their sample of members of the Division of Clinical Psychology declared an eclectic orientation. The rise in eclectic counseling is viewed by many as constructive responses to the wide range of client differences. Eclectic practice coincides with the current knowledge based on a growing body of empirical research that no one theoretical approach produces reliable counseling outcomes with a heterogeneous group of clients. Many researchers also have articulated the advantages of developing an eclectic approach (Brabeck & Welfel, 1985; Brammer & Shostrom, 1982; Hart, 1983; Rychlak, 1985) from the perspective that no single theory is comprehensive enough to be applicable to all individuals under all circumstances.

Eclecticism reflects our growing knowledge of people and the dynamics of change in counseling. Nicholson and Berman (1983) have contended that "Eclecticism is finally being appreciated for what it is—an essential perspective for dealing with the complexity of human problems" (p. 25). Nomenclatures such as *creative synthesis, emerging eclecticism, technical eclecticism, theoretical eclecticism, systematic eclecticism* (Herr, 1989), *pragmatic technical eclecticism*

(Keat, 1985) *eclectic psychotherapy* (Norcross, 1986), and *adaptive counseling and therapy—an integrative eclectic model* (Howard, Nance, & Myers, 1986) have been crisscrossing reams of research literature. For example, Simon (1989) distinguished between technical and theoretical eclecticism and suggested that general systems theory (GST) could provide the framework for pulling everything together. Simon (1991) defined technical eclecticism as a kind of eclecticism "based on the assumption that the primary task of an eclectic theory is to indicate in a systematic manner which particular intervention or style of intervening should be used in which particular counseling situation" (pp. 112–113). McBride and Martin (1990) proposed a "theoretical eclecticism" as opposed to "syncretism, or unsystematic, atheoretical eclecticism." Hershenson, Power, and Seligman proposed an "integrated-eclectic" model, a mental health counselor-specific eclecticism (1989a), and the need for a "skilled-based, empirically validated" model (1989b). In addition, many counselors and therapists are eclectic in their use of theory and techniques. An eclectic approach is the reported emphasis of some 25% of counselor education programs nationwide (Hollis & Wantz, 1986). Lazarus (1985, 1993), Lazarus and Folkman (1984), and Lazarus and Mayne (1990) maintained that systematic, technical eclecticism offers by far the greatest promise for the future, both of practice and research. From the diversity of eclectic and integrationist viewpoints, national and international societies, groups and professional associations of eclectic counselors and therapists have been formed, and journals are emerging that are devoted to the dissemination of systematic eclecticism (Lazarus & Mayne, 1990).

Embracing an eclectic approach to counseling and psychotherapy is not without its skeptics. Smith (1982) has cautioned

> Although the eclectic model allows for openness and flexibility, it also encourages an indiscriminate selection of bits and pieces from diverse sources that results in a hodgepodge of inconsistent concepts and techniques. Thus, rejecting a single-theory approach and adopting an eclectic stance does not always improve the therapist's intentions. (p. 102)

Slaveney and McHugh (1987) warned that eclecticism can promote a "methodological porridge in which all ideas are considered equivalent" (p. 4). Ward (1983) further argued for an integrative model of counseling. He stated

> Without guidelines to structure counseling and to govern the appropriate selection and applications of theoretical demands, strategies and techniques, the eclectic faces the danger of operating haphazardly, inconsistently, and less effectively than is desirable. (p. 23)

In an attempt to address these concerns, Cavanagh (1982) proposed a "healthy" eclectic approach to counseling that requires the counselor to have (a) a sound knowledge and understanding of counseling theories, (b) an integrative philosophy of human behavior, and (c) a flexible means of fitting the approach to the client. The critical prerequisite skills for a well-informed and integrative eclectic counselor is both the mastery of theory and an acute perceptibility of knowing what approach to use with whom.

Nonetheless, perhaps the greatest support for eclecticism comes from the recognition of the uniqueness and individuality of each client. Thus, according to Ivey and Simek-Downing (1980),

> The immense variety of clients faced in daily practice do not fit easily into theoretical pigeonholes. One client responds well to one approach, but another may resist the same techniques and leave counseling. Evidence is mounting that the professional of the future will require more than a single set of methodological and theoretical answers to meet the needs of an increasingly diverse clientele. (p. 1)

Fundamentally, no single theory can fully account for the myriad of phenomena characterizing the range of human experiences. Within the context of contemporary society, a systematic eclectic approach may be a constructive response to a wide range of client differences. Counseling approaches and client outcomes can be viewed as a matrix of possible interactions with the mutual goal of personal well-being and interpersonal adjustment. Systematic eclecticism embraces the perspective that no one theory-bound approach has all the answers to all the needs that clients bring to the therapeutic setting. Eclectic practice should resemble a "systematic integration" of underlying principles and methods common to a wide range of therapeutic approaches, integrating the best features from both multiple and diverse sources.

In conclusion, the resourceful, responsive, and responsible therapist of the next millennium would have within his or her therapeutic repertoire a full spectrum of counseling techniques and educational therapies to meet the demands of an increasingly diverse clientele. This perspective supports the observations of Garfield and Bergin (1986) who stated

> A decisive shift in opinion has quietly occurred; and it has created an irreversible change in professional attitudes about psychotherapy and behavior change. The new view is that the long-term dominance of the major theories is over and that an eclectic position has taken precedence. I would go even further and state that all good therapists are eclectic. (p. 7)

Perhaps the greatest outcome from this quiet revolution in counseling and psychotherapy is the shifting paradigm of openness and receptiveness to new approaches and creative integration of past and future perspectives. New theoretical developments are occurring that should be integrated into our theoretical frameworks, such as the following:

> Guidano and Liotti's (1983) *constructivist cognitive therapy,* which integrates cognitive and attachment theories.
>
> Greenberg and Safran's (1987) *information-processing theory* of affective experiencing and change processes.
>
> Ivey's (1986, 1989, 1990) and Ivey and Goncalves' (1988) *cognitive-developmental theory* of counseling and human development. In the developmental counseling and theory (DCT) model, personality styles or disorders are seen as generated in a life-span development context and reflect the logical result of failed developmental progression (Ivey & Rigazio-DiGilio, 1991).
>
> Attneave's (1990) *network model,* which recognizes that an individual's change can best occur when family and larger systems support that change, e.g., the critical roles of social networks, culture, gender, and value orientations of the client network need to change for optimum success.

To integrate or clarify counseling theories, a more germane approach may be to look at the new and unfamiliar rather than to embrace the past. Proponents like Freud, Skinner, Perls, and Rogers are perhaps as important historical referents rather than as absolute guides to counseling practice. In Sexton and Whiston's (1991) review of the empirical basis for counseling, they found little evidence that adhering to a theoretical model was related to client change. Counseling theories may assist counselors in organizing information, but those same theories do not substitute for an understanding of the elements of the counseling process and the ability to implement appropriate strategies to best meet client needs.

We have a professional obligation to ensure that every client receive optimal benefits from therapeutic services. Planned, systematic clinical approaches with accountable outcomes must be the therapeutic norm rather than the therapeutic exception. Perhaps more important, however, we must relinquish and retreat from the present competition among helping professionals. Negative competition and defensiveness are not helpful to the professional practitioner or to the client consumer. Interdisciplinary collaboration and the acceptance of individual diversity will create a climate of openness and growth for all who embrace the helping relationship and the responsibilities that come with it.

Chapter 2

BRIEF THERAPY AND SOLUTION-FOCUSED COUNSELING: A PARADIGM FOR THE MILLENNIUM

This is the age
Of the half-read page,
And the quick hash
And the mad dash.
The bright night
With the nerves tight
The plane hop
And the brief stop.
The lamp tan
In a short span.
The big shot
In a good spot.
And the brain strain,
And the heart pain,
And the cat naps,
Till the spring snaps
And the fun's done.

Author Unknown

In the last decade, a virtual explosion of interest in brief therapy has occurred. The paradigm shift has been the result of time-limited treatment policies and the

15

need for interventions that resolve problems in a more efficient manner. In retrospect, brief therapy has been around for three decades, pioneered by Milton H. Erickson with brief family therapy. Ironically, the earliest proponent of single session therapy was Sigmund Freud. In the 1990s, brief therapy is experiencing a revival, with a growing number of counselors and therapists practicing some form of brief therapy. Even certain aspects of brief time-limited psychodynamic therapies with their emphases on client selection, assessment, and active interpretive interventions seem to offer new possibilities within the cost-containment context of health care. Regretfully, many people who can benefit from therapy will never receive it unless it is brief. Herr (1989) stated that the pool of mental health resources available can at best meet only 5% to 10% of the needs for such services (p. 285).

Bloom (1981) conducted an extensive review of the literature on single-session therapy and found that condensed encounters between mental health professionals and their clients are remarkably common. He found that not only are they frequently underestimated, but more important, their therapeutic impact appears to be underestimated as well (p. 180). Clients who would benefit from single-session therapy, according to Talmon (1990), are individuals who are motivated, resourceful, insightful, and "worried well" clients with good support systems. Other successful cases included clients with problems such as separation, divorce, posttraumatic stress, and violence in families. Talmon maintained that most clients who quit after a single interview do so because they have accomplished what they intended. In addition, many individuals can summon a tremendous capacity for survival in the wake of what might be viewed by others as insurmountable stress. Malan (1975) identified nine mechanisms that seem to operate in most people to protect and foster their mental health even under the most adverse condition:

insight;
capacity for self-analysis;
working through feelings with the people involved;
normal maturation and growth;
therapeutic relationships, especially marriage;
taking responsibility for their own lives;
breaking the vicious cycle between the client and his or her environment;
genuine reassurance; and
direct learning.

Garfield (1980) asserted that therapists must rely on their clinical experiences and evaluate their interventions as therapy progresses. From this perspective, therapists must assume the responsibility to make an adequate appraisal of client needs and treatment plans. Instead of starting with theoretical preconceptions and then checking the list of the facts to the model, the therapist should proceed inductively, gathering and analyzing data and later attempting to construe explanatory theories.

With brief counseling, the counselor or therapist initiates what occurs during treatment by taking responsibility for planning a strategy that will empower clients to change self-defeating or self-destructive behavior. For example, time-limited therapy as developed by Mann (1973, 1981) focuses on a central issue and requires the therapist to assess, within the first session, the client's capacity to engage and disengage quickly. Sifenos (1979, 1981) cautioned that a client must be able to interact flexibly to handle *short-term anxiety-provoking psychotherapy* (STAPP), to have a motivation to change along with being more sophisticated psychologically and intellectually.

Fuhriman, Paul, and Burlingame (1986) developed "eclectic time-limited therapy" that is

time-limited on the amount of therapy provided;
specific, restricted, and goal focused;
expectation-sharing between therapist and client about the time limitation and the goals to be achieved;
more directive therapeutic intervention; and
selection of appropriate clients.

Eclectic, time-limited therapy, as portrayed in this model, permits the counselor to work from his or her own theoretical orientation while observing the overall goals prescribed for the delivery of services (i.e., 10 sessions, a problem-solving and focused approach [herr, 1989]).

SOLUTION-FOCUSED THERAPY

More recently, Gentner (1991) provided a guide for the delivery of short-term counseling through the unification of the unique contributions of Erickson (1954), Haley (1963, 1967, 1973, 1976, 1984), de Shazer (1982, 1985, 1988, 1991), O'Hanlon and Weiner-Davis (1989), the Milan Associates, and the Mental Research Institute (MRI). A recent development in short-term counseling, a solution-focused approach founded in systems theory, provides a brief seven-stage, step-by-step strategic model for effective short-term counseling. Practitioners have reported using this model with various clients in diverse settings, including community mental health centers, state and private hospitals, private psychiatric practices, schools, and private psychotherapy practices (de Shazer, 1985). As a form of brief therapy, solution-focused therapy has the following attributes:

> goals are chosen in part by the client;
>
> attention is directed to one focused issue;
>
> counseling is directed at clarifying feelings, thoughts, and behavior manifestations in the here-and-now;
>
> emphasis is placed on the client identifying the change that is needed or the coping goals as related to the problem; and
>
> the client is encouraged to (a) actively search for exceptions to the problem and (b) identify strengths in his or her coping repertoire.

Solution-focused counseling is active, focusing on the solutions to problems rather than focusing on the pathology of problems. The assumptions of the therapist is that problems are temporary and that the client has the resources to solve problems. It is dependent upon using the identified strengths of the client, empowering them for self-sufficiency and positive change. The de Shazer group has developed a set of correlates that guide the solution-based approach (Zimstrad, 1989). The major task of counseling is to help the client do something different. The focus on the problem is redirected toward solutions already existing within the client's coping repertoire. Goals are framed in positive terms with an expectancy for change (no matter how small) to create the context for further change.

The model consists of seven stages, which may take place in one session or over the course of 6 to 10 sessions, during intervals between sessions from 1 to 6 months. Some time between counseling sessions provides the client and his or her support network time to alter the system and integrate new behavior. The approach is pragmatic and specific, avoiding in-depth explorations of problems.

Stage I: Defining the Problem

The task of the counselor or therapist is to reconstruct the problem through a careful analysis of various frames of reference presented and perceptions provided by the client. The counselor also uses language to

> communicate an expectancy for change,
>
> reframe the problem situation as normal and modifiable, and
>
> change labels and diagnoses of the problem situation into action descriptions.

This can be accomplished by using transactional and systemic questions (Bergman, 1985) to search for exceptions to the problem (e.g., panic attack) such as

"What is different about the times when you are not having a panic attack?"
"How does it make your day go differently when you are having a panic attack?"
"Who else noticed that you were having a panic attack (boss, colleagues)?"
"How is that different from the way you might have handled it a year ago?"
"How do you respond when you have a panic attack during an important presentation?"

Additional information regarding the frequency, intensity, and duration (**FID**) of the problem also should be gathered. The goal is to have the client be more specific about his or her presenting problem.

Stage II: Establishing Treatment Goals

Setting therapeutic goals facilitates evaluation of progress and establishes a point of termination. Goals should be concrete, specific, and observable. If the client is resistant to being specific about goals, it may be more germane to address the client's paradoxical role of requesting change within the context of resistance. The process of setting goals initiates the intervention; however, they should be constantly monitored with a mechanism for revision, adaptation, and reassessment. Critical questions to ask would include

"What will be the very first sign that things are moving in the right direction?"
"Who will be the first to notice?"
"Are there small pieces of this that are already happening?"
"What do you need to do to make it happen more?"
"What else will you be doing differently when you no longer have panic attacks?"

Stage III: Designing the Intervention

Brief strategic therapy is designed to prevent repetitive, dysfunctional behavior patterns by introducing alternative ways of experiencing interactions associated with problem behavior (Madanes, 1981). The foundation of this counseling model is the perspective of introducing change, however small. Gentner (1991) outlined three integral step-by-step parts involved in the delivery of the intervention design: reframing, utilization, and strategic tasks.

Reframing refers to providing a positive new meaning, perception, or understanding of the problem that allows the client's behavior to be perceived as constructive and useful (Boscolo, Cecchin, Hoffman, & Penn, 1987). Reframing a problem in a more positive light provides the mechanism that encourages change.

Utilization refers to using whatever the client presented, including rigid belief systems, behaviors, demands, or characteristics to motivate the client to act differently. From this perspective solutions are seen as contained within the presenting problem. The role for the counselor or therapist is to use the same structures expressed by the client to introduce some alternative that can precipitate a different way of experiencing the problem. This process allows the client to generate solutions from the altered structure (Gentner, 1991).

Strategic tasks are assigned to be carried out between sessions. The primary goal is to help the client do something different to fulfill the goals that were outlined in the first stage. Strategic tasks are designed to build upon and interface with the treatment components of reframing and utilization. They serve as a conceptual map to guide the client through familiar boundaries and new behavior alternatives (Gentner, 1991, p. 234).

Stage IV: Delivery of a Strategic Task

The delivery of the strategic tasks should take place at the end of the session (de Shazer, 1982; Weeks & L'Abate, 1982). The task is clearly outlined. The therapist should check for client understanding encouraging the client to write certain instructions that may be critical to the task performance and completion.

Stage V: Emphasizing Positive New Behavior

The stage is enhanced by questions that are future orientated, encouraging positive change and solutions. It offers clients the opportunity to see themselves responding in new ways that are consistent with treatment goals and task assignments. Critical questions would include

"What is happening that you would like to continue to have happen?"
"Who else will notice your progress?"
"How did it make things go differently?"

"Is there anything that might happen in the next week or so which might present a challenge to keeping these positive things from happening?"

The most engaging intervention developed by de Shazer and his associates has been termed the ***miracle question*** (de Shazer, 1991). One account of the miracle question follows: "Imagine tonight while you sleep, a miracle happens and your problem is solved." "What will be happening the next day, and how will you know that your problem has been solved?" Often clients are able to give answers to questions that are specific and concrete because the focus is on what will be present in the client's life when the problem is absent. The primary tasks are to elicit news of a difference, to amplify the differences, and to help changes continue.

Stage VI: Stabilization

Restraint is another therapeutic goal integrated into the counseling process to promote and maintain change (Fisch, Weakland, & Segal, 1983). The catalyst for change is to move slowly. This approach to intervention serves to anchor the client to a framework for change that allows for gradual adjustment and to integrate the assimilation of the new behavior outlined in treatment goals and assigned tasks.

Stage VII: Termination

Typically, in solution-focused counseling, the client recognizes problem resolution and then initiates termination. This empowers the client to control behavior change and facilitates the client's view of how counseling should end. This promotes a smooth transition, necessary closure, as well as a sense of security in the change that has occurred. Finally, this model integrates theory and technique by providing a comprehensive, empirical approach from the proponents of strategic and solution focused counseling. Counselors and therapists have a growing interest in becoming more efficient in their practice through the development and use of various forms of short-term counseling (Gentner, 1991).

ADAPTIVE COUNSELING
AND THERAPY READINESS MODEL

Adaptive counseling and therapy readiness model (ACT) is a systematic form of eclecticism. The model matches the counseling approach to the nature

---

Prespective for the Therapist: On psychotherapy . . .

Formal psychotherapy is a specific personal individualized intervention focusing on the patient's sensitivities to life situations and his personal reactions to life experiences; on gaining insight into these susceptibilities in an effort to strengthen his ability to deal with himself and his reactions; and on gaining mastery of his life situation.

Philip May

---

of the problem and the readiness of the client rather than maintaining a single theoretical orientation preferred by the counselor (Nance & Myers, 1991). From a consumer's perspective, it is client-centered. ACT outlines criteria for selecting the most effective treatment approach for particular clients and/or therapeutic purposes, i.e., counselors and therapists must adapt the style of counseling and therapy to the client with whom they are working. A through description of the ACT model is found in Howard et al. (1987) and Nance and Associates (1995).

According to ACT, therapist style reflects two dimensions: **direction** and **support**, which interact with the client's **readiness** to accomplish therapeutic goals. Readiness consists of three specific elements: **willingness, ability,** and **confidence**. Willingness is converted into the client's level of motivation, amount of resistance, or receptiveness to change. Ability reflects past experience, current coping skill level, and capacity for improvement. Confidence can be viewed as the client's internal drive or assessment of ability or likelihood of success. The key elements of the ACT/Readiness model are outlined in Figure 1 (Nance & Myers, 1991).

Figure 1 illustrates that the therapist dimensions of direction and support consist of four quadrants or styles. Client readiness is concurrently divided into four parts, each of which corresponds to the therapist's style quadrant. The relationship of readiness to therapist style can be seen in the vertical arrows. The bell-shaped curve represents (a) the continuum of combinations possible within this therapeutic model and (b) the need to match a client at the current level of readiness. The goal is then to move with the client in the developmentally appropriate direction while systematically altering the amounts of direction and support. Effective counseling interactions require 100% direction and 100% support. Treatment decisions are based on answers to questions such as, "How much direction and how much support are supplied by the client?" "How much by the counselor?" Fundamental to the process is allowing the client to use his or her own resources as much as possible (Nance & Myers, 1991, p. 122).

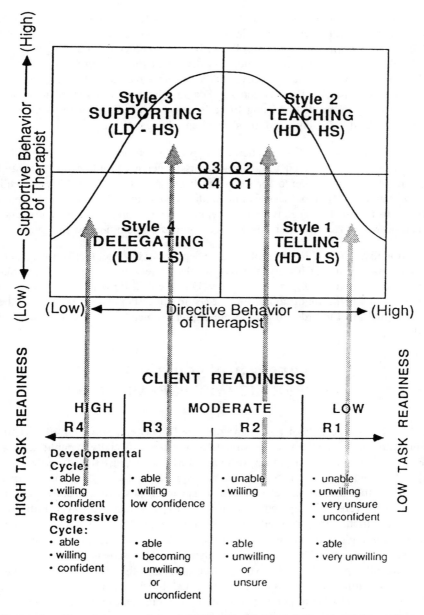

Figure 1. Key elements of the ACT/Readiness Model. Reprinted from Nance, D.W., & Myers, P. (1991). Continuing the eclectic journey. *Journal of Mental Health Counseling, 13,* 1. © 1991 ACA. Reprinted with permission. No further reproduction authorized without written permission of the American Counseling Association.

As an illustration, Nance and Myers (1991) portrayed their model as support for systematic eclecticism and related it to readiness variables for three clients. Client A is working on issues of self-worth. She has entered counseling willingly with the hope of developing a more positive, realistic self-perception. She has demonstrated abilities and positive qualities easily recognized by the therapist and others in the client's environment. For this client with this problem, change may best be accomplished using Roger's person-centered theory regarding the necessary and sufficient conditions for client change.

In contrast, Client B has a chemical dependency problem that he is unwilling to confront. He has been futile in attempts to get his problem under control. He has been court ordered for treatment because of two DWIs (driving while intoxicated). ACT/Readiness would predict that Client B would be far more likely to benefit from behavioral conceptualizations and intervention processes than he would from the person-centered approach recommended for Client A.

Finally, Client C has a bipolar manic depressive disorder that is transgenerational. Based on past history, the best level of intervention for this client may be pharmacological, i.e., lithium therapy. For Client C, if the problem is relieved by drug therapy, little or no need may exist to understand the client at any other conceptual level in order to get the presenting problem under control (Nance & Myers, 1991, p. 125).

PRESESSION SCREENING AND PRETHERAPY PREPARATION

According to Palmer and Hampton (1987), between 30% and 40% of first appointments with helping professionals are not kept especially in public settings. Pretherapy preparation has been recognized as one strategy to reduce the client dropout phenomenon. Clients who were prepared for their roles, prior to, or as a part of the initial stage of counseling had more positive outcomes than did those who were not prepared (Eisenberg, 1981; Friedlander, 1981). Luborsky, Cruts-Cristoph, Mintz, & Auerbach (1988) found that a long wait between seeking and beginning counseling was negatively related to outcome. Peiser (1982) also found that clients who missed one of their first four scheduled sessions were significantly more likely to have negative outcomes than were those who kept their appointments. This is further supported by the analysis of Sexton and Whiston (1991) who found that counseling sessions tend to be more successful within a framework that includes collaboratively structured roles for which the client is prepared ahead of time as well as sessions that begin soon after the client's initial request for services.

Talmon (1990) conducted presession preparation with the first phone call. He stated "Between now and our first session, I want you to notice the things that happen to you that you would like to keep happening in the future. In this way, you will help me find out more about your goals and what you are up to" (p. 19). This contains several messages:

The therapist is interested in natural changes (e.g., "notice the things that happen to you").

The focus is on the transition from the present to the future (e.g., "between now and our first session . . . that you would like to keep happening in the future").

The patient is active and soon can assume a "one-up position" with the therapist (e.g., "in this way you can help me"). This should be reinforced with a follow-up within 24 hours.

Fisch et al. (1983) found that using the following questions reduced pretherapy dropouts, increased participation of family members, and significant others. In addition, these questions alter the orientation of both client and therapist so that they can view the problem in a larger context:

"What else is stressful in the family?"

"Who else is involved with the family who could be helpful to counseling?"

"Therapy is most effective if all involved come in at least for the first session."

"Who will be attending the first session?"

Furthermore, Genter (1991) requested that prior to the first session the client and the referral source submit in writing their answers to three questions:

"From your perspective, what are the central issues or problems?"

"What are the factors (or circumstances) that seem related to the issue, or contribute to the problem?"

"What measures have been used so far in an attempt to solve the issues?"

Finally, Frayn (1992) developed assessment factors associated with premature psychotherapy termination. Premature termination is defined as any patient who unilaterally leaves intensive psychotherapy before the agreed-upon minimal treatment period, i.e., after less than nine months of beginning therapy. Frayn (1992) found that premature psychotherapy termination was associated with certain specific ego deficits and environmental circumstances that can be evaluated at the time of initial assessment. Introspection, frustration tolerance, motivation, positive countertransference, and life circumstances were factors that most highly discriminated between the termination and the continuation of therapy. A definition of specific ego functions included the following:

Introspection: the degree of psychological mindedness that includes self-awareness, curiosity, intuition, and capacity for insight.

Frustration tolerance: the degree of ego strength. i.e., adaptive ability, tolerance of anxiety, ability to function under stress.

Motivation: the degree of self-interest or commitment to understand self and sufficient suffering to bring about a desire to change.

Impulse Control: the ability to delay impulses, postpone immediate gratification, and discuss rather than act.

Frayn (1992) maintained that early recognition of significant assessment qualities should foster more significant selection of patients, and appropriate intervention strategies should lead to a more positive therapeutic outcome. Gaston, Marmar, & Thompson (1988) also reported that a high degree of defensiveness and lower environmental support were associated with decreased patient commitment and capacity to do therapeutic work. An inadequate therapeutic alliance also is a major predictor of early dropouts and poor clinical outcome. Collectively, client selection, therapeutic approach and setting, length of treatment, procedural and goal expectations, therapist experiences, and client attitude were all interactional influences on the potential for clients to terminate therapy prematurely.

Parenthetically, note also needs to be taken that brief therapy may not be for everyone. Clients who possess the following characteristics are more likely to benefit from brief therapy, if they

are motivated to understand themselves,
want to change,
have developed good relationships in the past,
are aware that problems have a psychological basis,
are able to interact flexibly with others, and
have a support network to encourage change.

Clearly, however, some individuals would not benefit from this therapeutic approach. They include clients who might require inpatient psychiatric care such as suicidal or psychotic individuals. Others who would not benefit would be those who have conditions that may have a biochemical aspect such as manic depression, schizophrenia, dementia, or Alzheimer's disease. Clients with the following disorders also may not benefit from brief therapy: anorexia, bulimia nervosa, attention deficit disorder, developmental disorders, agoraphobia, and hypochondriasis (Talmon, 1990, p. 31).

A CAVEAT ON USING COUNSELING TECHNIQUES

Specific techniques implemented by the counselor to elicit client change are an important component of the counseling process. Techniques in counseling and psychotherapy, however, are offered with the precaution that the acquisition of techniques alone merely produces a technician skilled in gimmicks, not a therapist whose intention is to effect change. The counseling experience is much more than the counselor's use of technique; the human dimension of the relationship as well as readiness and responsiveness of the client are very important.

Fundamentally, a technique may be conceptualized as a preferred strategy of the counselor and may be drawn from many available sources. The skillfulness with which the intervention is used and implemented is critical. A counseling technique must be organized around a fundamental principle of treatment and directed toward the ultimate goal of wellness. It should contribute to the total process, becoming an integral part of the therapeutic goal by becoming an assimilated force in the counseling relationship. Lambert (1989) suggested that the technically skilled counselor can have a major impact on the counseling process and therapeutic outcome.

Although a technique may or may not be associated with a specific theory of counseling, each theory or model has its own repertoire of techniques integrated into the total therapeutic process. Belkin (1988) maintained that most counseling interactions are universal regardless of theoretical orientation. A successful technique must be assessed in practice rather than in theory. To be effective, a technique must be flexible, appropriate, and pragmatic. Flexibility is a prerequisite to attending to diverse populations with varying expectations and needs. Furthermore, a technique that is too prescriptive and rigid will hamper the interaction between client and therapist, and may significantly impede progress.

This is perhaps best illuminated with the early work of Lieberman, Yalom, and Miles (1973) regarding encounter group experiences. They reviewed the activating techniques of encounter group leaders and compared them to outcome. Two important findings were revealed: (1) the more structured the exercises the leader used, the more competent did members deem the leader to be, and (2) the more structured the exercises used by the leader, the less positive were the results. These findings may seem like a contradiction because initially group members do want the group leader to lead and often equate a large number of structured exercises with competence. Yet, in the long run, many structured exercises become counterproductive, because they foster a dependent group who relies on the leader to supply too much to the process as members become resistant to working on their own issues.

Simkin and Yontef (1984) provided two guidelines for integrating techniques in the counseling session: (1) it has the aim of increasing awareness, and (2) it is within the bounds of ethical practice (Simkin & Yontef, 1984). Byrum (1989) further outlined ten components critical to a client's understanding and acceptance of techniques:

> State the purpose of the technique.
> Introduce the technique in familiar language that the client can understand.
> Support the use of the technique or the rationale.
> Relate the technique to the client's experience.
> Indicate how the technique has worked for other clients.
> Indicate that the technique is voluntary and that the client has the right to decline to participate in the experience.
> Give an overview of what will happen.
> Take the participant through the process.
> Process the experience with the client(s).
> Provide for action planning and follow-up. (pp. 196–202)

From this perspective, it becomes clear that techniques used in counseling or psychotherapy are guided by ethical responsibility and are not intended to be used haphazardly or capriciously.

This book does not assume full coverage of all the practical procedures with which counselors need to be familiar in selecting and assessing clients, implementing appropriate counseling techniques, and evaluating the therapeutic process. Counseling techniques are intended to be broadly applicable to a wide range of client problems—depression, phobias, sexual inhibitions, addictive disorders, school-related problems, stress, shyness, bereavement, crisis intervention, and family dysfunction. Moreover, this is not a comprehensive handbook covering all the strategies and tactics that a helping professional might want to assimilate in his or her therapeutic repertoire. However, with more than 250 systems of counseling and psychotherapy, and a plethora of counseling techniques, this book is perhaps a beginning.

Chapter 3

CLIENT-THERAPIST RELATIONSHIPS: COUNSELING INTENTIONS, INTERVENTIONS, AND THERAPEUTIC FACTORS

We all have a load; and we have to work with the load we've got, with the way we are. We could all use some time to think about ourselves. The routine time is fifty minutes, but that's ten minutes of getting started, twenty minutes of therapeutic alliance, ten minutes of work, and ten minutes of preparation to get back to reality.

Elvin Semrad

Within the therapeutic relationship, counselors and therapists often provide assistance in a short amount of time with the presenting problem remediated contingent upon the client's resources and the degree of counselor's expertise. For the most part, counselors and therapists find themselves gathering information, exploring feelings, generating alternatives, or merely providing unconditional support in a safe and secure environment. Budman (1988) concisely outlined the universal components of the therapeutic process as

naming the problem,
meeting client expectation,
establishing counselor credibility, and
techniques for relief.

Sexton and Whiston (1991) provided a conceptual three component model of counseling (see Figure 2, Conceptual Model of the Counseling Process). Their model consists of (a) existing factors, i.e., those characteristics clients and counselors bring to counseling such as race, sex, and psychological characteristics; (b) counseling process; and (c) intended outcome. Their model evolved after reviewing over 120 studies and significant meta-analyses (Lambert, Shapiro, & Bergin 1986; Luborsky, Crits-Christoph, Mintz, & Auerbach, 1988) in an effort to assess trends related to counseling that may be important to practitioners, students, and counselor educators.

Of all the characteristics in the model, the counseling process is perhaps the most critical. It begins with the relationship between counselor and client upon which organizational and experiential elements of the counseling session, as well as specific techniques and interventions are based (Sexton & Whiston, 1991, p. 331).

The existing factors and the counseling process result in the intended outcome of counseling—client action and behavioral change. The bi-directional arrows in Figure 2 represent the interactional and reciprocal relationships that occur throughout the process. Sexton and Whiston (1991) stressed that counseling effectiveness should be defined by the ability of an element in the counseling process to effect the client's change according to research that is data-based.

Fuhriman and Burlingame (1990) conducted a formidable and exhaustive meta-analysis of 167 studies comparing individual and group process research. They found broad therapeutic themes and dimensions in individual and group process. They termed their quest as a "comparative odyssey and a clearer realization of the commonalities and similarities of individual and group treatment of client maladies" (p. 36). The core therapeutic dimension capsulized focuses on the differences and similarities in group and individual counseling on the following dimensions: interactive client/therapist relationship, therapeutic interventions, and therapeutic factors. This is followed by factors that promote the efficacy of group counseling, curative factors in the group process, and counselor-therapist intentions in the counseling/therapeutic process. From these distinct dimensions are specific attributes that differentiate individual and group process.

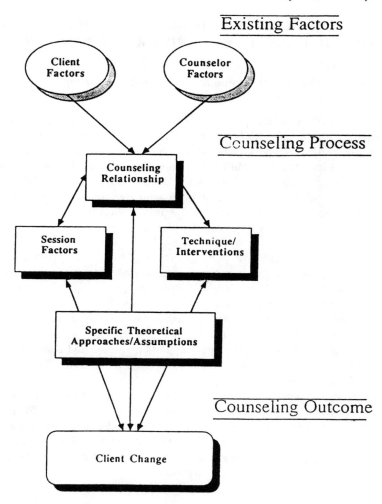

Figure 2. Conceptual model of the counseling process. Reprinted from Sexton, T.L., & Whiston, S.C. (1991). A review of the empirical basis for counseling: Implications for practice and training. *Counselor Education and Supervision, 30,* 6. © ACA. Reprinted with permission. No further reproduction authorized without written permission of the American Counseling Association.

INTERACTIVE CHARACTERISTICS
OF THE CLIENT-THERAPIST RELATIONSHIP

Characteristics That Are the Same for Individual and Group

The therapeutic relationship is the core of the helping process. The following characteristics are the same for both the individual and the group process. Relationships are reciprocal and collaborative. The importance of the counseling relationship is supported by empirical literature (Luborsky et al., 1988), client's involvement in the counseling process (Kolb, Beutler, Davis, Crago, & Shanfield, 1985), client's openness in the relationship with the counselor, and client's warmth and acceptance of the therapist. There are significantly related to positive or productive outcomes (Bent, Putman, Kiesler, & Nowicki, 1976).

> *Reciprocity.* Reciprocity is manifested through warmth, role implementation, comfortableness, trust, openness, expression of feelings, liking, respect, positive regard, and interpersonal attributes (Fuhriman & Burlingame, 1990; Ohlsen, Horne, & Lawe, 1988; Orlinsky & Howard, 1986).
>
> *Engagement.* Extent of engagement, involvement, and commitment by client and therapist is a contributing factor to the bonding component of the relationship. Substantial evidence supports therapists and clients engagement as a central construct of the therapeutic relationship (Fuhriman & Burlingame, 1990; Orlinsky & Howard, 1986).
>
> *Transference.* With transference, the client responds to the therapist as though he or she were a significant figure in the client's past, frequently a parent. Both individual and group process use the construct of transference as a significant variable of the therapeutic relationship. Transference can be positive or negative. Transference and countertransference of the therapist also is an important construct.

Characteristics That Are Unique to the Group Experience

The group is a social microcosm. The alliances between group members, between members and the therapist, and between the member and the group as a total unit yields multiple alliance possibilities.

> *Cohesion.* Cohesion is a multidimensional, interactive construct that has a curative influence in the group. Researchers have conceptualized cohesion as acceptance, unity, tolerance, support, attractiveness, liking, affection, involvement, belonging, solidarity,

closeness, attention, and acceptance. (Fuhriman & Burlingame, 1991, p. 23)

Fuhriman and Burlingame (1990) found that directive interventions appeared to have more empirical evidence and that they efficaciously effect the process and outcome of treatment. Evidence is clear that after a certain minimum level of activity the content, meaningfulness, and client's characteristic complementarily supersede a simple base-rate explanation for the efficacy for an intervention. Interventions and activities aimed at stimulating or facilitating one or more therapeutic factors (e.g., self-disclosure, insight, catharsis), which, in turn, mediate client improvement (p. 38).

THERAPIST INTENTIONS

Eighteen Therapeutic Intentions

Within the therapeutic relationship, counselors and therapists want to provide assistance effectively and efficiently. For the most part, counselors find themselves gathering information, exploring feelings, generating alternatives, or merely providing support in a secure environment. One means that counselors and therapists might utilize to clarify their intended purpose and to provide a focus for interventions could revolve around Hill and O'Grady's (1985) 18 therapeutic intentions:

Set limits. To structure, make arrangements, establish goals and objectives of treatment, and outline methods.

Get information. To find out specific facts about history, client functioning, future plans, and present issues.

Give information. To educate, give facts, correct misperceptions or misinformation, and give reasons for procedures or client behavior.

Support. To provide a warm, supportive, empathic environment; to increase trust and rapport so as to build a positive relationship and to help client feel accepted and understood.

Focus. To help counselee get back on track, change subject, and channel or structure the discussion if he or she is unable to begin or has been confused.

Clarify. To provide or solicit more elaboration; emphasize or specify when client or counselor has been vague, incomplete, confusing, contradictory, or inaudible.

Hope. To convey the expectations that change is possible and likely to occur; convey that the therapist will be able to help the client; restore morale, build the client's confidence to make changes.

Catharsis. To promote a relief from tension or unhappy feelings; allow the client a chance to talk through feelings and problems.

Cognitions. To identify maladaptive, illogical, or irrational thoughts or attitudes (e.g., "I must perform perfectly").

Behaviors. To identify and give feedback about the client's inappropriate or maladaptive behaviors and/or their consequences; to do a behavioral analysis, point out discrepancies.

Self-control. To encourage the client to own or gain a sense of mastery or control over his or her own thoughts, feelings, behaviors, or actions; help the client become more appropriately internal in taking responsibility.

Feelings. To identify, intensify, and/or enable acceptance of feelings; encourage or provoke the client to become aware of deeper underlying feelings.

Insight. To encourage understanding of the underlying reasons, dynamics, assumptions or unconscious motivations for cognitions, behaviors, attitudes, or feelings.

Change. To build and develop new and more adaptive skills, behaviors, or cognitions in dealing with self and others.

Reinforce change. To give positive reinforcement about behavioral, cognitive, or affective attempts to enhance the probability of change; to provide an opinion or assessment of client functions.

Resistance. To overcome obstacles to change or progress.

Challenge. To jolt the client out of a present state; shake up current beliefs, patterns, or feelings; test validity, adequacy, reality, or appropriateness.

Relationship. To resolve problems; to build or maintain a smooth working alliance; to heal ruptures; to deal with dependency issues; to uncover and resolve distortions.

Other Important Intentions

Objectivity. To have sufficient control over feelings and values so as not to impose them on the client.

Implementation. To help the client put insight into action.

Structure. To structure the on-going counseling sessions so that continuity exists from session to session.

Inconsistencies. To identify and explore with the client contradiction within and/or between client behaviors, cognitions, and/or affect.

Goals. To establish short and long range goals congruent with the client's potential.

Flexibility. To change long and short term goals within a specific session or during the overall counseling process as additional information becomes available.

Behavioral change. To develop specific plans, that can be observed, for changing the client's behavior(s).

Homework. To assign work to the client to reinforce change.

Problem solving. To teach the client a method for problem solving.

Hill, Helms, Spiegal, and Tichenor (1988) followed through on the initial efforts of Hill and O'Grady (1985), which delineated *counselor intention* by providing *client reactions* to support their initial proposal. These responses were gathered after immediate intervention rather than reporting more global strategies or reactions for the session. Client reactions were as follows:

Supported: "I felt accepted and liked by my counselor."

Understood: "I felt that my counselor really understood me and knew what I was saying or what was going on with me."

Hopeful: "I felt confident, encouraged, and optimistic; like I could change."

Relief: "I felt less depressed, anxious, or angry."

More clear: "I got more focused about what I was really trying to say."

Feelings: "I felt a greater awareness of or deepening of feelings or was able to express myself in a more emotional way."

Negative thoughts or behavior: "I became aware of specific thoughts or behaviors that cause problems for me or others."

Better understanding: "I realized or understood something new about myself, which helped me accept and like myself better."

Took responsibility: "I felt more responsibility for myself, blamed others less, and realized my part in things."

Challenged: " I felt shook up, forced to question myself, or challenged to look at issues I had been avoiding."

Got unstuck. "I felt freed up and more involved in what I was doing in counseling."

New perspective: "I got a new understanding of another person, situation, or the world."

Educated: "I gained a greater knowledge or information or learned something I didn't know."

Learned new ways to behave: "I got specific ideas about what I can do differently to cope with particular situations or problems."

Miscommunication: "I felt that my counselor didn't really hear me, or understand me. I felt confused or puzzled about what my counselor was trying to say. I felt distracted from what I was saying."

Felt worse about myself: "I felt sicker, more depressed, out of control, dumb, incompetent, ashamed, or self-conscious. I worried that my counselor would disapprove or not be pleased with me or like me. I wanted to avoid something painful. I was overwhelmed about what might happen."

Felt a lack of direction: "I felt that my counselor didn't give enough guidance. I felt impatient, bored, or dissatisfied with having to go over the same thing again."

Ineffective counselor intervention: "I felt attacked, criticized, judged, ignored, put down, or hurt by my counselor. I felt angry, upset, or disturbed about what my counselor was or was not doing. I questioned my counselor's ability or judgement. I felt pressured because my counselor was too directive and wanted things to go a certain way. I felt doubtful or disagreed with what my counselor said."

No particular reaction: "I didn't have a particularly positive or negative reaction to the counselor's statement. The counselor's statement was too short or unclear for me to react. I thought the statement was social conversation." (pp. 358–359)

THERAPEUTIC INTERVENTIONS

Strategies That Are the Same for Individual and Group Processes

Therapeutic interventions consist of therapist and client actions intended to facilitate the change process and therapeutic factors in counseling and psychotherapy. Outcome is enhanced when clients develop a problem-solving attitude (O'Malley, Suh, & Strupp, 1983) and become actively engaged in experiences that help them master problematic situations (Luborsky et al., 1988). Lambert et al. (1986) found that counselors who let the client ramble, did not focus the counseling session, and failed to integrate these issues and themes into counseling contributed to negative client outcomes. Sexton and Whiston (1991) also reported that 50% of the benefit of counseling seems to occur within the first 6 months of weekly sessions in which the client was involved, developed a problem-solving attitude with which he or she learned to master problematic situations in his or her life, and experienced a wide range of emotions while maintaining a positive expectation for change.

Confrontation. Confrontations focus attention on discrepancies between verbal and nonverbal behavior. Empirical evidence from both individual and group research reveal that confrontations are consistently associated with client improvement.

Interpretation. Interpretative intervention are normative and prescriptive in individual and group treatment and are defined as explanatory interventions to provide clients with insight. The overall effectiveness also may be a function of how interpretations interact with other variables such as content focus, patient characteristics, and timing (Beutler, Crago, & Arizmendi, 1986; Fuhriman & Burlingame, 1990; Orlinsky & Howard, 1986).

Content focus. Therapists are perceived as responsible for the topical boundaries of therapist-client interactions with support in the literature for focusing on client affect, cognition, and the therapeutic relationship. Content focus on the here-and-now receives more conceptual attention in group treatment.

Concrete rationale. Concrete rationale focuses on the importance of conveying a concrete rationale including a vocabulary for defining and describing client problems and pregroup preparation.

Guidance. Guidance and advice-giving in both individual and group context receives mixed reviews in the literature of being highly valued to less valued.

Therapist self-disclosure. Disclosure of a personal fact or experience by the therapist is often a technique to maintain therapist transparency; however, it is viewed as less appropriate when clients are more psychologically impaired.

Exploration. Exploration in the form of probes is an intervention to collect information and to focus on important aspects of the client's experience. Fuhriman and Burlingame (1990) found in group studies that exploratory interventions are most often incorporated into investigations of group structure where high-structure conditions include not only experiential activities but also more directive interventions such as focused questions and probes (p. 34).

Reflection. Reflection as an intervention involves repeating or rephrasing of a client's statement or nonverbal manifestations to clarify communication and to check for understanding.

Encouragement. Encouragement is used to establish and to maintain the supportive alliance of the therapeutic relationship ranging from minimal encouragers to more direct maneuvers of support, approval, and encouragement.

Experiential activities. Interventions advanced as "novel" means of fostering client improvement.

Pretherapy activities. Pretherapy activities are a growing professional trend advocated in both individual and group therapy by providing pretherapy preparation exercises that train the client to participate in treatment more effectively. Role preparation appears to affect early therapeutic processes positively and also seems to be linked to later client improvement (Fuhriman & Burlingame, 1990, p. 36).

Within-therapy activities. The analysis of the impact of specific within therapy activities for both individual and group therapy are not easily clarified. Fuhriman and Burlingame (1990), however, cited a number of studies that reveal that therapeutic structure is preferred (a) for clients who are severely disturbed (Dies, 1983), (b) for more dependent and externally oriented clients (Bednar & Kaul, 1978; Dies, 1983; Stockton & Morran, 1982), and (c) at early stages of treatment in order to negotiate particular developmental factors (Bedner & Kaul, 1978; Dies, 1983; Stockton & Morran, 1982, p. 37).

THERAPEUTIC FACTORS

Common Factors in Individual and Group Processes

Therapeutic factors are the mainstay of the therapeutic process. Garfield and Bergin (1986) maintained that the research indicated that counseling effectiveness can be explained best by "common factors" that are variables shared by many approaches and exhibited by a variety of skilled counselors and therapists regardless of their therapeutic school.

Insight. Insight is an integral process in both individual and group process, where the client makes connections between new information generated in therapy and present circumstances.

Catharsis. Catharsis is significant therapeutic process in both individual and group treatment. The nomenclature is synonymous with emotional ventilation, affective arousal, and release of tension, and it is sometimes used synonymously with abreaction.

Reality testing. Reality testing as feedback and confrontation are significantly and positively associated in client's outcome. The impact of feedback and confrontation, however, may differ in individual and group therapy. Bloch and Crouch (1985) maintained that "group therapy is unique in providing a forum for the mutual exchange of honest, explicit feedback. By contrast, feedback in individual therapy can only come from an authority figure—a radically different experience than from one's peers" (p. 51).

Hope. The instillation of hope and the expectation for improvement are the catalyst of the therapeutic process. Hope is also a variable that interacts with client improvement and premature termination. The instillation of hope is magnified by the vicarious learning that occurs in the group experience.

Disclosure. Self-disclosure is a prerequisite to growth and change. In the group experience, Fuhriman and Burlingame, (1990) cite Stockton and Morran's (1982) research, which documented that client self-disclosure is related to (a) reciprocal disclosures from other members, (b) greater liking and attraction, (c) higher levels of cohesion, and (d) more positive self-concept.

Identification. Identification involves relating oneself to others, resulting in a perception of increased similarity. The process of clients identifying with their therapist emerges as a primary ingredient in all theoretical orientations enabling the client to relinquish old values or behaviors and to replace them with new values based on their inherent identification with the therapist. At the group level, client identification with both the therapist and other group members fosters greater client improvement.

Factors That Are Unique to the Group Process

Fuhriman and Burlingame (1990) proposed four putative sources of learning unique to group treatment: (a) participating in a developing social microcosm, (b) giving and receiving feedback in the group, (c) consensually validating, and (d) reciprocal functioning of members in the group (p. 47).

Vicarious learning. Learning by observing others (or the process) has a unique and potent therapeutic aspect for the group process and is often termed "spectator therapy." Vicarious learning that occurs when members observe the therapist perform a difficult social interaction is often helpful in groups of shorter duration.

Role flexibility. The group process provides members greater role flexibility because they can reciprocally function as helper and helpseeker. Fuhriman and Burlingame (1990) conceptualized three consequences of role flexibility in group treatment: (a) enhancement of a member's self-esteem from responsible contributions to the therapeutic process, (b) dilution of the therapist power base so the client does not stay in a "one down" position with the therapist, and (c) attribution of change to self resulting in a healthier organizations of treatment effects (p. 49).

Universality. Universality is based on the notion that others are struggling with similar issues, that "we all are in the same boat," and that one's experiences are not unique. Universality is the most highly valued therapeutic factor in self-help groups.

Altruism. Altruism consists of unselfishly offering support, reassurance, suggestions, and insights to group members. Caring for others also empowers clients to relinquish their own self-absorption in exchange for curative factors of helping others. Altruism also has more therapeutic attributions in self-help groups.

Family reenactment. The group experience provides a microcosm of interpersonal interaction that resembles one's family. The group fosters an environment where a member can correctively relive and rework early familial conflicts. Yalom (1985) outlined several aspects of the group experience that resemble one's family of origin: male-female cotherapists (parental authority figures), member-member rivalry for therapist attention (sibling rivalry), and individual client-therapist interactions (early parental interaction patterns). Kerr and Bowen (1988) maintained that the family is always being dealt with even when just one person is present.

Interpersonal learning. Interpersonal learning involves clients' increasing their ability to socialize with others and behaviorally and attitudinally adapting to interaction within the group. Individuals who stay in a group longer may have more time to experience opportunities for social skill acquisition that group therapy is uniquely capable of providing (Fuhriman & Burlingame, 1990, p. 51).

Yalom (1985) and Hansen, Warner, and Smith (1980), as well as others, also have stressed the "curative" and "therapeutic factors" responsible for producing change in productive groups, such as

Development of social skills. The development and rehearsal of basic social skills is a therapeutic factor that is universal to all counseling groups.

Imitative behavior. Group members learn new behaviors by observing the behavior of the leader and other members.

Group cohesiveness. Group membership offers participants an arena to receive unconditional positive regard, acceptance, and belonging that enables members to fully accept themselves and be congruent in their relationships with others.

Catharsis. Learning how to express emotion reduces the use of debilitating defense mechanisms.

Existential factors. As group members face the fundamental issues of their life, they learn that they are ultimately responsible for the way they live no matter how much support they receive from others.

The reader should be cautioned that when trying to compare individual and group techniques other variables influence both modalities. These variables include the differences between and among therapists, clients, techniques, and interventions. From the perspective of accountability, it may become necessary to control for theoretical approach, counseling intervention, coping skills on the part of the client, and therapist style before the individual and group process can be validated. Nonetheless, a compendium of strategies, techniques, and divergent approaches are a beginning.

GROUP-FOCUSED FACILITATION SKILLS

Many helping professionals want to be able to identify group-helping behaviors to provide structure for service delivery. Gill and Barry (1982) provided a more comprehensive classification of counseling skills for the group process. Such a classification system can assist the therapist or counselor by delineating an organized, operational definition of group-focused facilitation skills. A classification of specific group-focused facilitation skills has a number of significant benefits such as clear objectives, visible procedures, competency-based accountability, and measurable outcomes.

Researchers have classified group counseling skills from their own group counseling experiences. Ivey (1973) proposed a taxonomy of group skills consisting of 10 skills appropriate to both individual and group counseling. He added four "phases" of skill focus: group, individual, self, and topic. Lieberman, Yalom, and Miles (1973) generated a list of what they considered to be critical group facilitation skills under the auspices of four basic leadership functions—emotional stimulation, caring, meaning attribution, and executive function.

Dyer and Vriend (1977) identified 20 behaviors for group leaders that could be viewed as important competencies for counselors in both one-to-one interactions and in group settings. Ohlsen (1977) outlined a classification system of ten facilitative behaviors for group leaders. Many of these earlier classification systems evolved from experiential rather than empirical data, with group leaders using individual counseling techniques to help one person at a time within a group setting. Gill and Barry (1982) recommended a more group-focused classification system providing a more practical and integrative framework that outlines what should be done. They outlined specific behaviors that are appropriate, operational, developmentally related, group-focused, and composed of progressive interdependent stages.

Gill and Barry (1982) proposed that if counselors wish to utilize the group as a medium for learning and change, dynamics such as group member interaction, group support, group decision making and group problem solving should receive greater emphasis. The researchers suggested the following selection criteria for building a system of group-focused counseling skills. Group-focused counseling skills should be

Appropriate. The behavior can reasonably be attributed to the role and function of a group counselor.
Definable. The behavior can be described in terms of human performances.
Observable. Experienced as well as inexperienced observers can identify the behavior when it occurs. The behavior can be repeated by different people in different settings.
Measurable. Objective recording of both the frequency and quality of the behavior can occur with a high degree of agreement among observers.

Developmental. The behavior can be placed within the context of a progressive relationship with other skills, all contributing to movement of the group toward its goals. The effectiveness of behaviors at one stage in the counseling process is dependent on the effectiveness of the skills used at earlier stages.

Group-focused. The target of the behavior is either the group or more than one participant. The behavior is often related to an interaction between two or more participants. The purpose of the group is to facilitate multiple interactions among participants to encourage shared responsibility for helping, to promote participation, or to invite cooperative problem solving and decision making (Gill & Barry, 1982, pp. 304–305).

Waldo (1985) further differentiated the curative factor framework when planning activities in structured groups. In a six-session structured group, activities can be arranged in relation to the group's development so that group dynamics can foster curative factors. The group can be structured as follows:

Session I: Establishing goals and ground rules (installation of hope) and sharing perceptions about relationships (universality).

Session II: Identification of feelings about the past, present, and future relationships (catharsis, family reenactment).

Session III: Demonstrating understanding of other group members' feelings (cohesion).

Session IV: Feedback between group members (altruism).

Session V: Confrontation and conflict resolution between group members (interpersonal learning).

Session VI: Planning ways group members can continue to improve relations with others, and closure (existential factors).

Each session involves lectures and reading materials (imparting information), demonstrations by the leader (initiative behavior), and within and between meeting exercises (social skills and techniques) (Waldo, 1985, p. 56). This model provides a conceptual map that can be utilized for structured groups on conflict resolution, decision making, interpersonal relations, or any intervention that needs to be structured in order to educate, learn, and integrate important life skills.

A FOCUS ON RELATIONSHIPS

Techniques presented in this book focus on improving relationships—relationships with ourselves, with our peers, with our families, and with our environment. Inevitably, clients engage in a relationship with a therapist because of current conflict or unfinished business with relationships in the past or the present. For example, we know that numerous dysfunctions or self-defeating ways of relating typically are learned in childhood, such as

how to remain superficial;
how to build facades;
how to play interpersonal games;
how to hide from ourselves and others;
how to downplay risk in human relating;
how to manipulate others (or endure being manipulated); and
how to hurt and punish others, if necessary (Egan, 1975).

An important point to realize is that every behavior is a communication, and often behavior that is self-defeating or dysfunctional often carries with it an underpinning of poor interpersonal relationships. This is acutely apparent when we examine the void in relationships among our young people today. The growing concern for American youth over adolescent suicide rates, alcohol and other drug abuse, alienation, depression, family dysfunction, teen pregnancy, gangs, and violence demonstrates the critical need for responsible adults to establish close, caring relationships with our young people. Children dropout of school because of poor relationships with teachers and authority. Children begin drinking when they start driving and dating because of the uncertainty and anxiety about interpersonal relationships with the opposite sex. Children have unintended pregnancies because of their need to have a relationship with someone who will depend on them. Children join gangs because of their need to belong and to have power and authority. Children attempt suicide because of difficulties in relating to others, feeling alone, and feeling depressed about either their relationships or lack of them. True, we are a technologically advanced society, but we are all walking around with a broken heart. This malady of poor relationships is pervasive and cuts through all ethnic, racial, and social strata. It is relentless, and it is devastating.

This book seeks to provide helping professionals with critical skills to assist their clients' interpersonal functioning. The focus is on improving relationships—those with others, our peers, our families, our environment, and ourselves. Each technique is followed by the counseling intention, as outlined in Chapter 2, and a description. The techniques in this book are not all-inclusive, but they do represent a beginning.

PART B
IMPROVING
RELATIONSHIPS
IN GROUPS

Chapter **4**

ECLECTIC TECHNIQUES

Many theorists such as Garfield and Bergin (1986), Corsini (1989), Andrews (1989), Kelly (1988), and Norcross (1986) collectively asserted that eclecticism and theoretical integration are emerging trends in counseling and psychotherapy. The rise of eclectic counseling and the development of metatheoretical eclectic models are viewed as a pragmatic response to the wide range of client differences. Any single theory and associated counseling techniques are unlikely to be universally effective with increasingly diverse client populations that reflect an equally diverse array of support systems. Part B of this book is divided into four sections: eclectic techniques, classic gestalt techniques, nonverbal and metaphorical techniques, and group energizers.

Group counseling is an interpersonal process where members explore themselves in relationship to others in an attempt to modify their attitudes and behavior. Reality testing within the group gives the individual a unique behavior-modifying experience. Carroll and Wiggins (1990) identified general goals for helping members in the group:

> become a better listener,
> develop sensitivity and acceptance of others,
> increase self-awareness and develop a sense of identity,
> feel a sense of belongingness and overcome feelings of isolation,
> learn to trust others as well as self,
> recognize and state areas of belief and values without fear of repression, and
> transfer what is learned in the group to the outside by accepting responsibility for solving one's own problems. (p. 25)

Perspective for the Therapist: On risk and the self . . .

Before all else, each of us must take a fundamental risk to be true to ourselves.

Jim Webb

•

Our lives improve only when we take chances—and the first and most difficult risk we can take is to be honest with ourselves.

Walter Anderson

Below is a compilation of group counseling techniques that facilitate group process, encourage self awareness, and foster greater communication among group members. Fuhriman and Burlingame (1990) found that directive interventions appeared to have more empirical evidence and that they efficaciously effect the process and outcome of treatment. Learning by observing others has a unique and potent therapeutic aspect for the group process and often is termed *spectator therapy.*

| Technique | *Opening Activities for Beginning Groups*

Counseling Intention: To break the ice; to help participants get to know one another

Description. The following activities provide a low-risk, structured activity to engage members in the process of getting to know one another.

Paired Introductions. Members pair in groups of two. Partners get to know each other and in turn introduce their partners to the group. Variations: (1) Partners get to know each other and instead of introducing each other to the group they join another pair of two and introduce their partners (this is sometimes less threatening), or (2) the leader can limit the topics that individuals use to introduce themselves, e.g., "tell your partner about yourself without mentioning anything about family, job, or school."

One-minute Autobiography. Members group in quartets. Using a time-keeper, each person is given 1 minute to tell about himself or herself. Again, dialogues can be restricted (e.g., nothing about job, school, family, place of birth, or hobbies). Limits such as these move members into sharing their values, goals, attitudes, and beliefs.

For any group to be successful, there must exist a sufficient sense of comfort among group members for them to speak freely, to express opinions, and to reveal the values they cherish without the fear of confrontation or ridicule.

•

One of the ways to overcome the fear of self-disclosure is to provide activities whose primary purpose is to build cohesiveness within the group on a less threatening level. Following the risk-taking/trust-building activity, it is essential to process the experience, to draw from the participants their feelings and thoughts about the activity.

Deeper Reaches.   In groups of four, members are given five minutes each to share deeper reaches of themselves. In the first three minutes, tell others in your group what has brought you to this point in your life. One minute is used to describe your happiest moment. The last minute is used to answer questions from others. The leader may model disclosure for the group to increase their comfort level.

Long and Winding Road.   Each person draws on a sheet of paper (newsprint, colored markers can also be used) a picture of his life using stick figures and symbols. The road can be divided into developmental stages (childhood, adolescence, adulthood) depicting critical stepping stones in one's life that brought the person to where he or she is today.

Name Circle.   Members sit in a large circle. The leader begins by stating the name of person seated on his or her right, followed by his or her own name. The person to the leader's right repeats the leader's name, his or her own name, and adds the name of the person seated to his right. The process is repeated around the entire circle.

Known/Not Known.   Sheets of paper or poster board are placed on the walls with headings of "Things I Know" and "Things I Want to Know" (about the content or purpose of the group). Nonverbally, members circulate around the room and write their concerns on the paper. Concerns are processed.

| Technique | *Risk Taking and Trust Building* |

Counseling Intention: To build trust within and among group members

Description. Each of the following activities may be used for initiating risk taking and building trust.

Trust Fall.   Partners stand, with back turned, and arms extended sideways, he or she falls backwards and is caught by the partner. Reverse roles and repeat.

Trust Walk.   One partner closes his or her eyes and is led around blind—through, around, and over things. Reverse roles and repeat. The role of the leader is to build trust in the led.

Trust Run.   Outside, one partner closes his or her eyes and is led by the other in a vigorous run. Reverse roles and repeat.

Tug-of-war.   Partners imagine a line between them on the floor and have a tug-of-war with an imaginary rope. One partner is to be pulled across the line.

Mirroring.   Partners stand facing each other. One becomes the mirror image of the other's bodily movements. With hands in front, palms toward partner, they move expressively. Then reverse roles and repeat.

Circle Pass.   Group participants stand in a tight circles. A volunteer or participant who wants to develop additional trust in the group is rolled around gently inside the circle.

Machine.   One at a time each participant stands up and imitates a part of a machine, using his or her body for active parts and uses voice for machine-like sounds. After one person is up, the next goes up, etc. The facilitator can ask the machine to quicken or slow down.

Eye Contact Chain.   Participants form two lines, facing each other about a yard apart. They hold hands, and the persons at the two ends hold hands. This forms a chain similar to a bicycle chain. Without talking, participants are instructed to look at the person opposite him or her in the eyes. When the group feels so, everyone takes one step to the right. Look the next person in the eyes. Take another step to the right. Continue until you return to your original position.

Personal Interview.   Dyad members interview each other. Possible questions are suggested here. A rule of thumb should be that any question one person asks, he or she should be willing to answer also. Each person has the right to decline to answer any question with which he or she feels uncomfortable.

| Technique | *Group Consensus on Where to Begin*

Counseling Intention: To provide a structure for the group as to where to begin

Description. As leader, define self-defeating behavior. Group members anonymously write on an index card a self-defeating behavior they would like to

---

The Dilemma

To laugh is to risk appearing a fool.
To weep is to risk appearing sentimental.
To reach out for another is to risk involvement.
To expose feelings is to risk rejection.
To place your dreams before the crowd is to risk ridicule.
To love is to risk not being loved in return.
To go forward in the fact of overwhelming odds is to risk failure.

But risk must be taken because the greatest hazard in life is to risk nothing.
The person who risks nothing does nothing, has nothing, is nothing. He may
avoid suffering and sorrow, but he cannot learn, feel, change, grow or love.
Only a person who risks is free.

Janet Rand

---

change. The leader collects completed cards and redistributes them instructing members to take any card but their own. Members read their new card aloud and the group assigns a rating to the problem from 1 to 10 (1 = low/10 = high). The leader tallies and ranks the problems for the group. The highest, collectively rated problem is identified. The individual who wrote it is identified, and the group counseling begins with the focus on that person's concern.

Technique | *Affirmations of Trust*

Counseling Intention: To build physical, intellectual, and emotional trust

Description. Each member is instructed to distribute as many statements from the *Trust Is* poem as he or she wishes that best describes his or her trust in another member in the group—to write the other persons name, the number of applicable statements, and his or her own signature on a slip of paper and to give it to the member. Each member is instructed to do this for every other member of the group. Members can discuss their reactions to this experience and focus on its goals.

Technique | *Controlling and Influencing Communication*

Counseling Intention: To facilitate communication and confront issues of control, dominance, or resistance

Description. Using a ball or other inanimate object, instruct group members that only the person in possession of the ball is permitted to speak. A member who

---

Perspective for the Therapist: On trust . . .

Trust Is

Trust is keeping your word.
Trust is the willingness to communicate.
Trust is being there.
Trust is consistency.
Trust is saying, "I understand,"
"I believe you."

Trust is not needing to explain.
Trust is a responsibility.
Trust is a compliment.
Trust is being open.
Trust is a willingness to be vulnerable.

Trust is a reciprocal thing.
Trust is knowing one another.
Trust is not taking advantage.
Trust is different things to different
people.
Trust is, above all, risky.

Anonymous

---

wishes to say something must gesture nonverbally to the individual in possession of the ball to receive it. This exercise may be used either as an icebreaker or with focus topics such as reaction to the group experience, dealing with ambiguity, dealing with life stressors. Focus topics are unlimited. Members who control, influence, dominate, or withdraw from communication in the group also could be processed.

| Technique | *One-on-one Risk Taking on a Scale of 1 to 10*

Counseling Intention: To encourage group self-disclosure

Description. Self-disclosure is a form of risk behavior that proceeds to different levels. Group or individuals can explore their own risk boundaries by listing or exchanging disclosure statements on a scale of 1–to-10. An individual lists, or partners exchange a statement that represents an attempt to disclose feelings, emotions, attitudes, experiences that represent a level of risk. Rank the levels of each statement on a scale from 1 to 10 (10 = high risk; 1 = no risk).

| Technique | *Sculpturing Repressed Feelings* |

Counseling Intention: To help a member express difficult feelings

Description. If someone in a group is experiencing difficulty expressing personal feelings to another member (to the point that it is interfering with his or her personal growth), nonverbal sculpturing of repressed feelings may be helpful. The individual who is having difficulty expressing feelings moves with the other participant to the center of the group circle. The recipient is to assume the role of a lump of clay. The individual who is having difficulty expressing feelings becomes the sculptor. The sculptor molds the statue of clay to reflect the way in which the sculptor is experiencing the individual and his or her behavior. Feedback should include facial expression, gestures, and posture.

After the sculpturing the statue holds the position. Next, the group leader instructs the sculptor to sculpt himself in relation to his feelings toward the other member and hold the position. Process both members' positions, feelings, and relation to one another. Encourage group members to share their insights.

| Technique | *Positive Perceptions* |

Counseling Intention: To focus the group on sending positive messages

Description. Each group member is to write a positive personal message to each other member of the group. The messages are intended to make the person feel positive about himself. Positive messages could reflect a positive attitude, appearance, success, or special message. Members can sign their positive perception or have the option of leaving it blank. Variations could include sending messages only to individuals for whom they have significant positive feelings. Another alternative could be providing two messages to the individual, one positive perception and one self-defeating perception.

Perspective for the Therapist: On group growth . . .

Trust is the pacemaker variable in group growth. From it stem all the other significant variables of health. That is, to the extent that trust develops, people are able to communicate genuine feelings and perceptions of relevant issues to all mmbers of the system.

Lorraine M. Gibb

| Technique | **Best Friend**

Counseling Intention: To project and introduce oneself in a less threatening manner

Description. Individual or group members are asked to identify someone who knows them better than anyone else, i.e., your *best friend*. He or she can be a mother, father, sister, brother, wife, or husband. He or she will be called your best friend. On a piece of paper, what would your best friend say about you such as the following: "He or she is a person who likes . . .," "One thing that he or she dislikes is. . . ." "If he or she could do one thing in life it would be? . . ."

Place a chair in the middle of the room or group. Stand behind the empty chair and introduce yourself as you would expect your "best friend" would do it. Process what was learned be one's self and others from this projected experience.

| Technique | *Choose an Object*

Counseling Intention: To project a perception of self

Description. A collection of objects of varying size weight, composition, color, and sensation are placed in container so that others cannot see the objects. Members are to move to the container and select one item that he or she can identify with from those within the container. Each member must identify with a single object. Members explore their respective object and their identification with it. Members should verbally share with the group their identification with their object. Others give feedback to each other as to whether the projected identifications matched or did not match their perceptions of each other.

| Technique | *Introspection for Individual Assessment and Feedback from Others*

Counseling Intention: To compare perceptions of self and those held by others

Description. Individual completes the Introspection Continuum according to the instructions. He or she writes his or her name on a second sheet and gives it to

---

Perspective for the Therapist: On risk . . .

If you expect to do something really special in your life by just following what other people have already done, you can forget about "being somebody." The losers in the world are content to travel on the beaten path. Their main distinction is that they're exactly like everybody else. That's how they're comfortable.

A.L. Williams

---

his or her partner to complete in terms of how that person sees him or her. Each member then compares his or her personal introspective continuum with the one completed by another member and discusses his reactions to the similarities and differences. Processing the experience could focus on why descriptions are different or similar from other people's descriptions in terms of congruency.

Introspection Continuum Scale

The following words were selected to enable you to record your perceptions of yourself. Place an "X" on one of the spaces between each pair of words. The distance from the "X" to a word indicates the degree to which it represents your view of yourself.

I Am

Impulsive						Cautious
Relaxed						Tense
Interesting						Boring
Self-confident						Self-conscious
Secure						Insecure
Happy						Sad
Industrious						Lazy
Compulsive						Flexible
Competent						Incompetent
Compassionate						Cold
Attentive						Preoccupied
Friendly						Aloof
Agreeable						Disagreeable
Mature						Immature
Modest						Flamboyant
Pleasant						Abrasive

Perspective for the Therapist: On hiding feelings . . .

To the extent you hide your feelings, you are alienated from yourself and others. And your loneliness is proportional.

Dorothy Briggs

•

Being authentic, being actually and precisely what you claim to be requires that your behavior prove your claim.

John Hanley

| **Technique** | *Life-o-gram* |

Counseling Intention: To bring the then-and-there into the here-and-now; to identify transgenerational issues and behavior patterns

Description. Write a one page autobiography that focuses on the things most important to your life up to the present. Reread it and then write a description of how the places, people, events, or crises that shaped who you are today, e.g., your values, your beliefs, and your goals.

| **Technique** | *Lifeline* |

Counseling Intention: To bring the then-and-there into the here-and-now; to identify behavior patterns significant role models

Description. Draw a horizontal line on paper. On the far left, place an "X" and indicate date of birth; on the far right, place a "X" for today's date. Divide the line into three parts: childhood, adolescence, and adulthood. Write in significant people and meaningful events along the lifeline. What significant events brought fond memories? Process what significant events brought painful memories. What messages did you hear? What values were imparted and assimilated by you?

| **Technique** | *Twenty Questions for the Chair Inside the Circle* |

Counseling Intention: To encourage self-disclosure; to provide an opportunity to focus on deeper levels of understanding

Description. A chair is placed in the middle of the group circle. Any group member may be invited to occupy the chair and assume the risk of answering

---

Perspective for the Therapist: On success and failure . . .

People can alter their lives by altering their attitudes.

William James

•

Perhaps the most important single cause of a person's success or failure . . .
has to do with the question of what he believes about himself.

Anonymous

---

any question group members ask the occupant of the chair. Questions can reflect various levels of self-disclosure such as family or interpersonal relationships, fears, expectations, unfulfilled dreams, or feelings toward other members or the group leader. Both questions that are answered or declined reveals the risk-taking capacity of the group member.

Vriend (1985) found that taking a risk in the controlled context of the group fosters more consequential risk-taking in the client's real world; appropriate risk-taking goals can be targeted in the intervals between group sessions. The chair in the middle (Vriend, 1985) also can be used in the introductory stage of the group.

Members can be asked to introduce themselves without reference to the roles they enact in their lives by answering the question, "What kind of person am I?" while seated in the chair in the middle. Two chairs in the middle can be used either between members who are in conflict or to process a psychodrama. All group members can turn outward of the circle (backs toward the center) in order to be less distracted when the leader wants to introduce a guided imagery for the group.

| Technique | *Superlatives* |

Counseling Intention: To bring closure to the group in a positive way

Description. To provide a structured opportunity for group closure, group members are asked to list the names of all participants including themselves and indicate what positive behavior each member is likely to accomplish as the result of the group experience by responding to the ***superlative*** "Most likely to. . . ." For example, John is most likely to stop procrastinating, Susan is most likely to charge less on her credit cards, or Tammy is most likely to finish graduate school. Positive affirmations and collective feedback provide a tremendous opportunity for group closure.

| Technique | **Strength Test**

Counseling Intention: To focus on individual strengths

Description. An index card for each group member is passed around the group, the leader asks each member to write a positive strength for every group member on his or her card. Incomplete Sentences. Completing stimulus statements about likes, dislikes, family, friends, goals, wishes, or focus topics can help the counselor understand clients, identify problem areas, and establish rapport. Some examples are as follows:

My greatest fear is _____.
The thing that creates the most difficulty for me is _____.
The thing I like to do most is _____.
The person in my family who helps me most is _____.
The nicest thing I ever did for anyone _____.
The nicest thing anyone ever did for me _____.
I used to be _____, but now I'm _____.
The thing I would like people to admire me for is _____.
Something I've never told anyone about before is _____.
The one thing I most want to accomplish is _____.

| Technique | **Actualizing Human Strengths**

Counseling Intention: To help actualize positive strengths of people in the group

Description. Each person writes his or her name on a piece of paper. One member's name is chosen at random. A volunteer is chosen as recorder of the member's strengths. The member who was selected at random expresses to the group all the strengths the person sees in himself or herself. He or she then asks the group to express the barriers they see that he or she must overcome.

| Technique | **Confronting Member Resistance with a Chair outside the Circle**

Counseling Intention: To encourage a greater self-disclosure; to confront resistance

Description. It is not unusual for a group member to engage the group in *circular counseling* by either rejecting facts or information, or becoming defensive excluding any possibility for helpful intervention. Members become frustrated with their attempts to mend a "broken record" (Vriend 1985). An intervention may resemble the following:

> Bill, I'd like to pause and ask you to look at yourself as a member of the group for a moment. Would you mind some feedback from myself and other members? You seem to be going on and on about your situation and have told us everything you would like us to know. You've also been repeating yourself and objecting to whatever suggestions you receive from anyone. Perhaps it would be helpful now if we gave you a reprieve, another chance to hear us and respond to our suggestions. I'm going to ask you to move your chair back out of the circle and turn it around so that you face away from all of us. We'll close you out of the circle for a moment. Then what we're going to do is go over what you have told us and figure out ways to be of help to you. Don't look around and don't respond to anything anyone says. When we're finished, we'll invite you back in. That's when you can tell us if you heard anything you think would work for you in this situation. You'll then get a chance to react, OK? (Vriend, 1985, p. 217)

When the client is situated outside of the circle, the counselor leads a review and evaluation of what has transpired during the group process. All members are involved in talking *about* rather than *to* the outside member and provide information about their perceptions, the member's needs, expectations, and self-defeating behaviors. The member is invited back into the circle and responds to what he or she has heard. This should resemble a gentle *carefrontation* (i.e., gently share cares and concerns with the member without hostility) between group members.

| Technique | *Role-playing*

Counseling Intention: To achieve catharsis; to bring about attitudinal change; to promote conflict resolution and self-awareness; to facilitate behavior change; to understand oneself and significant relationships

Description. The client reenacts oneself, another person, a situation, or a response to an interpersonal dilemma. Less difficult scenes are role-played first and may progress to more difficult scenes. Feedback is given to the client by the therapist or group members.

| **Technique** | **Role Reversal** |

Counseling Intention: To facilitate a change in attitude; to experience opposing beliefs; to reevaluate the intentions of another; to become more understanding of another's position or belief

Description. The client is requested to play a role opposite to his or her own natural behavior or to examine one's attitudes and beliefs about a situation (for example, "for gun control" vs. "against gun control"). The client may also play the role of another person he or she knows or switch roles with another person in a dyadic role-playing situation within a group setting. This allows the client to experience rather than talk about a situation. Members briefly state their position to each other about his or her belief. Members switch roles with the other and present his or her position as if the person were him or her. When reversing roles, members should be authentic and as accurate as possible in restating the other's position.

| **Technique** | **Journal Writing** |

Counseling Intention: To record experiences, feelings, and thoughts

Description. Journals may be used by the client to record innermost feelings, thoughts, or other events. Children often respond well to a homework assignment of keeping a diary, and it often provides a feeling of closeness to the counselor between sessions.

The journal or log provides the counselor and client with a record of feelings, thoughts, and events to be explored. It is also helpful to have group members write logs at the end of every group session. A 3″ x 5″ card entitled "Group Reflections" provides a useful format. The cards can be signed so that the leader can keep in touch with each member. These logs should never be read aloud to the group or referred to in the group by the leader.

Perspective for the Therapist: On trust and self-esteem . . .

Just trust yourself, then you will know how to live.

Goethe

•

Self-esteem is the reputation we acquire with ourselves.

Nathaniel Branden

| Technique | *The Three Most Important People in Your Life*

Counseling Intention: To focus on role models and transgenerational issues

Description. Have individual or group member identify who were three important people in his or her life at age 5, 10, 20. Then have them project into the future "Who will be the most important people in your life?" This technique helps the counselor gain valuable insights into the individual's world at various life stages, particularly in the dimension of psychological dependency.

| Technique | *Writing a Letter Aloud*

Counseling Intention: To focus on unresolved issues or on unfinished business in relationships

Description. The leader asks a group member to write an oral letter within the group setting. The recipient of the letter is an individual who is significant in the group member's life, someone to whom the group member is having some difficulty relating, with whom the group member has never resolved a conflict, or someone who is deceased.

The letter should contain whatever the group member would like to say that has not been previously said, the reason for any existing bitterness, and how the relationship should change. When the letter has been completed, everyone in the group is requested to react and to say what thoughts and feelings the letter elicited.

This technique is most appropriate when an individual expresses a concern about a significant other that is troublesome, agonizing, bitter, frustrating, and full of upsetting interactional demands and unreasonable behavior. The technique is most appropriately invoked after a member has emitted considerable data about the relationship's difficulties and has expressed obvious frustration about attitudes or abusive actions (Dyer & Vriend, 1977).

Rewriting the letter in the groups is very important to demonstrate what the group member can say in a more positive and effective manner. The contrast in letters will actively demonstrate differences in effective and self-defeating thinking patterns. "This is a very powerful tool; not a gimmick or a game" (Dyer, 1984).

Perspective for the Therapist: On goals and decisions . . .

He who chooses the beginning of the road chooses the place it leads to. It is the means that determines the end.

Harry Emerson Fosdick

•

When you have to make a choice and don't make it, that in itself is a choice.

William James

Technique | *I Have a Secret*

Counseling Intention: To explore self-disclosure; to confront irrational assumptions

Description. This exercise can be a method to explore fears, guilt feelings, and catastrophic expectations. Clients are asked to think of some personal secret. They do not actually share the secret with others but imagine themselves revealing the secret. Clients are to explore what fears that they have about other people knowing their secret and how they imagine others might respond.

Technique | *Here-and-Now Face*

Counseling Intention: To disclose feelings and emotions

Description. The here-and-now face (Kranzow, 1973) is an activity designed to help group members disclose and discuss their feelings and emotions. Instruct members to draw a face that represents the feelings they are experiencing at the present time. Below the face have them write a verbal description of those feelings and the reasons for them. The discussion should include both "what" the feelings are and "why" they exist in the person at the present time. For example, "I am feeling _____ because _____." This exercise is a means of generating a discussion of the importance of feelings in their lives and brings the group into personal contact.

Technique | *Life-Picture Map*

Counseling Intention: To bring the then-and-there into the here-and-now

Description. Ask group members to draw an illustrated road map that represents their past, present, and future. The map should pictorially depict experiences the members have had, obstacles they have overcome, what their present lives are like, what their goals are for the future, and what barriers stand in the way of accomplishing those goals. Upon completion of the drawings, have members share their maps with the group, explaining the various illustrations, and the experience is processed.

| Technique | *Paint a Group Picture*

Counseling Intention: To encourage group cohesiveness

Description. Divide the total group into groups of four to eight, and supply the subgroups with paper and markers. Ask them to paint a picture as a team that reflects the personality of the subgroup. The picture should be creative and integrate individual efforts. Members also could decide on a group name and sign the picture with it.

| Technique | *Competitive Thumb Wrestling*

Counseling Intention: To confront aggressive and hostile behaviors among group members

Description. This exercise is useful when the leader perceives that two members may be experiencing hidden aggression or hostility toward one another. Those involved should select their preferred hand and interlace their fingers, and hook their thumbs. One person then attempts to force the thumb of the other person down for a count of three. The leader then assists in processing the feelings of hostility between members.

| Technique | *Strength Bombardment*

Counseling Intention: To explore perceptions held by self versus those held by others

Description. One group member volunteers to tell his or her personal strengths; the group responds by telling the strengths they see in him or her. The member continues and asks "What do you see that is preventing me from using my strengths?" and the group responds again. Finally, group members construct a group fantasy in which they imagine what the focus member can be doing in five or more years if he or she uses his or her strengths to their full potential. The focus member reflects on this experience in the group.

Perspective for the Therapist: On feelings and attitude . . .

Ninety percent of the way you feel is determined by how you want to feel and how you expect to feel.

John Kozak

•

Everything can be taken away but one thing . . . to choose one's attitude in any given set of circumstances.

Victor Frankl

| Technique | *I Am Becoming a Person Who . . .*

Counseling Intention: To assess personal growth in the group

Description. Group members are given paper and pencils and are instructed to write their first names in large block letters on the top of the sheets. Then they are asked to complete the following sentence in as many ways as they can: "I am becoming a person who. . . ." They silently mill around the room reading each other's sheets, then they leave the group session.

| Technique | *Map of Life*

Counseling Intention: To review significant life events

Description. On sheets of newsprint, members draw maps of their lives, illustrating significant events. In an insert, they draw a map of the current week up to the here-and-now. Each member explains his or her map to the group.

| Technique | *Think—Feel*

Counseling Intention: To focus on cognitive-emotional issues

Description. Members are instructed to write on one side of a 3 x 5 index card a sentence beginning with the phrase "Now I am thinking . . ." and on the other side a sentence beginning with "Now I am feeling. . . ." Members are asked to process their thoughts and feelings from both sides of their cards.

| Technique | *Here-and-Now Wheel*

Counseling Intention: To identify and focus on feelings

Description. This can be used as a closure activity to enable people to get in touch with the emotions they are feeling, to put a label on them, and to try to determine why they are feeling them. Have group members draw a circle on a piece of paper and divide the circle into four parts (four quadrants). In each part, they are to write a word that describes a feeling they have at the moment. The leader can ask for five volunteers to share their wheels with the entire group.

| Technique | *Value Box*

Counseling Intention: To explore what clients value

Description. Each group member is to bring in a box containing three to six items. These items are those that hold special meaning or represent something that holds significant meaning for the individual. Group members take turns explaining the content of their boxes, each person revealing and explaining the objects he or she has selected.

| Technique | *Who Are You?*

Counseling Intention: To explore dimensions of the self

Description. Who are you? Take nine pieces of paper. Ask yourself "Who am I?" nine times, and write your answer each time on one of the sheets. Your reply may be anything that comes to mind that you feel may identify you such as your age, sex, profession, a symbol, image, and a value. After you have finished, go through your answers and rank order them in importance (1 being the highest and 9 the lowest). Then place each piece of paper face down in front of you. Turn up number nine and think about what it represents. Consider what your life would be like without number nine and proceed through each number to number one.

Process the filtering out of parts of you not essential to your self. Do you think you exist apart from your activities, titles, or career? Are there aspects of codependency with others regarding your identity and your meaning to others?

Perspective for the Therapist: On self-acceptance . . .

We spend so much time disguising ourselves from everybody that we end up disguising ourselves from ourselves.

Francois de Rochefocauld

•

The curious paradox is that when I accept myself just as I am, then I can change.

Carl Rogers

Technique | *Cued Sharing*

Counseling Intention: To promote more open dialogues among group members; to assess locus of control

Description. Cue the group to share with one another

an episode from childhood or adolescence that was very formative;
a personal secret;
feelings about a part of one's body, e.g., proud or ashamed;
feelings about occupation—satisfactions or frustrations;
about their financial situation;
about their love life, past and present, or marriage; or
feelings about other members in the group.

Technique | *Leave the Room*

Counseling Intention: To confront the worst kind of rejection—being completely cast away from the group, ignored, or not taken seriously by others.

Description. Lewis & Streitfeld (1970) provide the following confrontation strategy for processing the experience of rejection:

Out in the Cold. The group forms a circle. Each member in turn steps out of the circle. Each member wanders around the room exploring how he feels in different locations, focusing on how it feels to step away from the group. For example, he or she may feel intensely rejected, isolated, weak, or meaningless to the group. On the other hand, he or she may be relieved and may feel liberated.

The member then returns to the group and focuses on how he or she feels now. For example, do you feel whole or fragmented? Do you feel awkward or comfortable? Are you happy or sad? Other members should focus on how they felt when someone leaves. Are you sorry? Or do you feel rejected when someone moves away? Some members may feel that the group has annihilated the one who has left and that they can abuse him. Others may feel that the person who has left is freer and stronger than the group.

| Technique | *Actualizing Human Strengths* |

Counseling Intention: To actualize the positive strengths of people in the group

Description. Each person in the group writes his or her name on a slip of paper; one person's name is chosen at random. One group member is designated as the recorder to take notes on the strengths he or she sees in self.

> The person chosen expresses to the group all the strengths he or she sees in himself or herself.
> The person chosen then asks the group, "What other strengths or potentialities do you see in me?" "What do you see keeping me from using these strengths?"
> Group members share their perceptions of member's assets and liabilities.
> The group then fantasizes what the member would be like if he were using these strengths in the next five years.
> The recorder gives the notes to the focus member and the entire experience is processed.

| Technique | *Impressions of Self* |

Counseling Intention: To gain a fuller impression of how one sees self

Description. Build a representation of yourself in three dimensions. To do this empty a junk drawer or closet. Dump out a collection of heterogeneous materials such as papers, pictures, matchbooks, strings, scraps of wood, magazines, and any other miscellaneous finds. Gather some of these things from the pile and build a portrait of yourself out of them.

| Technique | *Group Reentry Questions* |

Counseling Intention: To check in with group members regarding their group experience

Description. Reentry questions help to reestablish the level of group rapport that has been developed as well as positively enhance self-concepts of group members. Questions such as these are useful:

What was the most exciting thing that has happened to you in the last week?
What was one of the most exciting things that you did?
Suppose you had a magic box. In it can be anything you want that will make you happy. What is in your box that makes you extremely happy?
If you could teach everyone in the world just one thing—an idea, a skill, a hobby—what would it be?

Chapter 5

CLASSIC GESTALT TECHNIQUES

Today, within the realm of more humanistic-existential psychotherapies, gestalt therapy is perhaps the most prominent. It is parallel to other "third force" approaches (Seltzer, 1986) with its strong conceptual emphasis on self-fulfillment and the development of authenticity and self-responsibility. Gestalt therapy stresses here-and-now awareness and the unity of mind, body, and feelings. "Lose your mind and come to your senses" (Perls, 1969) is a major tenet in this counseling approach.

Inherently, it is an experiential therapy designed to help people experience the present moment more fully and gain awareness of what they are thinking, feeling, and doing. Unfinished business from the past (such as unexpressed feelings of resentment, anger, guilt and grief) is viewed as needless emotional debris that clutters present-centered awareness. Gestalt therapy uses confrontational techniques as an invitation for the client to become aware of discrepancies between verbal and nonverbal expressions, between feelings and actions, or between thoughts and feelings.

Perls maintained that people often fragment their lives and sabotage their potential by losing touch with their inner selves, and by not coming to terms with unfinished business (i.e., unfulfilled needs, unexpressed feelings, or lack of closure to significant life events such as loss). Individuals often find themselves experiencing a split in their being between what they think they should do, and what they want to do. People also tend to flounder at times between existing polarities in their lives such as love/hate, internal/external, or real/unreal. Gestalt techniques are experiential exercises to bring clients in touch with the full range of their experiences. The process involves many of the following components:

Enhancing awareness. Clients are helped to attend to that which they are presently experiencing.

Changing questions to statements. Clients are encouraged to use statements rather than questions, which leads them to express themselves unambiguously, and to be responsible for their communication.

Assuming responsibility. The client is asked to substitute the use of the word won't for can't. Experimentation in this substitution often leads individuals to feel that they are in control of their fears.

Asking "how" and "what." Asking why leads to defensiveness and intellectualization rather than experiencing and understanding. How and what enable individuals to get into the experience of their behavior.

Bringing the past into the now. Much of that which is dealt with in counseling is concerned with past events. Rather than rehashing the past, previous experiences or feelings can be brought into the here-and-now.

Verbal and nonverbal congruency. The counselor observes the client's body language and focuses attention on discrepancies and brings them to the clients awareness.

| Technique | *Empty Chair*

Counseling Intention: To address conflict or relationship issues for the client

Description. A role-playing technique involving the client and an imaginal person in the empty chair. The client sits opposite the empty chair when speaking to the imaginal person; a technique in which the client plays his or her role and the role of an imaginal person or partner.

Perspective for the Therapist: On Gestalt Therapy . . .

The aim of Gestalt therapy is to develop more "Intelligent" behavior, that is, to enable the individual to act on the basis of all possible information and to apprehend not only the relevant factors in the external field but also relevant information from within. The individual is directed to pay attention at any given moment to what he/she is feeling, what he/she wants, and what he/she is doing. The goal of such direction is non-interrupted awareness.

Elaine Kepner
Lois Brien

| Technique | Hot Seat |

Counseling Intention: To confront a group member regarding interpersonal issues or resistance

Description. A technique to focus intensely on one member of the group at a time; the member sits opposite the group leader and dialogues on a life problem with intermittent input from other members upon request by the group leader.

| Technique | Mirror |

Counseling Intention: To provide feedback to the client regarding how he or she is perceived by the group or one member

Description. A technique employing role-playing. The role-playing group member with the problem is asked to remove himself or herself from the group setting while a volunteer group member comes forth to imitate the role player and also to provide alternative role-played behavior. The original role player observes as an objective, nonparticipatory learner.

| Technique | Monotherapy |

Counseling Intention: To facilitate awareness and a therapeutic dialogue

Description. In Gestalt therapy, a technique in which the counselor requests the client to write or create a dramatic scene and role play all characters involved; the client is encouraged to role-play personal fantasies or repressed wishes.

| Technique | Playing the Projection |

Counseling Intention: To gain a deeper awareness of one's own projections from the perspective of others

Description. The purpose of this exercise is to demonstrate how often we see clearly in others qualities or traits that we do not want to see or accept within ourselves. Group members are to make a direct statement to each person in their group, and then apply that statement to themselves. For example, one member might say to another member, "I think you are very manipulative" and then say "I am manipulative." Or one member might say to another member, "I don't think you really care about me" and then say "Then I don't care about me." This technique serves to create a deeper awareness of one's own projections.

| Technique | *Territoriality and Group Interaction*

Counseling Intention: To reveal a group sociogram of member interaction

Description. After the group has been in session for a time, ask them to change seats. Process the issues of territoriality, that is, did the group members tend to arrange themselves in the same seating order? How did they feel when they saw someone else sitting in their seat? Ask group members to diagram with arrows the interactions of a given period of group discussion. Discuss cross-currents in the group. Who are isolates? Who are stars? Is there ease of communication, direct eye contact, and equal air-time?

| Technique | *Think—Feel*

Counseling Intention: To focus on discrepancies between thoughts and feeling

Description. Members are instructed to write on one side of a 3″ x 5″ index card a sentence beginning with the phrase "Now I am thinking . . ." and on the other side a sentence beginning with "Now I am feeling. . . ." Members are asked to process their thoughts and feelings from both sides of their cards.

| Technique | *Making the Rounds*

Counseling Intention: To provide a structured opportunity to relay difficult feelings or thoughts

Description. In this exercise a person goes around the group and says something that is difficult to say. For example, one member might have mentioned that he or she does not trust the other group members enough to risk any self-disclosure. He or she may be given the opportunity to go around the group and say to each member: "I don't trust you because_____" or "If I were to trust you, then _____."

The person making the rounds completes the sentence with a different ending for each group member. The purpose of the exercise is to give participants the experience of confronting a given fear and concretely stating that fear in the group.

| Technique | *I and Thou* |

Counseling Intention: To enhance communication; to get in touch with barriers to communication as it is perceived by others

Description. Clients often respond as if they are talking either to a blank wall or *about* a person or persons rather than *to* them as if they did not exist. The client is asked, "To whom are you saying this?" He or she is led to discover the distinction between "talking to" or "talking about" another. The client is led to discover whether or not his or her voice and words are reaching the receiver. Awareness of how voice and verbal behavior may inhibit relating to others also can be explored.

| Technique | *The Principle of the Now* |

Counseling Intention: To relate experience in the here-and-now; to gain greater self-awareness

Description. To encourage communication in the present tense, the therapists asks, "What is your present awareness?" "What is happening now?" "How do you feel at this moment?" The client is taught to experience himself or herself in the now to gain awareness. Self-awareness is not a thought about the problem but is itself a creative integration of the problem.

| Technique | *Turning "It" Language into "I" Language* |

Counseling Intention: To empower the client to take responsibility

Description. It is not at all uncommon for individuals to refer to their bodies and their behavior in "it" language. (For example, "What are you experiencing

---

Perspective for the Therapist: On expectations . . .

I do my thing and you do your thing.

I am not in this world to live up to your expectations, And you are not in this world to live up to mine.

You are you and I am I, And if by chance we find each other, it's beautiful. If not, it can't be helped.

Fritz Perls

---

in your stomach?" The client answers, "It is upset.") The client is directed to change "it" into "I." Instead of "it is upset," "I am upset," and going a step further, "I am upsetting myself." The client begins to see himself or herself as an active agent who does something rather than as a passive recipient to whom things somehow happen. The client can see immediately the degree of responsibility and involvement that is experienced.

| Technique | *Awareness Continuum* |

Counseling Intention: To guide the client(s) into the present; to diminish the facade of rationalizations, verbalizations, explanations, and interpretations

Description. The client is diverted away from the emphasis on the "why" of behavior, as in psychoanalytic interpretation, toward the "what" and the "how" of behavior. Questions such as, "What are you aware of at this moment?" "How do you experience this now?" "Can you be your thoughts and your eyes and tell me the dialogue for them?"

| Technique | *Parallel Dialogue* |

Counseling Intention: To integrate personality and create a greater awareness of conflicting forces

Description. When a dichotomy is manifested in the perceptions or behavior of a client, the client is asked to have an actual dialogue between these two components, for example, aggressive versus passive, secure versus insecure, outgoing versus shy. The dialogue also can be developed between the individual and some significant person. The client simply addresses the person as if he/she were there, imagines the response, or replies to the response. An understanding of more satisfying behaviors can be outlined.

| Technique | *No Gossiping* |

Counseling Intention: To facilitate direct confrontation of feelings

Description. The "no gossiping norm" facilitates direct confrontation of feelings. Clients often gossip about others when they have not been able to handle directly the feelings they arouse. Gossiping is defined (Fagen & Shepherd, 1970) as "talking about" an individual that is present rather than "talking to them." For example, a group member might speak about another group member. Sue comments, "It frustrates me that we cannot begin on time because John is always late." The counselor intervenes and asks Sue to "talk to" John rather than about him. "John, I get frustrated when you come late because the group cannot begin on time."

| Technique | *May I Feed You a Sentence?*

Counseling Intention: To confront thematic issues; to clarify perceptions

Description. By listening and observing the client, the counselor may infer that a particular theme, attitude, or message is implied—a key sentence. He or she may suggest or say, "May I feed you a sentence?" The key sentence is proposed for the client to practice with others in the group or with others in the client's daily interactions.

The counselor proposes the sentence, and the client tests out personal reactions to the sentence. Although this technique may seem highly interpretive, the client is encouraged to make it his or her own experience through active participation. With the counselor's selective framing of the key issue, the client then can provide spontaneous development.

| Technique | *Can You Stay with This Feeling?*

Counseling Intention: To confront issues habitually avoided; to encourage self-confidence and autonomy

Description. This Gestalt technique is most effective when the client refers to a feeling, mood, or state of mind that is unpleasant, coupled with the defense mechanism of denial or avoidance. At a therapeutic junction the client may feel empty, confused, frustrated, or discouraged. The counselor says, "Can you stay with this feeling?"

The counselor asks the client to remain deliberately with his or her present experience. The counselor asks the client to elaborate on the *what* and the *how* of his or her feelings, for example, "What are your sensations . . . your perceptions . . . your fantasies . . . your expectations?"

| Technique | *Shuttle between Here and There . . . between Reality and Fantasy*

Counseling Intention: To discover what is missing in the "now"

Description. Close your eyes, and go away in your imagination to a place where you feel secure and happy. Come back to the here-and-now. Compare the two situations. You may be more aware of this world and have your goals more clearly in mind. Very often the "there" situation was preferable to the "here" situation. How was it preferable? What is it you want? Close your eyes and go away again, wherever you'd like to go. Notice any change since your last fantasy.

Come back to the here-and-now, and again compare the two situations. Has any change taken place? Continue to shuttle between the here and there until you feel comfortable in your present situation. Do this in any boring, tense, or uncomfortable situation. Very often Perls (1969) maintained that the there situation gives you a cue for what is missing in the now. The difference between your "there and here" can show you the directions in which you want to move. As a long range goal, the client may try making the real life more like his or her fantasy life.

| Technique | *Bringing a Dream Back to Life*

Counseling Intention: To use dreams as a way to reveal unfinished business; to understand images in dreams that represent aspects of the client's personality

Description. Relive your dream as if it were happening now. Act it out in the present. Say the dream aloud, using the present tense. Be aware of what you are feeling when you say it. List all the elements of your dream: the people, animals, objects, colors, moods. Be particularly aware of any situations, such as dying or falling, which you avoided in the dream by running away or waking up. Act out each of the elements. What does each part have to say? What do you have to say to it? What do the parts say to each other?

If in your dream there were situations you avoided, try to finish the dream by acting through frightening situations in fantasy. In acting out parts of your dream, you turn into a dreamer again and become one with your dreaming self.

Perspective for the Therapist: On support . . .

Sickness, playing sick, which is a large part of this getting crazy, is nothing but the quest for environmental support. . . . Regression means a withdrawal to a position where you can provide your own support, where you feel secure.

Fritz Perls

You may give words to characters whose emotions were unspoken in the dream, so that now they engage in a dialogue.

Keeping a "Dream Diary" may help a client remember dreams. The following guidelines may be helpful:

Before going to sleep the client should repeat aloud, "Tomorrow morning I will remember my dreams." Say it 10 times slowly, like a chant.

Keep a paper and pen next to your bed. Upon awakening, record your dream in the greatest detail possible. If you do not remember a dream, lie quietly and see what comes to you. Very often any images or pictures that come to you are often pieces of a dream.

After accumulating several weeks of notes on dreams, review them. What kinds of situations and which people occur most often? Notice images, sounds, colors, tastes, or smells that occur. Sort your dreams in any way that seems meaningful to you. A dream is a personal letter to yourself. Dreams are windows to the subconscious.

| Technique | *Mothers and Fathers/Husbands and Wives*

Counseling Intention: To evoke resentment and resolve conflict

Description. Perls called resentment "the bite that hangs on." Resentment is eclipsed in guilt. The two always go together. Any time you feel guilty, you resent the person you feel guilty toward. When you feel resentful, you also want the other person to feel guilty. This exercise seeks to destroy symbolically the object of resentment.

Close your eyes and picture your mother (father, husband, or wife) in your mind's eye. Take a pillow to be used to bang and scream until you have discharged completely the resentment held toward this individual. Seek to destroy symbolically this oppressive individual. Become so physical with the pillow that you could answer yes to the question, "Is the individual dead?"

Next, name all things that you hate a person for: "I hate him or her for beating me when I was a kid." "I hate him for embarrassing me in front of my friends." "I hate him for being so abusive toward my mom and for dying before I grew up." Then look at these resentments and forgive the person for it. If you get your feelings out, you will free the self from a demoralizing conflict. In addition, you can no longer go back and blame that individual again, because, symbolically at least, he or she is dead inside you.

Perspective for the Therapist: On forgiveness . . .

Forgiveness is the fragrance of the violet which still clings to the heel that crushed it.

George Roemisch

•

The weak can never forgive. Forgiveness is the attribute of the strong.

Mahatma Gandhi

Technique | ***Reviewing Past Experience in the Here-and-Now***

Counseling Intention: To assist clients who are suffering from posttraumatic stress disorder, unresolved conflicts, or unfinished business; to encourage the client to reenact stories from the past by bringing them in present-tense language (Levitsky & Perls, 1973)

Description. The therapist should encourage reexperiencing the emotion so that the confusion, the fright, and the panic are experienced again in the present recall of the past event. For example, if a client says, " I was walking down the street and I felt disoriented," the therapist may have the client restate this as though it were happening in the present and in greater detail so that the statement might be, "I am walking down Elm street. It is 10:00 a.m. in the morning. The air is humid and I feel hot and sticky. I am aware that I am lightheaded and confused. I realize that I am lost and I am feeling scared. Now I am feeling a sense of panic . . ." (Crose, 1990, p. 283).

This maneuver allows the client to relive the experience rather than merely report what had occurred. By bringing the incident into the here-and-now, the therapist can facilitate the client's closure on the disturbing past event. Bringing past feelings into present awareness can assist a client in the final development stage of ego integration.

Technique | ***Dialoguing***

Counseling Intention: To process or articulate feelings of resentment

Description. Identify someone for whom you have strong feelings of resentment. Sitting in a chair, get in touch with all the emotions, feelings, and behaviors that you resent about the individual. Verbally express your resentful feelings.

Perspective for the Therapist: On self-actualization . . .

From Freud we learned that the past exists now in the person. Now we must learn, from growth theory and self-actualization theory, that the future also now exists in the person in the form of ideals, hopes, goals, unrealized potentials, mission, fate, and destiny. One for whom no future exists is reduced to the concrete, to helplessness, to emptiness. For him, time must be endlessly "filled." Striving, the usual organizer of most activity, when lost, leaves the person unorganized and unintegrated.

Abraham Maslow

Next, switch chairs, think about what behaviors you demand they change. Identify your feelings toward the individual when they change the behaviors you resent. Verbally express your demands to that person. Finally, switch chairs again and think about the things that you appreciate about the individual.

Identify your feelings of appreciation to this individual. Verbally express all your feelings of appreciation to this individual. Shift back-and-forth switching chairs between resentment, demands, and appreciations. The therapist assists the client in processing the experience.

| Technique | *I Take Responsibility for . . .*

Counseling Intention: To help a client accept personal responsibility for his or her own feelings

Description. Aloud have the client make a statement describing personal feelings, and then add, "I take responsibility for it." For example, if the client often feels helpless, he or she might say "I feel helpless, and I take responsibility for it." Other feelings that can be the objects of this exercise are boredom, isolation, rejection, feeling unloved, and so on.

Chapter **6**

NONVERBAL AND METAPHORICAL TECHNIQUES

Nonverbal Communication can be defined as all messages other than words that people exchange (DeVito & Hecht, 1990). Nonverbal messages are used to send three primary meanings: immediacy, power, and responsiveness (Mehrabian, 1971).

We communicate about 60% of our meaning nonverbally. Many researchers maintain that another person's actual words contribute only 7% to the impression of being liked or disliked, while voice cues contribute 38% and facial cues contribute 55%. Nonverbal messages are usually more believable than verbal messages. When verbal and nonverbal messages contradict, most adults in the United States believe the nonverbal message.

Millions of dollars are spent annually to create impressions or special images. We strive to hide our negative feelings and disguise our bad moods. In addition, we often fake our real attitude to create the impression that what we feel is appropriate for the situation.

Technique	*Actions Speak Louder Than Words*

Counseling Intention: To facilitate awareness and self understanding of perceptions

---

Perspective for the Therapist: On experience . . .

Experience is a hard teacher because she gives the test first, the lesson afterwards.

Vernon Sanders Law

Description. The counselor interprets the nonverbal communication of the client. If the client nonverbally shows anger and hostility while telling about the need to provide for his ailing mother-in-law, the counselor points out the discrepancy.

> **Technique** | **Nonverbal Exaggeration or Verbal Repetition**

Counseling Intention: To confront verbal or nonverbal communication more directly and assertively

Description. Often a client's verbal or nonverbal communication may become fragmented or incomplete. Gestures may be undeveloped or a sentence may be incomplete. The client could be asked to exaggerate the movement repeatedly to make the inner meaning more apparent. A complementary technique of repeating a statement (that has been glossed over) is to have the client say the words over and louder to absorb fully the impact of repressed communication.

> **Technique** | **Break In**

Counseling Intention: To explore issues of inclusion and exclusion

Description. Members are asked to stand in a tight circle and one person is left outside the circle. He or she attempts to penetrate the group in any way that he or she can. Break In can be used as a springboard for members to explore their feelings of being rejected, isolated, or an outsider by the current group or as it is experienced in his or her own life at the present. The use of "territoriality" to define in group out group expectations also can be processed.

> **Technique** | **Meeting Someone Halfway**

Counseling Intention: To communicate nonverbally

Description. Divide the group into two sections at opposite sides of the room, facing each other. Members are instructed that when they choose (or if they choose), they may walk out to the center of the room and wait for someone on the other side to join them. When the two meet, whatever communication the two desire can take place, but communication is to be nonverbal. Members should process their reactions to the experience and explore their relationship with the person who met them and those who did not.

| Technique | Group Sociogram

Counseling Intention: To focus on communication, relationships, and attachments

Description. Group members participate to form a living sociogram by placing and moving themselves and each other around the room in ways that are meaningful to them. The final form of the sociogram could be drawn on a flip chart for processing and discussion.

| Technique | Sticks and Stones

Counseling Intention: To focus on issues of power, dominance, influence, and aggression

Description. Yardsticks and large stones are placed in the center of the group. The leader instructs the members to use them without talking to express their reactions to each other.

| Technique | Feedback through Posture

Counseling Intention: To focus on first impressions and perceptions versus reality

Description. Group members are focused on one-at-a-time to receive feedback from other members in the group. Each member assumes a body posture that indicates his or her impressions of the individual. After all members posture for one individual, the exercise is processed before the next member is focused upon.

| Technique | Beating Drums

Counseling Intention: To communicate emotions and feelings; to develop trust

Description. The leader plays a recording of drum music and instructs group members to dance freely along with the music. The leader stops the music and instructs the members to freeze. Members observe each other's figure and choose a partner to process the experience.

| Technique | *Nature Walk/City Streets*

Counseling Intention: To increase sensory awareness; to discuss environmental stress.

Description. Group members take a walk in the park or on the city streets. Members are instructed to explore in as much detail as they can their environment and to communicate their feelings to each other without talking.

| Technique | *The Eyes Have It*

Counseling Intention: To increase comfort levels, openness, and self-disclosure

Description. The group stands in a circle. A group member rotates clockwise around in the circle, establishing eye contact and communicating nonverbally with each other member. At the conclusion, the member returns to his or her spot in the circle. The next member follows the same procedure of eye contact and nonverbal expression until all members have contacted all others.

| Technique | *Talking with Your Hands*

Counseling Intention: To identify and communicate feelings

Description. Group members get a partner and move a comfortable distance from the other members. The leader instructs partners to communicate nonverbally feelings such as anger, frustration, hate, euphoria, love, grief, joy, contentment, and fear. Each feeling should be announced independently of the others with approximately one minute the pairs to process each experience.

| Technique | *Unwrapping the Problem*

Counseling Intention: To provide an opportunity to convey resistance or conflict

Description. A group member who may be experiencing resistance or interpersonal conflict is asked to curl into a tight ball. He or she may choose another

---

Perspective for the Therapist: On giving advice . . .

Advice is like snow; the softer it falls the longer it dwells upon, and the deeper it sinks into the mind.

Samuel Taylor Coleridge

•

I have found the best way to give advice to your children is to find out what they want and then advise them to do it.

Harry S. Truman

---

member (or ask a member to assume another significant person in his or her life) to unwrap or open him or her up completely. The member may succumb or resist.

| Technique | *Touch-Talk Blind Milling*

Counseling Intention: To communicate nonverbally

Description. Mill around the room with your eyes closed. As you come in contact with someone, explore that person with your eyes and hands. Touch his or her face, shoulders, hair, hands. Communicate only through use of touch and try to convey a message about how you feel about the person, allowing time for your partner to communicate back to you. Move on to another person in the group and repeat the process.

| Technique | *Eyes as Windows to the Soul*

Counseling Intention: To dismantle first encounter facades; to encourage genuine contact

Description. Sit facing a partner, and stare directly into each other's eyes for five minutes. Tell your partner something important with your eyes. See what your partner has to say to you. Follow-up with five minutes of talking to learn as much as possible about each other.

| Technique | *Pantomimes*

Counseling Intention: To express feelings toward oneself and others that may not be ordinarily verbalized

---

Metaphorical communication has been used in the form of stories, myths, parables, fairy tales, allegories, and anecdotes. In counseling and psychotherapy, it can serve as a technique to access resources within the client that may not be recognized or utilized. Towers, Wollum, Dow, Senese, Ames, Berg, & McDonald (1987) found that metaphors arouse client interest in the counseling process and increase the client's view of the counselor as a trustworthy person. Metaphors also can be used to illustrate specific interpersonal issues, suggest solutions, help clients recognize themselves or clarify their circumstances, and reframe problems (Barker, 1985).

Description. Sit with your partner. Stand and pantomime your impression of that person. Show your feelings with gestures and facial expressions. Then pantomime how you feel your partner feels about you. Reverse the process, then discuss revelations about individual impressions.

| **Technique** | *Self-metaphors (Goodman, 1985)*

Counseling Intention: To evoke a more creative perspective on one's self

Description. Metaphors are powerful tools that people can use to enjoy new and creative perspectives on themselves, their values, and their world. This exercise provides an opportunity for validation from self and others focusing on what they prize or value for themselves. The leader suggests that this activity will be an opportunity for each member to reinforce feelings of "I like me," by completing the statement, "I am like . . . because. . . .", thereby creating a positive self-metaphor. Members should be directed to write in first person (i.e., "What do I like about myself and what from my environment is most like me?") Read the examples below to the group:

> "I am like a snowman. People think of me as a really cool guy, but I have an emotional side of me that people don't always see. When someone else gets all hot and bothered, I can melt quickly. I really do feel for someone who is upset."
>
> "I am a stream. I have a surface that everyone can see. But there are many things going on underneath that surface. I am one stream; within that stream are many different currents which flow at different speeds and in different directions. I hope to get in touch with my flow."
>
> "I am like the wind. I can be as noticeable as a hurricane or as unassuming as a light breeze. I can go anywhere. It's

my choice. People are concerned about me and like to hear the daily forecast. Yet, I'm unpredictable and like myself that way."

After each person has completed a metaphor, place all the papers together in a pile. Shuffle them, and then redistribute them to people at random. Each person then writes a validating response to the self-metaphor he or she has received. This validation should reflect empathic listening—expressing ways that person supports, identifies with, and/or appreciates the individual who wrote the self-metaphor. The response should speak directly to the metaphor itself, as in the samples below:

"Hello Snowman! You are a very refreshing person! I always have enjoyed being around you. You are so versatile. I admire your ability to stand your ground when it's rough outside; and I appreciate how you can "flow" with the situation when things heat up. Your quiet presence is reassuring. The delight you bring to young people is wonderful to watch. Take care, be cool, The House."

"Dear Stream: It must be exciting to be a steam, to have the different speeds and directions to pick from. To choose what fills your needs, when you are needing. Getting in touch with your flow probably will make you more aware of what choices you have—smooth flowing! Yours truly, The Bee."

"Hi Wind! I enjoy the feeling your description of yourself imparts to me. I can feel your looseness and freedom and feeling about yourself. You seem spontaneous and open and happy and have a clear understanding of yourself and your relationship to others. I like you, too. Sincerely, The Leaf"

When everyone has finished, put the papers back into one big pile. Each person can then fish out his or her original metaphor with the response written below it. Volunteers can read their metaphors or response papers aloud to the whole group (Goodman, 1985).

| Technique | *Friends as Metaphors* |

Counseling Intention: Describing friends at a deeper level

Description. Images are more experiential than other forms of communication as they move the client closer to his or her feelings. Use metaphors to describe friends and family members.

Chapter 7

GROUP ENERGIZERS

These simple and enjoyable games can serve a variety of purposes. The most obvious is that if used the first thing in the morning, immediately after lunch, or even after a rather lengthy discussion, they help the group to "wake up" and become energized for the work to follow. They also provide an opportunity for the group to function together in a light activity which is generally nonthreatening. In addition, the activity itself can be processed after it has been completed, providing another opportunity for the group, or the individual, to become aware of the feelings and behaviors of others.

| *Technique* | *Tiger—Gun—Man (Fluegelman, 1976)* |

Description. This is a variation of the childhood game, rock-paper-scissors. The group is divided into two teams, which stand in a line facing one another, with a space of 5 feet between them. The teams huddle and quickly decide if they are to be a tiger, a man, or a gun. The teams return to their line, and on the signal of the leader, each person in the line makes the sound and movement appropriate for the choice they have made. If they are the tiger, they would lunge forward (as if clawing) and growl viciously; if they are a man, they would pose as a Mr. America showing their muscles; if they are the gun, they would point and shout, "Bang." If both teams make the same choice, it is a draw. Otherwise, the tiger beats the man, the gun beats the tiger, and the man beats the gun.

Source for Chapter 7: Fluegelman, A. (Ed.). (1976). *The new games book.* Garden City, NY: Doubleday & Company. Adapted with permission.

Perspective for the Therapist: On humor . . .

Laughter is inner jogging.

Norman Cousins

•

If you lose the power to laugh, you lose the power to think.

Clarence Darrow

Technique | **Humdinger** (*Fluegelman, 1976*)

Description. This is a way of dividing the members into groups. First, determine the number of groups you need. If, for example, you need four groups, you'll need to choose four songs people know well, such as "Row, Row, Row, Your Boat," "Twinkle, Twinkle, Little Star," "Mary Had a Little Lamb," and perhaps a familiar contemporary song. Give each person in each group a slip of paper with the name of the song written on it. When everyone has a song title, ask the members to walk around the room, humming their song. The humming must continue until everyone has found the appropriate group. Then, have the group introduce themselves by singing their song to the other groups.

Technique | **Are You Really Looking at Me?** (*Fluegelman, 1976*)

Description. Have members pair off, then sit back-to-back. Have each one change at least four things in his or her appearance. After two minutes, direct the members to face each other. The object is to see if each member can identify what the other has done to change in appearance. Give them a couple of minutes to identify what has been changed, but explain that no one is to correct/alter what has been changed. This activity will help the members sharpen their sense of observation as they are working on listening skills. They may find an endless number of ways to change by adding to themselves rather than taking away, such as borrowing a ring or pin or watch. Other ways to change appearance include switching a ring to another finger, putting a watch on the other wrist, taking off glasses, messing up hair, rolling up sleeves or pants legs, etc.

Technique | **Clay Dough** (*Fluegelman, 1976*)

Description. Have each member choose a partner. Ask the partner to think of four emotions he or she has felt today. Now, explain that each pair is to choose one person in the pair to be Person A and the other Person B. Person A whispers one of his or her emotion words into Person B's ear. Person B "sculpts" Person A to look as if he or she is feeling that emotion. Each pair then links up with another pair to guess what the "sculpted" person represents. Once they have guessed correctly, have the members switch roles. The activity helps members think of feeling words and the nonverbal behaviors that accompany them.

| Technique | *Mirroring (Fluegelman, 1976)*

Description. This energizer can be done with partners or in small groups. Have the participants stand facing each other. Designate one in each pair as the leader, the other as the follower, or "mirror." The leader is to begin to move his or her head, arms, and body slowly and smoothly. The movements do not have to mean anything. The follower mimics everything the leader does. After a while ask them to switch roles. Emphasize the symmetry and precision of the mirror-im age. Switch leaders again and again, finally asking each pair to pursue the activity without having a designated leader.

| Technique | *Amoeba Tag (Fluegelman, 1976)*

Description. This tag game is played in slow motion. Begin with one "It." "It" chases (in slow motion) another person and links arms with that person when "It" catches him or her. At that point the two of them are young amoeba. The young amoeba chases another person and links arms with that person, thus becoming a teenage amoeba. The teenage amoeba chases another person and links arms with that person to become an adult amoeba. Immediately, the adult amoeba lets out the amoeba cheer (**AM! ME! BA!**) and splits in half to become a young amoeba. The young amoeba becomes a teenager, then an adult, which lets out the amoeba cheer, and so on, until everyone has become part of someone else's amoeba.

PART C
IMPROVING
RELATIONSHIPS WITH
OURSELVES AND OTHERS

Chapter 8

COGNITIVE TECHNIQUES

Millions of individuals suffer from a wide range of emotional distress because they hold harmful, mistaken beliefs about themselves and the world around them. This directly or indirectly impacts their relationship with others. Cognitive behavior therapy (CBT) and cognitive restructuring therapy (CRT) are the most contemporary approaches used in counseling and psychotherapy today. Cognitive behavior therapy (Beck, 1976; Burns, 1989; Ellis & Harper, 1975; McMullin, 1986; McMullin & Giles, 1981; Meichenbaum, 1977) is a model for client reeducation. It is built on the premise that all behavior is learned and that new behaviors can be learned to replace faulty patterns of functioning.

Inherently, individuals' thoughts mediate between feelings and behaviors. Individuals experience emotional distress because of distorted thinking and faulty learning experiences. Thoughts always come before our emotional reactions to situations. This approach emphasizes individuals' capacity for creating their emotions; the ability to change and overcome the past by focusing on the present; and the power to choose and implement satisfying alternatives to current patterns.

Further, from a person-centered approach, individuals can learn better ways of communicating and listening to others. Many of the problems individuals experience today have the source of discomfort that revolves around a fragile relationship. Part C is divided into four sections: cognitive techniques, rational-emotive techniques, behavior techniques, and person-centered techniques.

TWELVE DISTRESSING MYTHS

Psychologist Albert Ellis maintained that people worry and become upset because of the way they interpret their stressors. He believed that people can choose to react *rationally* (reasonably) or *irrationally* (unreasonably) to a stressor. Roberts and Guttormson (1990) listed twelve irrational beliefs (myths) to which people commonly cling.

Myth #1:   "I must be loved by everyone, and everyone must love everything I do."

Myth #2:   "I must be intelligent, competent, and capable in everything I do."

Myth #3:   "Some things in the world are bad, wrong, or evil, and I must be punished severely if I see, do, think or feel them."

Myth #4:   "The world is over when things don't turn out the way I want them to."

Myth #5:   "I have no control over my own happiness. My happiness depends on what happens to me."

Myth #6:   "Worrying about something bad keeps it from happening."

Myth #7:   "It's always easier to run away from problems than it is to deal with them."

Myth #8:   "You need someone else to depend on. You can't function independently."

Myth #9:   "If something bad happened in your past, it must affect you forever."

Myth #10:   "If someone else doesn't live his or her life in the way you think he or she should, you must do everything you can to change that person."

Myth #11:   "There is only one correct answer to any problem. If that answer isn't found, the consequences will be terrible."

Myth #12:   "You can't help feeling the way you do."

These distressing beliefs are complicated when unreasonable demands emerge as unrealistic expectations. Schriner (1990) aptly stated that "disappointment is the caboose on the train of expectation." Many clients spend a tremendous amount of time and energy wrestling with distorted perceptions of themselves made up of self-criticisms, comparisons with others, apprehension, unrealistic expectations of the future, relentless demands for improvement, defensive excuses for failures, and an array of accompanying self-defeating thoughts and feelings.

| Technique | *Eliminating the "Big Ten" Cognitive Distortions*

Counseling Intention: To confront irrational thought and related anxiety; to counteract depression, stress, and panic attacks

Description. Crawford and Ellis (1989) have classified irrational beliefs into one of five categories:

self-defeating beliefs that interfere with basic goals and drives,
highly rigid and *dogmatic beliefs* that lead to unrealistic preferences and wishes,
antisocial beliefs that cause people to destroy their social groups,
unrealistic beliefs that falsely describe reality, and
contradictory beliefs that originate from false premises.

DESCRIPTIONS AND SOLUTIONS

Most people who suffer from panic disorders also are depressed. Handly and Neff (1985) outlined and provided solutions to the "big ten" cognitive distortions that affect most anxious people:

Perfectionism. Often, a high achieving client may set unreasonably high standards for himself or herself but credit accomplishments to mere luck. *Solution:* Don't strive to achieve unrealistically high levels in everything attempted.
Rejectionitis. This is the tendency to exaggerate a single rejection by someone to the point that it effects every dimension of one's life. *Solution:* To prove that this assumption is not true, have the client list his or her good qualities, and make another list of people who are like them.
Negative focus. This is the tendency or habit of letting a negative experience obliterate all the positive dimensions. *Solution:* Go to alpha and picture all the good things about oneself, then select some positive affirmations

---

. . . the desire to be in control of our lives is entirely human; it is hardly irrational. But it can lead to irrational behavior, when we are unconsciously manipulated by our self-destructive and self-sabotaging beliefs. To be "in control" means to understand the facts of reality that bear on our life so that we are able to predict, with reasonable accuracy, the consequences of our actions. Tragedy occurs when, out of a misguided notion of control, we attempt to "adjust" reality to our beliefs, rather than to adjust our beliefs to reality. Tragedy occurs when we cling to our beliefs blindly and manipulate events without awareness of doing so, insensitive to the fact that alternative possibilities exist. Tragedy occurs when we would rather be "right" than happy, when we would rather sustain the illusion that we are "in control" than notice that reality is not the way we have told ourselves it is.

Nathaniel Branden

---

and repeat them throughout the day. (See Chapter 13, the section on meditation to reach the alpha state of awareness.)

Refusing the positives. Refusing the positives expands the "negative focus." A client may tell himself or herself that even "good" things in life are negatives, that is, choosing to be uncomfortable with thinking one is successful, refusing the positive, and inviting depression. *Solution:* When the client receives a compliment or recognition for something well done, direct the client to say "thanks" and not another word.

The white-is-black phenomenon. This occurs when a client uses neutral or even positive facts to make negative conclusions about his or her own relationships to others. For example, when someone interprets another's action as being particularly hostile to them, when in actuality the person is experiencing some discomfort (e.g., assuming that someone didn't return your call because they don't like you, when in reality they were out of town and wouldn't receive your message for another week). *Solution:* Think rationally and check reality. Have the client remind himself or herself that he or she is not responsible for another person's behavior.

Stretch-or-shrink thinking. This is the tendency of either stretching the truth into an "anxiety-producing fiction" (i.e., overreacting when one has done something that he or she is less than proud of) or shrinking from attention and accolades until one is invisible when something is done extraordinarily well. *Solution:* Apologize for human mistakes. Acknowledge self aloud, send good messages to your unconscious, which can result in pleasant dreams and positive imagery.

Creating fictional fantasies. This means letting your emotions substitute for the truth about what is happening. *Solution:* Counter fictional fantasies with the acknowledgement that distorted thoughts create negative feelings. Use emotional transfusion to change feelings at the unconscious level.

"Shoulds and oughts." These cause clients to act in ways they would prefer not to act by misconstruing responsibilities, expectations, or obligations. *Solution:* A client will need to recognize that he or she alone is responsible for his or her actions.

Mistaken identity. This is the tendency to tell oneself that he or she is bad because of a mistake. *Solution:* Try saying "I made a mistake," and let it go.

Saying "my fault." This assumes all blame and responsibility for a negative event even when the responsibility is not one's own. In reality no one can control another person. *Solution:* Express your concern, but do not accept responsibility.

| Technique | *The Cognitive Therapy Process* |

Counseling Intention: To introduce the client to specific steps in resolving problems using cognitive therapy

Description. Guide the client through the following steps:

- Make yourself aware of precisely what you are thinking when you feel anxious.
- Write or record in some way those thoughts down so that you can read them, so that you can study the exact words you are using.
- Analyze your thoughts for errors in thinking. For example, "Are you using all-or-nothing thinking, comparative thinking (I'm not as good as . . .), perfectionism, or overgeneralizing?"
- Brainstorm goals to change your unwanted behavior. A SMART goal is:

  S = Specific (Clarify and identify steps.)
  M = Motivating (Self-motivating; state the goal as "I will.")
  A = Achievable (It has a time frame and it is realistic.)
  R = Realistic (Set yourself up to win.)
  T = Trackable (Change can be measured and progress can be monitored.)

- Break the problem down to workable parts.
- Analyze possible courses of action by making separate lists of the advantages and disadvantages of pursuing and/or not pursuing each one.
- Prepare a backup plan (Plan "B") going through the same steps as required for the first plan.
- Take action (Freeman & DeWolf, 1989, pp. 18–19).

| **Technique** | *Cognitive Focusing* |

Counseling Intention: To help clients crystallize their emotional reactions to certain stimuli; to help clients clearly identify the causes of their personal unhappiness; to shift core beliefs that are irrational and replace them with a more rational belief

Description.

1. Ask the client to relax briefly, clearing the mind and focusing inwardly for the next few minutes. Changing the focus from an external to internal focus narrows attention, increasing the likelihood that images will form.
2. Present the client with an analogy to help uncover the major sources of discomfort. McMullin (1986) provided the "storeroom analogy" as follows:
   Imagine that you are sitting in a storeroom cluttered with boxes. In each box is one of your problems. Each problem has a different box, and the largest boxes contain the largest problems.

Now picture that you move the boxes, one at a time, into the corners of the room, so that you can have space to sit down. From a relatively comfortable perch in the middle of the room, survey the boxes around you carefully. Pull out the box that you most want to open, and open it.

Lift the problem out of the box and look at it. Turn it from side to side so that you can see every aspect of it. Try to step outside yourself and watch your reactions to it. (pp. 144–145)

3. Once that client has selected a problem from his or her "storeroom," ask the person to focus upon how he or she feels about the problem.
4. Instruct the client to focus on the overall emotion that best captures how he or she feels about the problem.
5. Once the overall emotion has been defined, involve the client in a careful analysis of various aspects and components of that feeling.
6. Have the client recall, in detail, other similar situations in which he or she has felt that same emotion. Have the client resonate those situations with the feelings, so that you can confirm that an association has been made between the anxiety and the situations (past or present).
7. Probe to determine what thoughts sparked the same emotion in each of these similar situations. In each setting, determine what the client has been saying to himself or herself. What meaning does the client assign to these situations.
8. Next, try to help the client switch the emotion. First, ask the client to focus on similar situations that did not incite the negative emotion. Remind him or her to not simply recall what was experienced but to try to recreate the same feelings.
9. Then, instruct the client to focus on his or her thoughts, beliefs, or what self-talk occurred during similar situations when the overall emotion was different. Guide the client through an analysis of these feelings.
10. Finally, have the client practice replacing those initial feelings (Steps 4 and 5) with those feelings in the other situations (Step 8). McMullin (1986) maintained the key to switching the emotions is switching the

---

Perspective for the Therapist: On perceptions . . .

It all depends on how we look at things, and not on how they are in themselves.

Carl Jung

•

There is a positive side and a negative side; at each moment you decide.
Bernard Gunther

thoughts. Have the client imagine those thoughts when he or she was not anxious (Step 9, rather than Step 7). Teach the client how to practice this shifting technique at home, using a variety of concrete examples from the client's own experiential repertoire. Continuous rehearsal of shifting from negative to positive emotions is necessary to assimilate the new behavior.

| Technique | *Alternative Interpretation*

Counseling Intention: To encourage the client to suspend judgement until he or she has obtained more information and to perceive the situation more objectively

Description. A client's first impression of an event is usually not the best; later judgements are often more rational. The intent of this exercise is to get the client to suspend judgement until he or she obtains more information and perceives situations more objectively. Between counseling sessions, have the client keep a written log of the worst emotions experienced during a one-week period identifying (a) the activating event and their first interpretation of this event and (b) the about the event.

After the next session, for the next week have the client continue the log, finding at least four interpretations for each event. At the next counseling session, help the client rationally decide which of the four interpretations has the most objective evidence to support the belief. The client should then be instructed to continue to find alternative interpretations and to actively suspend judgement until some time and distance provide a more objective assessment. This process should be continued for a month until the client can assimilate the procedure automatically (McMullin, 1986, p. 11).

| Technique | *Anti-catastrophic Reappraisals*

Counseling Intention: To overcome the negative emotion caused by catastrophizing (thinking the worst) situations and events

---

Perspective for the Therapist: On courage . . .

Courage is grace under pressure.

Ernest Hemingway

Description. Clients often distort reality; their exaggerations become habitual causing chronic anxiety and chronic dread of unpleasant situations. The therapist frames a new interpretation to overcorrect the negative emotion caused by catastrophizing. List the situations the client catastrophizes.

Record the damage the client anticipates for each situation on a continuum from 1-to-10.

Discuss counter-catastrophizing with the client and record the best possible thing that could happen in each of the situations. Mark the extent of the damage for this outcome.

Have the client decide, based on past experience, whether the catastrophic or best possible outcome is most likely to occur.

Have the client use the continuum to predict danger in upcoming situations that are feared. After the event actually occurs, have the client check the scale to see whether the anticipated level of damage occurred.

The client should practice counter-catastrophizing regularly until he or she can more realistically assess anticipated damage.

| Technique | *Changing Thinking Patterns and "Internal Conversations"* |

Counseling Intention: To change distorted thinking and negative self-talk

Description. Emery (1981) outlines the following procedures for changing dysfunctional thinking patterns:

maintain a continuing quest for greater self-awareness—assess your goals, dreams, feelings, attitudes, beliefs, and limitations;

recognize, keep track and challenge your "automatic thoughts," that is, the involuntary inner dialogue that occurs especially in stressful situations;

use critical thinking skills to clarify emotional reactions to an event (e.g., "Is my reaction logical, based on evidence?");

Perspective for the Therapist: On control . . .

I was a control freak. I had life by the throat, and I was saying, "You're going to give me what I want," and it wasn't. When you exercise every ounce of control in your human capability, when you will things to happen and you force them to happen and you fight for them to happen and they do not happen, you have only two choices—you can go insane, or you can relax your death grip on life.

Robert Cohen

---

when looking at a situation, consider alternative explanations and another perspective;

try to substitute positive images for negative ones, and view challenges or criticism as opportunities for change rather than condemnation; and

do something specific to change negative thoughts, keep a journal, make a plan, and monitor your progress.

Technique | *The Anxiety Formula: Knowness Versus Importance*

Counseling Intention: *To reduce the level of anxiety*

Description. With the anxiety formula, anxiety is the ***degree of known*** multiplied by the ***importance of loss.*** Have the client think about an anxiety provoking situation. (1) Rate its degree of knowness and importance from (0 to 10) to find the anxiety score. (2) Generate ideas that would help lower the unknown aspect of the situation. (3) Generate ideas that would make the event less important, then go back and redo Step 2 (Emery & Campbell, 1986). An example is as follows:

Situation: Airplane Flight
Rate degree of knowness and importance: Unknown x Importance = Level of Anxiety
                                                    9   x   10   =   90% Anxiety
What would make the event less important?   Course on fear of flying
Rate knowness and importance again: 4   x   10   =   40% Anxiety

---

Technique | *The ACT Formula: Accept, Choose, Take Action*

Counseling Intention: *To help the client focus on personal choice (Emery & Campbell, 1986)*

Description. If a client is experiencing painful, overwhelming anxiety, introduce the ACT formula:

"Accept your current reality."
"Choose to create your own vision, that is, your picture of what you want in life."
"Take action to create it."

Technique | *Create What You Want*

Counseling Intention: *To assist the client in planning for his or her vision for the future*

Perspective for the Therapist: On failure . . .

What is failure?

It is a word used to define a stage.
It is not a condemnation of character.
It is not a permanent condition.
It is not a fatal flaw.
It is not a contagious social disease.

It is a judgement about an event. How well you cope with that event in large part determines what kind of person you become. The point is to remember that it is the way you cope with failure that shapes you, not the failure itself.

Carole Hyatt
Linda Gottlieb

Description. The client should be instructed to keep a journal and to write in it 10 experiences he or she wants to create. Make each item specific and measurable. (For example, "I will walk 2 miles a day for the next month.") Put an "I choose to have" in front of each vision and say the sentence aloud. (For example, "I choose to walk 2 miles a day for the next month.") Have the client update the list as he or she reaches each desired vision (Emery & Campbell, 1986).

| Technique | *Alternative Solutions* |

Counseling Intention: To assist the client in understanding that alternatives are usually unending

Description. A client is asked to list all of the possible alternatives to a situation without any initial judgements of these alternatives. Then the counselor can assist the person in placing various value judgements on the most reasonable possible solutions. From this more limited list, the individual then can begin to weigh and select an ultimate choice.

| Technique | *Giving Constructive Criticism* |

Counseling Intention: To resolve conflict in a more positive way

Description. A formula for giving someone constructive criticism involves six steps:

Perspective for the Therapist: On psychic reality . . .

Psychic reality will always be structured around the poles of absence and difference; and human beings will always have to come to terms with that which is forbidden and that which is impossible.

Joyce McDougall

Step 1:   Give the person two compliments. Be honest, sincere, and specific.
Step 2:   Address the person using his or her name.
Step 3:   In a pleasant tone of voice, and with a pleasant look on your face, state your criticism in one or two short, clear sentences.
Step 4:   Tell the person what you would like him or her to do. Keep it simple. Set a time limit if it is appropriate to do so.
Step 5:   Offer your help, encouragement, and support.
Step 6:   Thank the person for their time and for listening.

In reality, when confronting another individual, the client should be cautioned that they may be interrupted. He or she should be encouraged to listen and acknowledge the other person and adhere to the formula. A helpful procedure is to role-play or practice the formula ahead of time.

| Technique | *Brainstorming*

Counseling Intention: To generate alternative solution to a problem

Description. The purpose of brainstorming is to generate as many ideas as you can, as fast as you can, without stopping to think about any of them. As long as you write your ideas down, you can sort them out later and decide which ones seem workable. Brainstorming guidelines:

You can brainstorm alone either with a pen and paper or on a computer screen. Or you can brainstorm with other people—a friend, a group, a class at school, your family.
Set a time limit—for example, five or ten minutes. Then write down every idea that comes to your mind, no matter how crazy or impossible it seems. Stop when time is up.
Sort the ideas, discarding the useless ones. Prioritize the rest into a list.

| Technique | *The ABCs of Stopping Unhappy Thoughts (Maultsby, 1975)*

Counseling Intention: To keep a journal on negative thoughts and feelings

Description. The client is directed to record the following in a journal when he or she notices being upset following a situation or an event:

A—Facts and events. Record the facts about the unhappy event.

B—Self-talk. Record the things you tell yourself about the event.

C—How you felt. Record how you felt.

D—Debate. Debate or dispute any statement in A that is not logical or objective.

E—Examine the future. This is how I want to feel in the future in this kind of situation.

Chapter 9

RATIONAL-EMOTIVE
AND RATIONAL BEHAVIOR
TECHNIQUES

Rational-Emotive Therapy (RET) theorizes that emotional and behavioral problems are not caused directly by events but rather by how one perceives those events. RET theorizes that emotional and behavioral problems are caused primarily by irrational beliefs that arise when clients intensify strong desires into absolute demands, that is, "musts" and "shoulds." Irrational beliefs impede some clients from working toward their goals, beliefs, and values; rational beliefs help individuals work toward their goals (Ellis, 1979, 1989).

RET employs a variety of cognitive, emotive, and behavioral techniques aimed at diminishing emotional and behavioral problems (Ellis, 1985; Ellis & Dryden, 1990). RET's main intervention is the disputation method, which has been outlined as "any process where a client's irrational beliefs and cognitive distortions are challenged and restructured for a more positive outcome" (Ellis, Sichel, Yeager, DiMattia, & DiGiuseppe, 1989, p. 49).

Two of the foremost cognitive-behavioral interventionists are Maultsby and Ellis. Maultsby is recognized for rational behavior therapy (RBT) and Ellis for rational emotive therapy (RET). In 1993, Ellis changed the name from Rational-Emotive Therapy (RET) to Rational-Emotive Behavior Therapy (REBT).

Maultsby (1975) and Ellis (1973) articulated the role of *interventionist* by demonstrating to troubled clients that through (a) their own thinking, and (b) the use of a structured strategy they can reorder their perceptions and behavior to remove the source of their difficulties.

Essentially, Ellis (1979,1985,1990) has developed an ABC theory of personality that holds that activating events (A) do not directly cause emotional and behavioral consequences (C). Rather, the emotional and behavioral consequences (C) are largely caused by one's beliefs (B) about the activating event (A). The disputation method involves identifying, debating, and challenging irrational beliefs and replacing them with rational beliefs (Ellis, 1975). Thoughts, feelings, and behavior are all interrelated.

The classic model for examining the relationships between thoughts, feelings, and behavior was developed by Ellis (1989): the A-B-C model. Point A = the activating event; point C = feelings about the event. The critical component between A and C is point B, one's self-talk. Our self-talk influences our feelings and behavior. It can be rational or irrational, functional or dysfunctional. Self-statements can become habitual responses to stress or conflict. By cognitively restructuring, the client can learn specific "coping skills" to restructure thoughts, reduce stress, and increase relatively positive or negative feelings.

| Technique | *Ellis's A-B-C-D-E Paradigm* |

Counseling Intention: To correct distorted thinking or self-defeating belief systems

Description. Albert Ellis maintained that people upset themselves via their own belief systems. Clients are taught how they falsely attribute their own upsets to outside or activating events. When feeling upset, clients are directed to examine their B's (beliefs) instead of blaming the A's (activating events).

Perspective for the Therapist: On fear and irrational beliefs . . .

Nothing in life is to be feared, it is only to be understood.

Marie Curie

•

While one person hesitates because he feels inferior, the other is busy making mistakes and becoming superior.

Henry C. Link

They are shown that activating events (A's) do not result automatically in emotional and behavioral consequences (C's), but that it is mainly the beliefs about A (i.e., B's) that are responsible for the impact at point C. By disputing (D) the irrational beliefs at point B, the effect (E) is the elimination of negative consequences (C's.)

The client may be provided with a homework exercise to begin identifying self-defeating feelings such as anger. An example is as follows:

A = (Activating event) Describe a situation about which you became angry.
B = (Beliefs) What do you tell yourself about the situation?
C = (Consequences: behavioral or emotional) Describe the upset feeling. Describe what you did because of being angry.
D = (Dispute) Question your angry thoughts, expectations, disappointments. Is there a different way of looking at the situation?
E = (Effect) What would you like to see happen? What can you change and what should you accept?

| **Technique** | *Identifying Unpleasant Emotions* |

Counseling Intention: To identify antecedents to subsequent feelings

Description. Identify the last time you were feeling a strong, unpleasant emotion. Write the emotion under "C." Under "A," write in the event before the emotion occurred. Under "B," identify what you were thinking between the event and the emotion.

A (Activating event): "My clients do not implement the action plans developed in therapy."
B (My thinking): "Maybe I come on too strongly." "Maybe I'm really a poor therapist." "She really doesn't know what is best for her."
C (My feelings and behavior): Self-doubt about skills; anger about client's lack of initiative.

Next, analyze the accuracy of the facts and events written in "A." This can be accomplished through rational self-analysis (i.e., "Where is the evidence that what you believe is true?"). In addition, one can differentiate between rational and irrational beliefs by answering the following questions:

Do the client's beliefs reflect an objective reality? Would a second party perceive the situation in the same way? Are the beliefs exaggerated and personalized?

Are the beliefs helpful to the client? (Self-destructive thoughts are usually irrational.)

Are the beliefs helpful in reducing conflicts with others or do they foster a "us versus them" mentality?

Do the beliefs help or get in the way of short- or long-term goals?

Do the beliefs reduce or enhance emotional conflict?

Write the objective version of the facts and events at "D" below. Only the event that can be recorded visually or auditorially should be listed into the "D" section (recording visually or auditorially means that it can be reproduced by camera, video camera, of tape recorder). Essentially, if the event can be recorded, it is a fact. If the event cannot be recorded, it is probably an opinion, a feeling, or an evaluation. This strategy should help the client see how misperceptions of situations can alter one's self-talk or inner dialogue that in turn affects one's emotional response. Irrational thoughts lead to negative emotional feelings. Negative emotional feelings ultimately lead to depression (Wilde, 1992, 1996).

Finally, have the client decide how he or she would like to feel in the situation you described in "D," and enter the feeling under "F." Is it realistic to have a positive emotional response to a stressful situation or is it more appropriate to accept a neutral feeling. Now have the client attend to the "E" section and develop a more rational alternative to the irrational thoughts at "B." The rational alternatives should be acceptable to the client and meet at least three of the five criteria for rational thinking. This exercise merely outlines some strategies for developing a rational plan of action and changing unwanted feelings and behaviors. This could be reframed in the following manner:

D (Objective event): "My client did not carry out his action plan."
E (My rational thinking): "He is responsible for his own behavior."
F (Desired feeling or behavior): "Relaxed with continued therapeutic interactions."

Perspective for the Therapist: On consequences . . .

Every man is his own ancestor, and every man is his own heir. He devises his own future, and he inherits his own past.

H.F. Hedge

| *Technique* | *Cognitive Restructuring* |

Counseling Intention: To recognize and stop self-defeating thoughts; to substitute self-defeating thoughts with positive, self-enhancing, or coping thoughts

Description. The client is instructed to note what he tells himself or herself before, during, and after a problem situation or setting. Further, the client is instructed to note and record his or her negative thoughts before, during, and after stressful or depressing situations for one or two weeks. The client's log should be analyzed for self-defeating and illogical thoughts and the location of negative thoughts (i.e., before, during, or after the experience).

The therapist helps the client work toward identifying more positive coping thoughts that can replace the negative ones (coping thoughts should be incompatible with self-defeating thoughts). Coping thoughts can be practiced and applied using imagery and role-playing exercises.

| *Technique* | *Perceptions Versus Reality* |

Counseling Intention: To assist the client in assuming personal responsibility for choices and actions; to shift the center of responsibility

Description. Have the client think of an incident that really made him or her angry or resentful, one that he or she still has some feelings about.

Have the client, in writing, describe the incident as if *others* were completely responsible for bringing about the event. Blame them. Make it clearly their fault.

Have the client rewrite the incident as if he or she were *solely* responsible for starting, developing, and getting with the problem. Take full account of what you could have done so that the whole problem would not have arisen.

Although the client may feel a sense of unreality about both points of view,

---

Perspective for the Therapist: On attitude . . .

Our attitude is not determined by circumstances, but by how we respond to circumstances. Our minds determine our attitude. We can respond positively or negatively. It is how we react to events themselves, that determines our attitudes.

Anonymous

---

have him or her reexamine them and see which one he or she feels most comfortable with, if it altered the opinion originally held, if he or she blames or feels like a victim.

| Technique | *Daily Activities to Help the Client Give Up Irrational Thinking*

Counseling Intention: To keep the client focused on strategies taught in counseling sessions

Description. The following activities can be assigned to clients between counseling sessions:

Pleasurable Pursuits—committing time each day to pleasurable pursuits,

Rational-Emotive Imagery—vividly picturing difficult events and practicing thinking rationally about them,

Shame-attacking Exercises—performing "silly" or "embarrassing" acts in public to demonstrate that there is no need to feel ashamed,

Courting Discomfort—deliberately doing uncomfortable things, or staying in uncomfortable situations a little longer,

Risk Taking—doing things anxiously feared,

Behavioral Rehearsal—practicing unskilled or fearful things, and

Rewarding and Penalizing—rewarding or punishing for doing or not doing something (Grieger, 1986).

| Technique | *Overcoming Resistance to Change*

Counseling Intention: To get the client to confront irrational beliefs and self-defeating behavior

Description. Resistance often exists that impedes the client from risk taking or taking responsibility for change. Examples of resistance are as follows:

Fear of Discomfort—believing that the effort to change is too difficult, that it is easier to drift along with problems than to make the effort to change them;

Fears of Disclosure and Shame—believing present feelings, actions, thoughts are inappropriate, that it would be terrible if anyone else knew it;

Feelings of Powerlessness and Hopelessness—believing that one is unable to change, that problems are too big to overcome;

Fear of Change—believing that the safety and security of present self-defeating behaviors are less risky than change;

Fear of Failure and Disapproval—believing that one must always succeed, fearing that symptoms may lead to risk failure and disapproval;

Self-punishment—believing one is a bad person and deserves to suffer; and

Discouragement—believing that disturbances can not be overcome (Grieger, 1986).

| *Technique* | *Rational-Emotive Imagery (REI)* |

Counseling Intention: To help the client think more rationally and to become less emotionally upset

Description of Negative Imagery. Picture yourself or fantasize, as vividly and intensely as you can, the details of some unpleasant activating experience (A) that has happened to you or will likely occur in the future. As you strongly imagine this event, let yourself feel distinctly uncomfortable—for example, anxious, depressed, ashamed, or hostile—at "C" (your emotional consequence). Get in touch with this disturbed feeling and let yourself fully experience it for a brief period of time. Don't avoid it; confront it, face it, and feel it.

When you have actually felt this disturbed emotion for a while, push yourself to change this feeling in your gut, so that instead you *only* feel keenly disappointed, regretful, annoyed, or irritated but *not* anxious, depressed, guilty, or hostile. Do not think that you cannot do this. You *can* get in touch with your gut-level feelings and push yourself to change them so that you experience different feelings.

Perspective for the Therapist: On life experiences . . .

We must insist on talking to patients only about what they actually experience. In other words, go right through the defenses, rather than lose our efforts in helping them strengthen their already strong defenses. The only thing we really deal with in our relationships with patients is their actual life experience—not the stock they came from, their heredity, their genes, the biological propensities to growth. All we deal with is their reaction to their life experience; how much of it isn't integrated; how much they can handle and how much they can't handle, but have to postpone or avoid or deny. And the more infantile the personality, the more they handle by avoidance.

Elvin Semrad

Push yourself only to feel disappointed or irritated; look at what you have done in your head to *make yourself* have these new, appropriate feelings. Upon close examination, you will recognize that you have in some manner changed your *Belief System* (or B.S.) at "B," and have thereby changed your emotional *Consequences,* at "C," so that you now feel regretful or annoyed rather than anxious, depressed, guilty, or hostile.

Let yourself clearly see what you have done, what important changes in your Belief System you have made. *Become fully aware of the new beliefs (B) that create your new emotional consequences (C) regarding the unpleasant Activating Experience (A) that you keep imagining or fantasizing.* See exactly what beliefs you have changed in your head to make yourself feel badly but not emotionally upset.

Keep repeating the process. Make yourself feel disturbed; then make yourself feel displeased but not disturbed. Keep repeating the process. See exactly what you did in your head to change your feelings. Keep practicing until you can easily, after you fantasized highly unfortunate experiences at "A," feel upset at "C"; change your feelings at "C" to one of disappointment but not disturbance.

Practice REI for at least 10 minutes every day for the next few weeks. You will get to the point where whenever you think of this kind of unpleasant event, or when it actually occurs in practice, you will tend to feel easily and automatically displeased rather than emotionally upset (Ellis, 1975, pp. 211–212).

Description of Positive Imagery. To employ positive imagery and thinking, picture to yourself as vividly and intensely as you can the details of some unpleasant activating experience (A) that has happened to you or will likely occur in the future. Picture the situation at "A" at its very worst. Let yourself feel distinctly uncomfortable—anxious, ashamed, depressed—at "C," your emotional consequence. Fully experience this disturbed feeling.

As you feel upset at "C," notice what you keep telling yourself at B (your belief system or B.S.) to make yourself feel disturbed. When you clearly see these Beliefs, Dispute them at "D" as you would in the usual kind of Disputing that RET or rational behavior training (RBT) teaches you to do.

Now, as you see these irrational beliefs and vigorously dispute them, strongly fantasize how you would feel and behave *after* you started giving them up and *after* you started believing, instead, rational beliefs about what keeps happening to you at "A." Intensely picture yourself (a) disbelieving your irrational beliefs and believing your rational ideas about obnoxious events that may occur at "A"; (b) feeling appropriately displeased and disappointed rather than inappropriately depressed and hostile at "C"; and (c) acting in a concerned instead of an upset manner at "E."

Keep practicing this procedure so that you first imagine something unfortunate or disadvantageous; then make yourself feel depressed, hostile, or otherwise disturbed about your image. Then see what irrational beliefs you hold to create your disturbance; then work on changing these beliefs. Then strongly picture yourself disbelieving these ideas and feelings and acting in accordance with your new rational philosophies of being only concerned and displeased rather than depressed and hostile (Ellis & Harper, 1975).

| Technique | *Disputing Irrational Beliefs (DIBS)*

Counseling Intention: To teach clients to seek out, discover, and dispute their irrational beliefs

Description. If you want to increase your rationality and to reduce your irrational beliefs, you can spend at least 10 minutes every day asking yourself the following questions and carefully thinking through the appropriate answers. Write each question on paper, or record the questions and answers on a tape recorder.

What irrational belief do I want to dispute and surrender? "I must always be liked by others."

Can I rationally support this belief? "No."

What evidence exists of the falseness of this belief? "Many indications exists that this belief is false." "No law of the universe says that everyone must like me." "No evidence exists for any absolute must that others should like me."

Does any evidence exist of the truth of this belief?

What worst things could actually happen to me if I don't get what I think I must?

Perspective for the Therapist: On loneliness . . .

People are lonely because they build walls instead of bridges.

Joseph F. Newton

Perspective for the Therapist: On fear . . .

The world is really not so unknowable. If I but keep my eyes from seeing too much, my ears from hearing too much, my mind from thinking too much, it becomes quite reasonable. I can even persuade myself I see all there is. If I but worship this deity, adhere to this virtue, suffer that pain, insist on that plan, the world becomes quite manageable. If I but hush the voice of possibility both within and about me, the fears grows quieter, I am no longer afraid, so much.

James F.T. Bugental

| Technique | *Disputing Irrational Beliefs by using "A-FROG"*

Counseling Intention: To provide a five-step thought process to think and behave more rationally

Description. Use the acronym A-FROG to decide if one is thinking rationally.

A—Does it keep me *a*live?
F—Do I *f*eel better as a result?
R—Is it based on *r*eality?
O—Does it help me get along with *o*thers?
G—Does it get me to my *g*oals? (Beck & Emery, 1985)

| Technique | *Rational Self-analysis (RSA)*

Counseling Intention: To provide a systematic way to change unpleasant emotions and to follow up on inappropriate behavior (Sabatino & Smith, 1990)

Description of Event or Situation. Record (write or tape record) just what happened—not what you think about it, just a description of the event. Address the following:

Self-talk or opinion—Record what you said to yourself about the event.
Emotions and actions—Record the emotions and actions that you experienced.
Rational challenges—Take each statement you made and substitute a rational statement based upon what you know to be fact. Ask why you tell yourself each of these things.
New ways of thinking and feeling—Record new feelings and the thinking that might lead to solving the problem.

Chapter **10**

CLASSIC BEHAVIORAL TECHNIQUES

The basic principles of learning and behavioral change are classics in the school of behavior therapy. Behavioral techniques have been used with much success to eliminate undesirable behavior such as smoking, overeating, nail-biting, losing weight, improving study skills, and coping with stress. Krumboltz and Thoresen (1976) outlined behavior principles for strengthening and developing appropriate as well as principles for eliminating inappropriate behavior.

Expanded behavior intervention programs will increasingly incorporate a variety of efficacious strategies and techniques, some operant, some cognitive-mediational, some observational. Cognitive-behavioral approaches can be integrated to provide the optimal combination of strategies to enhance the adjustment of the client.

| *Technique* | *Affirming New Positive Behavior* |

Counseling Intention: To strengthen or teach a new behavior

Description of Positive Reinforcement Principle. To increase or enhance a certain activity, provide a reward immediately after each correct performance. The reward is something the person values; it may have material value (e.g., clothes or money), social praise by a support group (e.g., compliments or encouragement), or an opportunity to participate in a pleasant activity (e.g., dining out). The positive reinforcement cycle is "response-then-reward" with the distinct prerequisite that reward does not occur unless the behavior occurs first.

Description of Token or Point Reward Paradigms. To maintain the behavior until it is well established in the client's repertoire of positive responses, a point or token system can be established. The token or point system is set up as a contract where the recipient receives points for positive behaviors, accumulates them, and cashes them in for a desirable behavior. This is applicable for increasing such behaviors as assertiveness, weight loss, and nonviolent behavior. For example, after losing so many pounds (such as two pounds a week) and accumulating so many points, one might "cash in" the points for new clothes. The point system gives the client small rewards for the small successes toward the larger goal.

| **Technique** | *Developing New Positive Behavior* |

Counseling Intention: To develop new behavior

Description of the Successive Approximations Principle or Shaping. Each small successive step toward the final behavior is rewarded. This is most applicable when teaching a behavior that someone had never attempted before such as learning the motor skills of riding a bike or learning to ski (e.g., the new skier begins on the beginner's slopes and upon mastery, proceeds to the intermediate and then to the advanced slopes).

Description of the Principle of Modeling. Modeling is essentially learning by example or learning by observation. It is teaching a new way of behavior by showing how an effective person performs the desired behavior. This strategy has been successful in assertiveness training, teaching teachers to teach, fear-related behaviors, delinquents, addicts, and helping professionals.

Description of the Principle of Cueing. To establish new behavior for a specific time, a cue can be established to signal for the appropriate behavior just before the action is expected.

Description of the Discrimination Principle. To encourage a particular behavior under a particular set of circumstances but not another, the client should be assisted in identifying the cues that differentiate the circumstances and establish the reward only when the action is appropriate to the cue.

| **Technique** | *Maintaining New Positive Behavior* |

Counseling Intention: To maintain new behavior

Description of Intermittent Reinforcement. To encourage an individual to continue performing an established behavior with few or no rewards, gradually and intermittently decrease the frequency with which the correct behavior is rewarded.

Description of Contingency Contracting. To facilitate a client's goal for behavior change, contingency contracting may be helpful. It can be broken down into six steps:

1. The therapist and client identify the problem to be solved.
2. Data are collected to verify the baseline frequency rate for the occurrence of the undesired behavior.
3. The therapist and the client set mutually acceptable goals.
4. Specific counseling techniques and methods are selected for attaining the goals.
5. The counseling techniques are evaluated for observable and measurable change.
6. Step 4 is repeated if the selected counseling techniques are not effective. If the techniques are effective, a maintenance plan is developed to maintain the new behavior.

| Technique | *Stopping Inappropriate Behavior*

Counseling Intention: To stop inappropriate behavior

Description of the Principle of Extinction. Extinction is removing a pleasant consequence, resulting in decreased responding. To stop someone from acting in an undesirable way, try to arrange conditions so that the person receives no rewards following the undesired act.

Description of the Principle of Alternative Behavior. This principle for eliminating undesirable behavior involves rewarding an alternative action that is inconsistent with or cannot be performed at the same time as the undesired act. An example could be substituting positive self-talk in the place of negative self-talk.

Perspective for the Therapist: On power . . .

Most powerful is he who has himself in his own power.

Seneca

Description of the Principle of Satiation. To decrease a behavior allow the individual to continue (or insist he or she continue) to perform the undesired act until he or she tires of it.

| **Technique** | *Anger Expression*

Counseling Intention: To get in touch with one's anger; to take responsibility for anger expression

Description. A prerequisite to expressing anger is the acknowledgment that it does exist. Once the anger is owned, it can be either eliminated through rational disputation or channeled into appropriate more assertive expression. Teaching the client to state "I am angry" over and over, louder and louder, can be used to bring the client in touch with his or her anger.

This process is particularly successful in a group setting. Pounding rubber dolls, cushions, pillows, or other indoor-safe toys can be used to express anger in a less threatening way. Behavioral rehearsal then can be taught to the client for future encounters. By rehearsing the desired behavior through role-play with the therapist, the client often feels more competent and successful in future relationships.

It may be helpful to the client to develop a relaxation response when beginning to feel angry or annoyed. Learning stress-inoculation techniques or learning how to express anger assertively may be beneficial. Developing a rational belief system and overcoming irrational beliefs, such as the world should be fair, would be another intervention.

| **Technique** | *Anxiety Management Training*

Counseling Intention: To develop self-control, self-confidence, and self-management of anxiety

Description. Relaxation training and goal-rehearsal are prerequisite skills in which the client should become proficient prior to anxiety management training.

Perspective for the Therapist: On defenses . . .

A man can fail many times, but he isn't a failure until he begins to blame someone else.

John Burroughs

The client is directed to generate anxiety and the concomitant sensations, cognitions, and emotions. Following this anxiety provoking experience, the client is directed to perform the opposite behavior, that is, to elicit relaxation and to dwell on calm sensations, to picture peaceful images, to dispute irrational ideas, and to concentrate on tranquil and relaxing thoughts.

Technique | *Behavior Rehearsal*

Counseling Intention: To assist the client to assimilate new behavior

Description. Clients often need to practice new behaviors in the confines of a secure therapeutic setting. Through role-play the therapist assumes the role of the individual. The client then can confront (e.g., therapist is the employer; client is the employee), and the client practices the new behavior as an actual encounter. The dialogue should be video-taped so that the therapist and client can critique the playback. Roles are reversed and the same procedure is followed. Behavior rehearsal and video playbacks are continued until the therapist and client are satisfied with the client's performance. To help the client meet his or her goal, the therapist should plan an intervention as follows:

Specify the target behavior, what the client wants to change.
Identify the setting or situation for which the skill is needed.
Construct a hierarchy (from least threatening to most threatening) of settings or situations to practice the targeted skill.
Beginning with the least threatening setting or situation, have the client engage in a rehearsal (role-play) of the targeted skill. Give the client feedback about the strengths or weaknesses of the assimilation of the targeted skill. Feedback can be enhanced with a video playback. Assign homework consisting of in vivo rehearsal of the targeted skill.
Determine when the client has satisfactorily demonstrated the assimilation of the targeted skills and proceed up the hierarchy to client mastery.

Technique | *Thought-Stopping or Thought-Blocking*

Counseling Intention: To eliminate self-defeating or illogical thinking (one that is based on unrealistic fears and assumptions); to control or eliminate negative ideas

Description. Thought stopping has proven effective in helping clients who obsessively ruminate on the same thoughts all day long. Clients can learn to cope more effectively in an anxiety-producing situation by practicing what he or she

---

Perspective for the Therapist: On wellness . . .

Healthy people, research shows, see themselves as liked, wanted, acceptable, able and worthy. Not only do they feel that they are people of dignity and worth, but they behave as though they were. Indeed, it is in this factor of how a person sees himself that we are likely to find the most outstanding differences between high and low self-image people. It is not the people who feel that they are liked and wanted and acceptable and able who fill our prisons and mental hospitals. Rather it is those who feel deeply inadequate, unliked, unwanted, unaccepted, and unable.

Donald E. Hamachek

---

will say the next time it occurs. They should be encouraged to rehearse appropriate replies, mentally practicing the response. A simple method of combatting certain obsessive and intrusive thoughts is simply to scream "STOP" (subvocally) over and over again. The client is instructed to imagine himself or herself in a situation or setting that produces an irrational thought sequence (e.g., I am in my boss' office with a new idea to present, he won't give me the time; he really thinks I'm stupid). The procedure is as follows:

Ask the client to verbalize the thoughts that are occurring as he or she imagines the scene.

When the client starts to verbalize nonproductive thinking, the therapist interrupts the client with a loud "stop" and handclap or the flicking of the wrists with a rubber band.

The client processes what happened in this self-defeating chain when it was abruptly interrupted by the therapist.

The procedure is repeated with the client interrupting the nonproductive thinking overtly (aloud) and covertly (imagined).

The client is instructed to continue covert and overt interruption to self-defeating thoughts as they occur in his or her daily experiences.

Rathus and Nevid (1977) modified the thought stopping technique listed above by using a tape recorder. The procedure is as follows:

Have the client outline clearly the content of the negative ruminative thoughts.

Construct two or three statements that oppose the helplessness and self-defeating nature of the ruminations.

Have the client record in his or her own voice, the strongly stated command "STOP!" followed immediately by the assertive, counterruminative statements, spoken clearly and affirmatively.

Sitting in a comfortable position, have the client purposefully ruminate the distressing thoughts. Press play on the recorder. The recording disrupts the ruminations and provides assertive, counterruminative statements.

Repeat the procedure ten times in a row, three or four times a day for two weeks. After that time frame, use the procedure ten times in a row once daily for another couple of weeks (pp. 33–34).

| Technique | *Self-management* |

Counseling Intention: To empower client to master and manage their own behavior

Description. The major difference between self-management and other procedures is that the client assumes major responsibilities for carrying out the program including arranging own contingencies or reinforcements. To benefit from self-management strategies clients must use the strategy regularly and consistently. The client should be instructed to do the following:

Select and define a behavior to increase or decrease.

Self-record the frequency of the behavior for a week to establish a baseline measure (i.e., the present level before the implementation of self-management procedures). Record (a) the setting in which it occurs, (b) the antecedent events leading to the behavior, and (c) the consequences resulting from the behavior.

Using self-monitoring, the client should proceed either to increase or to decrease the baseline of behavior, depending on the client's goal. The self-monitoring should occur for two weeks. A contract with the client will reinforce this process.

Change the setting and the antecedent events leading up to the target behavior.

Change the consequences that reinforce the target behavior.

Evaluate the use of self-management on the targeted behavior at the end of the contractual period. Arrange a plan to maintain the new, more desirable behavior.

Perspective for the Therapist: On failure . . .

Error is discipline through which we advance.

William Ellery Channing

| Technique | *Goal Rehearsal or Coping Imagery* |

Counseling Intention: To rehearse a new skill or situation

Description. Goal-rehearsal implies the deliberate and thorough visualization of each step in the process of assimilating a new behavior. The deliberate picturing or coping imagery of a new situation enhances transfer to the actual event. Clients should be encouraged to be realistic in reaching their goal (i.e., not expect perfection). For example, an individual may experience a severe panic attack when called on to speak in public. He or she may picture the audience scene vividly, replete with all the anxious feelings toward the situation that may emerge with a feeling of accomplishment if three out of five symptoms are reduced.

| Technique | *The Step-up Technique* |

Counseling Intention: To decrease anxiety and panic attacks to upcoming events

Description. Some clients can be paralyzed by anxiety or panic about upcoming events such as a public speech, job interview, or a blind date. The step-up technique consists of picturing the worst thing that can possibly happen and then imagining oneself coping with the situation—surviving even the most negative outcome. Once the client successfully pictures himself or herself coping with the most unlikely catastrophes deliberately called into the imagination, anticipatory anxiety tends to recede. When the real situation occurs, the individual may feel less anxious. Difficult cases may require self-instruction training (Lazarus, 1977, p. 240).

| Technique | *Self-instruction Training* |

Counseling Intention: To directly influence clients to change what they say to themselves

Description. To break a chain of negative feelings and sensations such as fear, anger, pain, and guilt. Meichenbaum (1977) and Ellis (1962) have shown empirically that negative self-talk contributes to many peoples' failures and anxiety. On the other end of the continuum, the deliberate use of positive, self-creative statements can facilitate successful coping.

Lazarus (1977) cited the following sequence of self-instruction to use with a client who is experiencing anticipatory anxiety over an upcoming event: "I will develop a plan for what I have to do instead of worrying. I will handle the situation one step at a time. If I become anxious, I will pause and take in a few deep breaths. I do not have to eliminate all fear; I can keep it manageable. I will focus on what I need to do. When I control my ideas, I control my fear. It will get easier each time I do it" (p. 238).

| Technique | *Systematic Desensitization*

Counseling Intention: To teach anxiety reduction strategies and self-control skills to clients

Description. Clients experiencing public speaking anxiety, test anxiety, nightmares, fear of flying, fear of death, fear of criticism or rejection, acrophobia (fear of heights), agoraphobia (fear of open places), or other anxiety-provoking situation can often benefit from this approach.

Desensitization should not be used when the client's anxiety is vague or free-floating (Foa, Stekette, & Ascher, 1980). Clients with many fears or with general, pervasive anxiety may benefit more from cognitive change strategies.

Perspective for the Therapist: On fear . . .

There are all kinds of fear:

Fear of being laughed at
Fear of being different
Fear of being left out
Fear of appearing too smart
Fear of being stupid
Fear of being rejected
Fear of success
Fear of failure
Fear of being weak
Fear of being alone

Fear can be a killer.
It can kill:
love, humor, enthusiasm, warmth, growth, curiosity, sensitivity,
understanding, and compassion.

Anonymous

Description. According to Wolpe (1982) systematic desensitization is "one of a variety of methods for breaking down neurotic anxiety response habits in piecemeal fashion. A physiological state inhibitory of anxiety is induced in the patient by means of muscle relaxation, and he or she is then exposed to a weak anxiety-evoking stimulus for a few seconds. If the exposure is repeated several times, the stimulus progressively loses its ability to evoke anxiety. Successively "stronger" stimuli are then introduced and similarly treated" (p. 133).

Systematic desensitization consists of the gradual replacement of a learned fear or anxiety response with a more appropriate response such as the feeling of relaxation or a feeling of being in control. The three basic steps involved in systematic desensitization are (a) construction of hierarchy of anxiety-provoking scenes, (b) training in deep muscle relaxation or coping response, and (c) the visualization of scenes from the hierarchy while experiencing deep relaxation. Components of systematic desensitization consist of the following:

1. **Identification of Anxiety-Provoking Situations.** The counselor and client must ascertain the specific anxiety-provoking situations associated with the fear; specific emotion-provoking situations must be identified. The client can be instructed to observe and to keep a log of the anxiety-provoking situations as they occur during the week, noting what was going on, where and with whom, and rating the level of anxiety on a scale of 1 (low) to 10 (high).

2. **Construction of a Hierarchy of Stimulus Situations.** A hierarchy typically contains 10 to 20 items of aversive situations. The client and the counselor can begin generating items during the session. The client can be instructed to generate items during the following week on 3″ x 5″ index cards. The cards then can be rank ordered from the least stressful situation at the bottom and successfully more stressful items in an ascending order (i.e., from least to most anxiety provoking).

3. **Selection and Teaching of Counterconditioning or Coping Responses.** For desensitization to be successful, the client must learn to respond in a way that either inhibits anxiety or creates response to cope with anxiety. The counselor selects the most appropriate counterconditioning or coping response and trains the client in the procedure. The anxiety-inhibiting or counterconditioning response most used in desensitization is deep-muscle relaxation. Other examples of counterconditioning or coping responses include emotive imagery (focusing on pleasant scenes during desensitization), meditation (focus on breathing and counting), assertion responses, music, and coping thoughts (whisper or subvocalize coping statements, e.g.,"I can do this.").

Teaching muscle-relaxation response will take several sessions to complete. Identification of hierarchy items should not occur simultaneously with relaxation; however, teaching counterconditioning or coping response can occur simultaneously with hierarchy construction. Teaching should be continued until the client can discriminate different levels of anxiety and can achieve a state of relaxation. It is helpful to have the client rate the felt level of stress or anxiety on a scale of 1 to 10 before and after each teaching session. Daily homework practice also should be a requirement.

4. **Evaluation of Client's Capacity to Generate Images.** The client's capacity to generate images is critical to the success of this procedure. Marquis, Morgan, & Piaget (1973) proposed four criteria for creating effective imagery:

- the client must be able to imagine the scene completely with detail to touch, sound, smell, and sight sensations;
- the scene should be imagined in such a way that the client is a participant not an observer;
- the client should be able to switch a scene on and off upon instruction; and
- the client should be able to hold a particular scene as instructed without drifting off or changing the scene (p. 10).

Each scene in the hierarchy is paired with the counterconditioning or coping response so that the client's anxiety is inhibited or diminished. Each scene-presentation session should be preceded by a training session involving the designated counterconditioning or coping response. Successive scene presentation always begins with the last item successfully completed at the preceding session. Typically, when the client visualizes an item and reports anxiety associated with the visualization, the client is instructed to remove or stop the image, then to relax away the tension.

A helpful procedure is to have a signaling system between the counselor and the client. One method advocated by Wolpe (1982) is to instruct the client to raise the left index finger one inch as soon as a clear image of the item is formed. Wolpe presents the item for a specified time (usually between 7 to 10 seconds) and then asks the client to stop the image and to rate the level of anxiety felt during the visualization on a scale of 1 to 10. An alternative approach is to have client imagine the scene and to indicate when anxiety is felt by raising an index finger.

5. **Steps in Gradually Prolonging Exposure to an Anxiety-provoking Situation.** Rathus and Nevid (1977) suggested reducing some fears by gradually prolonging exposure to the anxiety-provoking situation. Fears

amiable to these conditions include fear of being in a small room, fear of hospital rooms, and fears of handling sharp tools.

- First, ascertain that the target situation or thing meets two requirements: (a) the client can tolerate brief exposure to the target, and (b) the client has complete control over the duration of exposure to the target.
- Create a situation in which the client can readily expose himself or herself to the target and then readily remove self.
- The client then places himself or herself in the target situation until he or she begins to feel discomfort. The client should maintain self in the situation for only a few moments longer.
- The client leaves the situation and relaxes, breathing deeply and focusing on a peaceful scene.
- After re-achieving relaxation, the client should return to the fear-inducing situation until discomfort is experienced. Remain a few minutes longer and then leave.

Through gradually prolonging exposure to a fear-inducing situation, and then allowing the physical sensations of fear either to dissipate or to be replaced by the physical sensation of relaxation, ability to remain in the anxiety-provoking situation will become stronger (p. 57).

6. **Homework and Follow-up.** Homework should include daily practice of the selected relaxation procedure, visualization of the hierarchy items completed to date. The client also should be encouraged to participate in real-life situations that correspond to situations covered in hierarchy-item visualization during counseling sessions.

Sample Hierarchy: Test Anxiety

(Least Anxiety-provoking situation = 1; Most anxiety-provoking situation = 18)

1. Taking a course examination three months from now.
2. Two months before taking course examination.
3. One month before taking course examination.
4. Three weeks before taking course examination.
5. Two week before taking course examination.
6. One week before taking course examination.
7. Four days before taking course examination.
8. Three days before taking course examination.
9. Two days before taking course examination.

10. One day before taking course examination.
11. Morning of taking course examination.
12. Three hours before taking course examination.
13. Two hours before taking course examination.
14. One hour before taking course examination.
15. Thirty minutes before taking course examination.
16. Entering building where course examination is to be given.
17. Entering room where course examination is to be given.
18. Examiner walks in the room with course examination.

| *Technique* | *Confronting Shyness* |

Counseling Intention: To assist the client in becoming more assertive

Description. Three simple guidelines can be considered when assertive behavior has implications:

1. The best way to get what you want is to ask for it.
2. The best way not to get what you do not want is to say no to it.
3. The best way to get someone to stop doing something you do not want the person to do is to tell him or her how those actions make you feel.

Assertiveness implies a special type of self-disclosure. Do not avoid expressing "negative" feelings. Negative feelings are just as important as positive ones. Focus on first person "I" language to signify that the statement you are making is an indication of your own feelings (Wassmer, 1978).

| *Technique* | *Cost and Benefits* |

Counseling Intention: To assess missed opportunities for growth

Description. Does shyness cost anything? Has the client missed any opportunities or passed by any unique experiences because he or she is shy? Have the client make an itemized cost.

Perspective for the Therapist: On assertiveness . . .

I have an absolute right to be who I am, to think what I think, to feel what I feel, and to want what I want.

Robert Wassmer

Shyness Costs

Time of Your Life	Valued Event, Opportunity That Was Delayed or Diminished	Personal Consequence to You
1.		

Technique	*Shyness Journal*

Counseling Intention: To evaluate dimensions of shyness

Description. Keep a journal of the times you feel shy. Write down the time, what happened, your reaction, and the consequences for you.

Shyness Journal

Time	Situation or Setting	Physical Symptoms	Mental Notation Reactions	Consequences (+) (-)
3rd bell	U. S. Government class—discussion of daily current events	Heart pounding, nervous, look down, avoid eye contact	"I can't remember anything I read this morning. I'm going to fail this class; I'll have to go to summer school."	"I've lost another opportunity for my grade. Time is running out." Panic.

Technique	*Undoing Negative Self-talk*

Counseling Intention: To identify circumstances around negative inner dialogue

Description. Have the client make a list of his or her weaknesses. Put them on the left side of the page. Then put the opposite positive statements on the right side. An example is shown below:

Weaknesses	**Truth**
"No one who knows me likes me."	"Everyone who really knows me, like Jake, Jan, and Jessica, likes me."
"There are few things about me that are attractive."	"I have a lot of attractive features—my eyes, my hair, and my teeth."

| Technique | *Write Yourself a Letter* |

Counseling Intention: To identify and validate personal attributes that are positive

Description. Write yourself a letter focusing on your positive attributes or record a message about your successes, hopes, and possibilities and play it back to listen to it.

| Technique | *First-time Talking* |

Counseling Intention: To focus on critical social skills

Description. If you find that you have a difficult time talking to "anyone," try some of the following less threatening experiences.

Call information and ask for the telephone numbers of people you want to call. Thank the operator and note his or her reaction.

Call the local discount department store and check on the price of something advertised in the paper.

Call a radio talk show, compliment their format and then ask a question.

Call a local movie theater and ask for the discounted show times.

Call the library and ask the reference librarian some question about the population in your town or the United States.

Call a restaurant and make reservations for four, then call back within the hour and cancel them. Thank the reservation desk and note their reaction.

| Technique | *Saying Hello* |

Counseling Intention: To begin an experiential hierarchy of anxiety-provoking situations

Description. On campus, in hallways at school, or at work, smile and say hello to people you do not know.

Perspective for the Therapist: On merit . . .

If you wish your merit to be known, acknowledge that of other people.

Oriental Proverb

| Technique | *Beginning a Dialogue with a Stranger*

Counseling Intention: To continue structured interpersonal experiences

Description. An ideal way to practice initial conversational skills is to initiate a safe conversation with strangers in public places, such as grocery store lines, theater lines, the post office, a doctor's waiting room, lottery lines, the bank, the library, or the lunchroom. Start a conversation about a "common experience" such as "It looks like mystery meat for lunch again." "I hope this will be my lucky lotto ticket." "Have you seen "Sleepless in Seattle" [or recently released movie]?

| Technique | *Giving and Accepting Compliments*

Counseling Intention: To provide an opportunity to integrate social skills into interpersonal relationships

Description. Giving and accepting compliments is an easy way to start a conversation and make the other person feel good about themselves. Yet it is probably the most overlooked "ice breaker" between people. Suggestions on items about which to comment include the following:

> What a person is wearing—"That's a cool jacket."
> How a person looks—"I like your haircut."
> A skill—"You sure know how to catch those waves."
> Personality trait—"I love your laugh."
> Possessions—"That car is awesome!"

To get further into the conversation, simply ask a question: "What an awesome car. How long have you had it?"

| Technique | *Starting a Conversation*

Counseling Intention: To identify comfort levels in interacting with others

Description. A conversation can be started in a number of ways. Choose the one that is most appropriate and comfortable for you.

> **Introduce yourself.** "Hello, my name is _____." (Practice this in a mirror at home.) This is best practiced when you are at gatherings where everyone is a stranger to you.

Give a compliment and then follow it up with a question. "That's a terrific suit. Where did you get it?"

Request help. Make it obvious you need it and be sure the other person can provide it. "Last time I went to this library, I used the card catalogue. How can I find the works of Carl Rogers with this computer terminal?"

Try honesty and self-disclosure. When you make an obviously personal statement, it will create a positive, sympathetic response. Be honest and say, "I'm not sure what I'm doing here. I'm really quite shy."

Cultivate your normal social graces. "Looks like you need a refill; let me get it for you; I'm headed that way." "Here, let me help you with those groceries."

| Technique | *Keeping the Conversation Going* |

Counseling Intention: To provide the client with strategies to sustain a conversation

Description.   Once you have initiated a conversation, there are several techniques you can use to keep the conversation going:

Ask a question that is either factual—"Can you believe how poorly the Redskins look this year?"—or personal—"How do you feel about gun control?"

Offer one of your own personal stories or opinions. Read a lot about some political or cultural issues and become knowledgeable about them, for example, the national deficit or violence in society. Come up with a few interesting things that have happened to you recently and turn them into brief interesting stories, for example, registering for classes, incidents on the job, a new video game, learning to surf or rollerblade, or encounters with teachers, parents, brothers, and sisters. When you meet people, be ready with several stories to tell or interesting comments to make. Practice ahead of time in the mirror or on a tape recorder.

Get the other person to talk about himself or herself—his or her interests, hobbies, work, education, etc.

Express interest in the other person's expertise—"How were you able to land a job like that?" "How did you make it through Gaskin's class?"

Above all, share your reactions to what is taking place at that moment while you are interacting. Relate your thoughts or feelings about what the other person has said or done (Zimbardo, 1977, p. 180).

| Technique | *Becoming More Outgoing*

Counseling Intention: To increase the client's interpersonal repertoire of experiences

Description. Start with the easiest reaching-out exercise and progress to those more difficult. Record your reactions to each of these opportunities.

Introduce yourself to a new person in one of your classes.

Invite someone who is going your way to walk with you.

Ask someone you do not know if you can borrow 25 cents for a phone call. Arrange to pay them back.

Find someone of the opposite sex in your class. Call him or her on the phone and ask about the latest class assignment.

Stand in line at a grocery store. Start a conversation about the line with whomever is near you.

Ask three people for directions.

Go to the beach, swimming pool, or sports stadium and converse with two or three strangers you meet.

Notice someone who needs help in school or class. Offer to help.

Invite someone to eat with you.

Say "Hi" to five new people during the week. Try to provoke a smile and return "Hi" from them.

| Technique | *Making a Date with the Opposite Sex*

Counseling Intention: To decrease irrational thoughts of rejection

Description. Dating is a social contact that is anxiety provoking for many. Shy daters feel more vulnerable to irrational thoughts of rejection.

Make your date by telephone initially. Be prepared ahead of time and have two specific activities in mind.

When you contact the person by phone, identify yourself by name and explain when you met (if applicable). "This is Jim Thompson. I met you at the yearbook signing party."

Be sure you are recognized.

Pay the person a compliment related to your last meeting, one that recognizes their talent, values, or position on an issue. "You really did a great job designing the cover of the yearbook."

Perspective for the Therapist: On potential . . .

Joy is the feeling that comes from the fulfillment of one's potential.
Fulfillment brings to an individual the feeling that he can cope with his
environment; the sense of confidence in himself as a significant, competent,
lovable person who is capable of handling situations as they arise, able to
use fully his own capacities, and free to express his feelings.

William C. Schutz

Be assertive in requesting a date: "I was wondering if you'd like to come
to a movie with me this Saturday?" Be specific in your request, state the
activity in mind, and state the time it will take place.

If "yes," decide together on the movie and the time. End the conversation
smoothly, politely, and quickly.

If "no," suggest an alternative such as a more informal get together. "How
about meeting for drinks after work on Monday—my treat?"

If the answer is still "no," politely end the conversation. Refusal is not
necessarily rejection. There may not be enough interest or there may be
previous commitments—school, work, or family commitments.

Chapter 11

PERSON-CENTERED TECHNIQUES

Person-centered counseling assumes that each individual is endowed with the urge to expand, to develop, to mature, and to reach self-actualization (Hansen, Stevic, & Warner, 1986). It is the only major therapeutic approach that relies on the counselee's innate movement toward growth. Individuals are viewed as self-healing, needing a warm, supportive environment to reach higher levels of self-fulfillment.

The counselor-client relationship continues to be considered a vital ingredient in psychotherapy (Gelso & Carter, 1985; Henry, Schacht, & Strupp, 1986). Counseling relationships differ from other relationships. In daily relationships between family and friends, for example, communication is reciprocal, focusing on give-and-take statements that may offer advice, judgements, or personal perspectives.

The major barrier to interpersonal communication lies in our inherent tendency to judge others, that is, to approve or to disapprove of the statements of the other person. In the counseling relationship, however, communication is focused on the person experiencing difficulty and is nonreciprocal. Rogers (1986) described the three facilitative conditions as (a) "genuineness, realness, or congruence;" (b) "acceptance, or caring, or prizing-unconditional positive regard;" and (c) "empathic understanding." Rogers maintained that

> There is a body of steadily mounting research evidence that, by and large, supports the view that when these facilitative conditions

are present, changes in personality and behavior do indeed occur. Such research has been carried on in this and other countries from 1949 to the present. Studies have been made of changes in attitude and behavior in psychotherapy, in degree of learning in school, and in the behavior of schizophrenics. In general they are confirming. (p. 198)

A number of studies have reported improved psychological adjustment, greater tolerance for frustration, decreased defensiveness, accelerated learning, and less tangible improvements such as increased self-esteem, and congruence between one's ideal and real self. The works of Carkhuff and Berenson (1967) and Truax and Carkhuff (1967) have validated the important contributions that the variables of empathy, respect, and genuineness make to the counseling process.

Researchers have acknowledged that conditions proposed by Rogers for counseling are sufficient to bring change to the client. Through person-centered counseling, clients have enhanced their self-esteem and also "tend to shift the basis for their standards from other people to themselves" (Corsini & Wedding, 1989, p. 157). One major difference between person-centered counseling and other approaches is the increased responsibility placed upon the client compared with that assumed by the counselor (Brammer & Shostrom, 1982).

Core conditions or communication strategies from this perspective are presented in the following paragraphs.

Unconditional Positive Regard

Possessing unconditional positive regard is accepting the client without judging the behavior, event, or feeling as good or bad. Verbal sharing responses to communicate positive regard might include, "I really look forward to our talks together."

Empathy

Empathy is the ability to sense and identify the feelings of others and to communicate it to the client from his or her point of view, that is, entering the client's frame of reference. The conceptual importance of empathy is not unique to Rogerian-related approaches. It has been adapted by others under a different nomenclature. Special references to empathy are apparent in approaches such as

---

Perspective for the Therapist: On low levels of empathy . . .

Low levels of empathy is related to a slight worsening in adjustment and pathology. If no one understands me, if no one can grasp what these experiences are like, then I am indeed in a bad way . . . more abnormal than I thought.

Carl Rogers

Adlerian psychotherapy (Dinkmeyer, Pew, & Dinkmeyer, 1979) and developmental counseling and therapy (Blocher, 1974; Ivey, 1986).

In addition, even though behavioral therapy (Krumboltz & Thoresen, 1976) and cognitive therapy (Bedrosian & Beck, 1980) put less emphasis on counselor-client relationships, they do focus on the use of empathy to understand the client's problem accurately. Even Ellis's rational emotive behavioral therapy regards empathy as an important counseling component. Finally, Patterson (1986) emphasized empathic understanding as one of the core elements in relationships common to most therapeutic systems.

Brammer & Shostrom (1968) delineated that responding with empathy is "an attempt to think with rather than for or about the client" (p. 180). For example, if a client says, "I've tried to get along with my boss, but it never works out. She's too hard on me," an empathic response could be, "You feel discouraged about your unsuccessful attempts to get along with your boss." In contrast, if the counselor responded with, "You should try harder," the counselor is responding from his or her own frame of reference. The communication formula for basic empathy (Egan, 1990), for responding verbally to the client's feelings about the concern, uses a statement that identifies the client's feelings and the content of the situation:

> "I feel _____" (fill in the right category of emotion and the right intensity) "because _____" (fill in the experiences, behaviors, or both that elicit the feeling or emotions).
>   *"You feel frustrated because your boss doesn't trust you to run the operations when he is out of town."*

Genuineness

Genuineness is the ability to be authentic or "real" with others. The counselor does not distort communication, hide motives, operate from hidden agendas, or

---

Perspective for the Therapist: On relationships . . .

The degree to which I can create relationships which facilitate the growth of others as separate persons is a measure of the growth I have achieved in myself.

Carl Rogers

---

become pretentious or defensive. Genuineness means being oneself, not playing a role. The counselor's actions and words match his or her feelings both verbally and nonverbally.

Active or Reflective Listening

Listening is an art. Full attention is given both to what the client is saying and to other nonverbal cues such as posture and facial expression. Attending is a precondition to helping. An active listener feeds back what has been said in his or her own words for three reasons: (a) to make sure that he or she understands correctly, (b) to reassure that he or she was heard, and (c) to facilitate more disclosure on the part of the client.

Identifying feelings communicates to the client that the counselor is listening and encourages the client to express himself or herself more freely. This facilitates the focus on key issues for working out a satisfactory solution. McKay, Davis, and Fanning (1983) maintained that active listening requires the counselor's participation as a collaborator in the communication process. It includes *paraphrasing, clarifying,* and *feedback.*

Paraphrasing Responses.   This means to state in your own words what the client has actually said using such lead-ins as "What I hear you saying is" . . . "In other words" . . . "So basically now your feeing is" . . . "Let me understand what is going on with you which is" . . . "Do you mean . . . ?" The counselor

---

Perspective for the Therapist: On client responsibility . . .

First of all, the client in therapy moves toward being autonomous. By this I mean that gradually he chooses the goals towards which he wants to move. He becomes responsible for himself. He decides what activities and ways of behaving have meaning for him, and what do not.

Carl Rogers

Perspective for the Therapist: On giving personal attention . . .

The principle form that the work of love takes is attention. When we love another, we give him or her our attention. . . . By far the most common and important way in which we can exercise our attention is by listening.

M. Scott Peck

---

should paraphrase when the client says something of any importance to him or her. The benefits of paraphrasing in the counseling relationship are that

clients deeply appreciate feeling heard;

paraphrasing stops escalating anger and cools down crisis;

paraphrasing stops miscommunication (False assumptions, errors, and misinterpretations are corrected in the counseling session.);

paraphrasing helps the counselor remember what was said; and

paraphrasing inhibits blocks to listening on the part of the counselor such as judging, comparing, advising, or the preoccupation of other thoughts (McKay, Davis, & Fanning, 1983, p. 24).

Clarifying Responses. This compliments paraphrasing responses by asking questions to clearly understand the client beyond vague generalities. The counselor uses these clarifying responses to understand events in the context of how the client thinks and how the client feels about the problem.

Feedback. During the counseling interview, feedback provides the counselor an opportunity to share what was thought, felt, or sensed, and to check perceptions. To check perceptions, the counselor frames what was heard and perceived into a tentative description. For example, "I want to understand how you feel. Is this (giving a description) the way you feel?" "As I listened to what you said, it seems like (counselor description) is what is really happening in this situation." Feedback is nonjudgmental and should be honest, supportive, and in the here and now.

Congruence

Congruence requires the counselor to be transparent to the client; that is, if the counselor is feeling angered by the client's communication, it would be incongruent to deny these feelings or to try to hide them from the client. Sometimes trying to be congruent may conflict with trying to be nonjudgmental, illustrating how difficult it is to provide relationship conditions that are facilitative. To be an effective communicator the counselor must attend to both verbal and nonverbal communication. Collectively,

70% of what we communicate is through *body language,*
23% of what we communicate is through *tone of voice,* and
7% of what we communicate is through *words* (Glasser, 1985).

Listening for Feeling

Effective communication involves the thorough understanding of the other person's world (listening) and conveying that understanding to that person (responding). Through accurate listening and responding, barriers that hinder mutual understanding can be broken down (Dinkmeyer & Losoncy, 1980). Identifying and verbalizing the feelings in messages are framed with responses such as "sounds like," "you are kind of feeling," "your feeling now is that" "if I'm hearing you correctly."

Listening with Empathy

This means that the counselor recognizes that "This is hard to hear, but this is another human being trying to live." The counselor should ask himself or herself: "How did this belief or this decision, though it eventually may fail, lower this person's anxiety or get some needs met?" McKay, Davis, and Fanning (1983) suggested that if listening with empathy is difficult, the counselor should ask these questions:

What need is the self-defeating behavior coming from?
What danger or anxiety is the person experiencing?
What is he or she asking for?

Listening with Openness

The counselor needs to hear the whole communication before judging; more information may be disclosed later and all the information may not be present.

Listening with Awareness

This is accomplished by comparing the client's verbal and nonverbal communication with tone of voice, emphasis, facial expression, and posture for any mismatch between expression and content. Brigman & Earley (1990) maintained that, in order to have a satisfying relationship with others, a client must learn to communicate effectively. Much of our ineffective communication practices involve nagging, reminding, criticizing, threatening, lecturing, advising, and ridiculing.

Respect

Respect is an interpersonal skills that demonstrates an appreciation of the uniqueness of others, tolerance of differences, and willingness to interact with others equally.

Concreteness

Concreteness is demonstrated with specific, clear, and unambiguous communication—one uses **"I Messages"** rather than **"You Messages."** One uses I Messages and takes responsibility for feelings, emotions, and actions. Effective communication messages involves three components: (1) owning feelings, (2) sending feelings, and (3) describing behavior. Sending a feeling message adheres to the following communication formula: **Ownership + Feeling Word + Description of Behavior = Feeling Message.** For example: "I (ownership) am anxious (feeling word) about sending in my tax return on time (description of behavior)."

"I Messages"	**Versus**	**"You Messages"**
respect the individual's integrity		do not respect the individual's integrity
reflect one's feelings		promote blame and anger
reflect the individual's needs in the here and now		criticize and focus on the then and there

The use of I Messages is especially beneficial for responding assertively and for resolving interpersonal conflicts. Alberti and Emmonds (1986) identified a three-step empathic assertive response model:

Let the person know you understand his or her position: *"I know it's not your fault."*

Let the person know your position (what the conflict is): *"But, I ordered my steak well done not medium rare."*

Tell the person what you want or what you plan to do: *"I would like you to take it back and have it cooked some more."*

The communication formula for an assertive response is *"I know (the other person's position) but (your position) and (what you want)."*

Immediacy

Immediacy is the ability to discuss openly what is happening in the here and now as well as the ability to use constructive confrontation.

Self-disclosure

Self-disclosure is the willingness to share personal experience with others without being critical or judgmental. Self-disclosure facilitates intimacy and self-exploration. Self-exploration also can occur on three levels of depth:

Level I: At this level clients talk of others and things related to themselves such as general events and ideas, global conceptual ideas, universal and public issues, and historical perspectives in the "there and then."

Level II: At this level the client will talk of self and ideas as related to others such as personal events and opinions, personal goals, perspectives for the future with significant others or peers in the "there and then."

Level III: At level three, the client begins to talk about self and related feelings as they impact on self-experience with attention to personal meanings, feelings and perceptions in the "here and now."

Confrontation

Confrontation is the ability to tell others about their behavior and its impact on them without being aggressive, critical, judgmental, or defensive. Confrontation is an open sincere identification of one's self-defeating patterns, behavior, thoughts, feelings, or actions that may interfere with his or her interpersonal relationships. Confronting an individual's discrepancies, at the minimum, leads to greater awareness of the reality that the particular behavior is helping or hindering his or her interpersonal relationships.

Warmth

Warmth is the ability to be open, friendly, and accepting of others with nonverbal communication that conveys congruent signals of openness and readiness to listen. The person-centered approach of Rogers has the potential to be applied to a variety of educational, psychological, political, industrial, managerial, recreational, medical, and other settings (Purkey & Schmidt, 1990, p. 129). This counseling model is especially important for self-acceptance by those who have a physical disability. In particular the self-acceptance of children who have disabilities is needed to assist this population in their efforts to move toward greater use of the potential they possess (Williams & Lair, 1991, p. 202).

| Technique | *The Companion*

Counseling Intention: To feel the personal presence of a loving, caring companion; to fulfill a profound emotional need (Schriner, 1990)

Description. Imagine that a deeply caring and insightful person is standing beside you, touching you in a reassuring manner, and offering words of encouragement. You listen, perhaps writing down the suggestions. Then you go on with your activities, knowing you can come back for advice and support any time you choose (p. 77).

| Technique | *Repeating the Obvious*

Counseling Intention: To clarify our thinking or redirect our feelings about a problem situation (Schriner, 1990)

Description. Two kinds of obvious statements are especially valuable to repeat:

1. "I understand" statements—statements that explain why we have a problem or an unhappy feeling: "Of course I'm feeling anxious—I always feel nervous speaking in front of people. This always happens to me." "My client's boss is prone to mood swings; this just must be one of my boss' days."
2. "I can" statements. Repeating what we do to alleviate our problems is empowering and reassuring: "I can remind myself to breathe deeply and to recall how I have been successful in past situations." "If my boss is still irritable after three days, I can request a personal conference."

Several writers have developed lists of more than 100 "assertive rights." The most basic ones include:

The right to act in ways that promote your dignity and self-respect as long as others' rights are not violated in the process.

The right to be treated with respect.

The right to say no and not feel guilty.

The right to experience and express your feelings.

The right to take time and to slow down and think.

The right to change your mind.

The right to ask for what you want.

The right to ask for information.

The right to make mistakes.

The right to feel good about yourself.

| Technique | *Technique Assertiveness Skills*

Counseling Intention: To be in control; to ignore irrational fears or anxieties; to express feelings; to ask for support or assistance

Description. The following are different ways to be in control:

1. Don't be afraid to say "no." Saying "no" is acceptable.
2. Make eye contact and maintain an open posture.
3. Repeat your request to reinforce your position. State your demand over and over again to transcend the barrier of resistance or the barrier of avoidance.
4. State your goal clearly. Be sensitive to the needs of others, but be firm in expressing what you need and what you want.
5. Recognize the needs of others and reassure them that you are aware of their position or their point of view.
6. Regulate your pitch and tone of voice to communicate a firm, controlled position.
7. Stand straight and thank the person for listening to your request.
8. Creating more assertive dialogue is represented in the following statements:

From	To
"I'm going to. . . ." "I will. . . ."	"I've decided to. . . ."
"One day I'm going to. . . ."	"My goal is to _____ by _____."
"I don't think. . . ."	"I think that. . . ." "My thoughts are. . . ."
"I can't do it. . . ."	"I want to do it. . . ."

| Technique | "I Language" Assertion |

Counseling Intention: To help the client express difficult feelings

Description. "I Language Assertion" involves a four-part statement in which you

1. objectively describe the other person's behavior or the situation that is creating concerns with you;
2. describe how the other person's behavior or the situation concretely affects your life, for example, in terms of additional time, money, or effort;
3. describe your own feelings; and
4. describe what you want the other person to do, for example, provide an explanation, change behavior, or apologize. Offer suggestions for solving the problem, get his reaction to what you've said (Jakubowski & Lange, 1978, p. 165).

| Technique | Different Ways to Refuse a Request |

Counseling Intention: To provide alternatives to saying "no" to a request

Description. The following are different ways to refuse a request:

1. Simply say no.
2. Use an "*I want*" *statement,* for example, "No, I don't want to loan you my car, I may need it."
3. Use an "*I feel*" *statement,* for example, "No, I just wouldn't feel comfortable parting with it right now."
4. Use an "*empathetic assertion statement,*" for example, "I can see you're in a bind, but I can't loan you my car tonight."
5. Use a "*mixed feelings statement,*" for example, "Part of me says let you have my car this evening, and the other part is saying 'No, I may need it and you will be stranded'" (Jakubowski, & Lange, 1978, p. 221).

Chapter **12**

CONFLICT MEDIATION AND CONFLICT RESOLUTION TECHNIQUES

The point here is that, while my emotions are throbbing with these fears, angers, and self-defensive urges, I am in no condition to have an open-minded, honest and loving discussion with you or anyone else. I will need . . . emotional clearance and ventilation . . . before I will be ready for this discussion.

John Powell

Individuals who witnessed or experienced excessive conflict in their families, such as in abusive or alcoholic homes, are particularly prone to view conflict as only destructive. They either may become aggressive themselves when resolving conflicts or retreat completely from a conflict situation.

Conflict is destructive when it results in

no decision or new coping behaviors and the problem remains;
diverts energy from more important activities and issues;
destroys the morale of individuals and groups;
reinforces poor self-concept;
divides people even more and polarizes groups; and/or
produces irresponsible behavior.

151

Conflict is constructive when it

increases the involvement of everyone affected by the conflict;
opens up discussion of issues resulting in clarification;
identifies alternative solutions;
results in the solution of a problem;
serves as release of pent-up emotions, anxiety, and stress;
builds cohesiveness among group members; and/or
helps individuals and groups to grow personally and apply their knowledge
    to future conflicts.

Main and Roark (1975) and Roark (1978) outlined a five-step process of
onflict resolution for dealing with emotion-laden interpersonal conflict:

1. At the beginning, each conflictee describes the situation from his or her
    perspective. Participants should restrict their account of the situation
    with cognitive descriptions, strictly avoiding emotional connotations.
    The outcome of this step is to achieve consensus and mutual understand-
    ing regarding the description of the conflict situation as starting point
    for conflict resolution.
2. Next, each conflictee describes his or her feelings regarding the conflict.
    It is important to avoid escalating the conflict with statements of blame.
    The outcome of this statement is to have conflictees understand one
    another's feelings and needs.
3. Prefaced by information and understanding from the first two steps,
    conflictees formulate and describe a situation acceptable to everyone.
    The outcome of this step should be
    a agreement on perceptions of the conflict,
    b understanding one another's feelings regarding the conflict, and
    c agreement on what the situation would be if the conflict was signifi-
    cantly reduced.
4. At this juncture, changes necessary to achieve the desired situation are
    agreed upon. Each conflictee should list the changes he or she is willing
    to make as well as verbalize and understand of what the other is willing
    to do.

Perspective for the Therapist: On hatred . . .

Hatred does not cease by hatred, but only by love; this is the eternal rule.

Buddha

Perspective for the Therapist: On conflict . . .

> *Today, let me be an instrument of peace.*
> *Where there is hatred, let me sow love;*
> *Where there is injury, pardon;*
> *Where there is discord, union;*
> *Where there is doubt, faith;*
> *Where there is darkness, light;*
> *Where there is sadness, joy.*
>
> *May I not so much seek*
> *To be consoled, as to console;*
> *To be understood, as to understand;*
> *To be loved, as to love.*
>
> *For it is in giving that we receive.*
> *It is in pardoning that we are pardoned.*
> *And it is in dying to self*
> *That we are born to eternal life.*
>
> the prayer of St. Francis

5. Finally, a detailed agenda should be formulated, including follow-up plans and specific dates for the accomplishment of all tasks (Roark, 1978, p. 402).

| Technique | *DESC Script (Describe, Express, Specify, Consequences)* |

Counseling Intention: To develop a formula for conflict resolution, negotiation, and assertiveness

Description. Bower and Bower (1976) provided the following technique or guidelines for handling interpersonal conflicts. It consists of four key elements: (D) describe, (E) express, (S) Specify, and (C) Consequences:

Describe: Begin your dialogue by describing as specifically and objectively as possible the behavior or situation that is bothersome to you. Use concrete terms. Describe a specified time, place, and frequency of action. Describe the action not the motive.

Express: Say what you feel and think about this behavior. Explain the effect of this behavior on you. Empathize with the other person's feelings. Express them calmly. State feelings in a positive manner, for example, as relating to a goal to be achieved.

Specify: Ask for a different, specific behavior, or specify what behavior you would prefer or need in this particular situation. Request only one or two changes at one time. Specify the concrete actions you want to see stopped and those you want to see performed. Take into account whether or not the other person can meet your request without suffering large losses. Specify (if appropriate to the situation) what behavior you are willing to change to make the agreement.

Choose consequences: State concretely and simply what positive and negative consequences you are prepared to carry through if your preferences are not met. Make the consequences explicit. Give a positive reward for change in the desired direction. Select something that is desirable and reinforcing.

Consider the impact of these consequences on yourself and on others involved in the situation. Sometimes you have to specify the negative consequences of not following changes. In one example situation, Jessica's father tries to give her advice (to the point of nagging) about what she should do in school, who she should and should not date, and who she is to have as friends, etc. Jessica loves and respects her father's concern for her, but she would like to make her own decisions without her father's constant nagging and interference. Jessica decides to outline a **DESC script** to use in dealing with her dad.

Describe: (The description should be concise, accurate,and directed toward a single point, carefully worded, objective and nonaccusing.) "Dad, you have been giving me detailed advice about what you think I should study in school, how you think I should choose my friends, and what guys I should date."

Express: (Express how it makes you feel; be positive and focus on common goals; do not provoke feelings of guilt.) "I know you want the best for me, and your intentions are well meaning. I feel like you are treating me like a child. I'm older now, and I can think for myself."

Specify: (Specify an alternative behavior instead of the current one.) "Please stop giving me advice unless I specifically ask for it. Trust me to be responsible for myself and allow me to learn on my own."

Consequences: (Let the other person know how you intend to follow through on your request for behavior change. The consequences consist of two parts: rewards if he or she accedes to your request and punishments if the individual fails to go along with it.) "We will get along much better if you will let me have more freedom to make my own decisions. I think you will be proud of how responsible I can be" (positive consequences). "If you continue to give me advice when I don't ask for it, I will gently remind you of our agreement, the first time. If you continue after this, I will just turn and leave the room" (negative consequences).

In most cases, if a DESC script is prepared and followed through with a clear calm statement, the other person will listen and probably respond favorably. If the script does not provide the desired result, the client can follow through on the consequences without feeling frustrated or helpless.

| Technique | *Locating "Pinch Points" That Provoke Aggressive Responses*

Counseling Intention: To help the client stop the internal process that triggers aggressive behavior

Description. One way to keep track of aggressive behavior is to keep a log. In the daily log, the client should note the following:

1. aggressive comments or actions;
2. a precise description of what the other person did or said just before the aggression;
3. in addition to anger, any other feelings experienced;
4. thoughts and internal dialogue;
5. and body language just prior to the aggressive reaction.

| Technique | *Guided Conflict Imagery*

Counseling Intention: To facilitate awareness of strategies for dealing with conflict situations; to examine methods of responding to conflict

Description. Ask the client to get comfortable, close his or her eyes, get in touch with himself or herself at the present moment, and relax. The guided imagery is as follows:

> *You are walking down a long hallway and begin to notice a familiar face coming in your direction. Suddenly, you recognize that it is the person with whom you are in most conflict at the present time. You realize that you must decide quickly how to respond to the person. As he or she comes closer, a number of alternatives flash through your head. Decide right now what you will do and then imagine what will happen.*

(Pause to allow the images and the response to develop.)

> *It's over now. The person has gone. How do you feel? What did you say? How satisfied were you with how the interchange went? What did you say to yourself?*

Perspective for the Therapist: On inferiority ...

To be a human being means to possess a feeling of inferiority which
constantly presses towards its own conquest. The paths to victory are as
different in a thousand ways as the chosen goals of perfection. The greater
the feeling of inferiority that has been experienced, the more powerful is the
urge to conquest, and the more violent the emotional agitation.

Alfred Adler

(Pause to allow the client to process and identify the
internal dialogue.)

Return to the present. Gradually become aware of any
tension in your body ... your breathing ... the sounds in
the room ... and finally open your eyes when you feel ready.

Ask the client (or group members) to spend five minutes writing (a) the
alternative ways of acting they had considered, (b) the one the client chose to
act upon, and (c) the level of satisfaction he or she felt as to the outcome of the
choice.

| Technique | *Resolving Conflicts Cooperatively*

**Counseling Intention: To assist clients in conflict to express feelings and inter-
personal conflict**

Description. The two individuals who are angry with each other sit opposite
each other with knees touching. Instruct them to look at each other in the eyes
as they talk, talking directly to each other and not about the other. Each will
state his or her viewpoint and feelings. One person begins by stating the problem
as he or she sees it and also says how he or she feels—"I feel _ when you _."
The other person is not to share his or her viewpoint at this time. He or she is
only to repeat what he or she heard the other person say. The listener who repeated
the problem and feelings is to confirm with the other person that everything was
stated basically as the other said it.

The second person is provided with the same chance to state the problem.
Encourage the two to do any of the following: agree to disagree, compromise
and come to a solution, seek forgiveness if wrong or forgive if wronged, or
accept the other's viewpoint.

Perspective for the Therapist: On self-expression . . .

Self-expression leads to growth and expanded awareness. Those who stifle themselves for fear of criticism "pay the piper" in "dis-ease" and the stunted growth of personality and psyche. Those who express themselves unfold in health beauty and human potential. They become unblocked channels through which creativity, intuition, and inspiration can flow.

Christopher Hills
Robert B. Stone

| Technique | *Assuming Responsibility for Choices and Actions*

Counseling Intention: To shift the center of responsibility or ownership to a problem

Description. Direct the client to think of an incident that really made him or her angry or resentful, one about which he or she still has strong feelings. In writing, describe the incident as if others were completely responsible for bringing about the event. Blame them. Make it clearly their fault. Now rewrite the incident as if you were solely responsible for starting, developing, and getting stuck with the problem. Take full account of what you could have done so that the whole problem would not have arisen. Process with the client the issues of blame, responsibility, and victimization.

| Technique | *Resent, Expect, Appreciate*

Counseling Intention: To work with bipolarities, or splits in the personality, by bringing each side into awareness; to become aware of expectations and mixed feelings held about others

Description. Have the client list three of his or her closest friends. For each individual, have the client think of one thing that he or she resents, one thing that is expected that the offending person change, and one thing that is appreciated about the person. Process how to resent and appreciate a person at the same time, how to be aware of the mixed feelings he or she may have toward others, and how to integrate opposing thoughts or feelings.

I Resent	**I Expect**	**I Appreciate**
"that you break a lot of promises."	"you to keep your word."	"how easygoing you are and your sense of humor."

PART D
IMPROVING
RELATIONSHIPS
WITH OUR ENVIRONMENT

Chapter 13

STRESS
AND STRESS-RELATED
TECHNIQUES

The twentieth century is the age of noise. The din penetrates the mind filling it with a babble of distraction—news items, mutually irrelevant bits of information, blasts of music, continually repeated doses of drama that bring no catharsis merely create a craving for daily emotional purging.

Aldous Huxley

The world is moving so fast these days that the man who says it can't be done is generally interrupted by someone doing it.

Elbert Hubbard

LINK BETWEEN LIFE STRESS
AND PSYCHOPATHOLOGY

The National Institute of Mental Health has concluded that the link of "life stress" to psychopathology is well supported in the literature. The current quest, however, is to delineate how life stress impairs one's health and well-being. As a conceptual framework, Klerman and Weissman (1985) provided a working definition of stress and its related nomenclature:

Stress—hypothesized psychological, emotional, or physical changes as the result of the stressor.

Stressors—stressful environmental changes, particularly circumstances requiring changes in patterns, routines or interactions.

Stress response—the behavioral, psychological, emotional, physical, or cognitive responses experienced in an attempt to cope, adapt, or survive.

Adverse health consequences—increased susceptibility to physical illness or emotional disorders. (p. 56)

Stressors become a causative or moderating influence, interacting with personal dispositions and factors in the social environment (Dohrenwend & Dohrenwend, 1985). The role of stress management, stress reduction, and stress relief procedures are viable intervention strategies. An individual's risk of psychopathology is intensified by the presence of debilitating stress and physical handicaps and is diminished if an individual has reliable coping skills, a positive sense of self, and perceives the existence of social support in their immediate environment.

From the perspective of the *individual*, Albee (1982) provided the following equation:

$$\text{Incidence of behavioral and emotional disorder} = \frac{\text{stress} + \text{physical vulnerability}}{\text{coping skill} + \text{social support} + \text{self-esteem}}$$

There also is an environmental-centered analogue to this equation that focuses on risk of psychopathology in a *population*:

$$\text{Likelihood of disorder in a population} = \frac{\text{stressors} + \text{risk factors in the environment}}{\text{socialization practices} + \text{social support resources} + \text{opportunities for connectedness}}$$

Psychopathology is less likely to occur in a population if there are socialization practices that teach and promote social competence, supportive resources available in the environment, and opportunities available for people to form constructive, positive social bonds and identities connected with the mainstream of society. Both equations are interdependent and reflect the paramount need for stress-related interventions that are multidimensional (Elias, 1989).

Symptoms of stress include but are not limited to the following:

Nervous tic
Muscular aches
Increase or decrease in appetite
Increased smoking
Sleep disorder
Increased perspiration
Stammering or stuttering
Nausea or gastrointestinal distress
Grinding teeth
Headaches
Skin Disorders
Crying spells

Constipation or diarrhea
Decreased libido
High blood pressure
Dry mouth
Irritability
Lethargy or fatigue
Cold, clammy hands
Depression
Fear, panic or anxiety
Restless
Other manifestations to cope with
  stress

STRESS OF THERAPEUTIC WORK

Psychotherapy often creates stress for practitioners. Among the most stressed aspects of therapy according to Hellman, Morrison, and Abramowitz (1986) were doubt about one's effectiveness, problems in scheduling, becoming too involved in work, becoming depleted, and having difficulties in managing relationships with clients. The five types of client behaviors that causing the most stress for therapists were suicide threats, resistance, expression of negative feelings, passive-aggressive behavior, and psychopathological acts.

Concurrently, the growing concern for American youth over adolescent suicide, substance abuse, alienation, depression, family dysfunction, teen preg-

---

Perspective for the Therapist: On the therapeutic role . . .

In the face of incredible emotional arousal—anger, sadness, panic, despondency, conflict—the therapist is expected to maintain neutrality, detachment, frustration tolerance, empathy, alertness, interest, and impulse control without feeling depleted, deprived, and isolated. As if such demands are not enough, we are also supposed to be charming and invigorated by the time we get home. Since our friends and family know what we do for a living, they have greater expectations that we will be inhumanly patient, forgiving, and compromising during those instances when they have us locked in battle.

Sigmund Freud

---

nancy, HIV/AIDS, violence, and escalating dropout rates demonstrates the critical need for responsible adults to establish close, caring relationships with young people. Debilitating stress accompanies all of these conditions, which in turn foster adverse health consequences (William T. Grant Commission on Work, Family, and Citizenship, 1988).

IMPROVING RELATIONSHIPS
WITH OUR ENVIRONMENT

Seasonal Affective Disorder (SAD)

Seasonal Affective Disorder (SAD) is a mood disorder characterized by recurrent fall and winter depressions alternating with nondepressed periods in spring and summer (Rosenthal, Sack, Gillin, Lewy, Goodwin, Davenport, Mueller, Newsome, & Wehr, 1984). Experts believe 10 million Americans may be severely afflicted with these symptoms, whereas 25 million others may suffer to a milder degree. Rosenthal and Wehr (1987) provide the following operational criteria for a diagnosis of seasonal affective disorder:

a history of at least one major depressive episode, according to Spitzer, Endicott, and Robins (1978);
regularly occurring fall-winter depressions (at least two occurring during consecutive winters) alternating with nondepressed periods during spring and summer;
no other major psychiatric disorder; and
no psychosocial variables accounting for the regular changes in mood.

These criteria have been modified and included in DSM-IV (American Psychiatric Association, 1994) as "seasonal pattern," a descriptor that may qualify any recurrent mood disorder. Seasonal depressions are accompanied by a distinctive constellation of symptoms such as: hypersomnia, overeating, carbohydrate craving, weight gain, fatigue and social withdrawal. It is triggered by light deficiency and responds to a novel type of treatment, phototherapy. Researchers have shown a strong association between the seasons and the incidence of depression, mania, suicides, and suicide attempts.

TECHNIQUES FOR DEPRESSED CLIENTS

Downing (1988) provided a multi-dimensional intervention system based on a learning theory approach for countering depression. Learning life skills to change debilitating behavior is much more productive than merely a lot of rhetoric about the problem. Clients can be taught depression-coping and control techniques such as recognizing depressive feelings, ways to increase activity level, the use of daydreams, ways to relax, and positive self-talk. The desired outcome of coping and control techniques is an improvement of the level of functioning in all aspects of a child's or an adolescent's life. This is best achieved through a multi-faceted support system involving an intervention team who maintain consistent, frequent, and regular monitoring of the helping process.

| Technique | *Success Experiences*

Counseling Intention: To systematically manipulate success and positive feedback for the client by ensuring daily successful experiences

Description. Members of the intervention team should determine appropriate and reasonable success objectives by establishing small attainable goals.

| Technique | *Increased Activity Levels*

Counseling Intention: To control depression by increasing the client's activity level

Description. Cantwell and Carlson (1983) found that depression can begin to be controlled by increasing the client's activity level. Client involvement in selecting and planning the activities will improve the likelihood of a more successful intervention. When the activities are fun, the probability of a positive response will be enhanced.

The major obligation for adolescents, for example, is one of attending school and should be a priority. Parents should insist gently that the child do chores and participate in family activities as well as think small and accept small gains (Downing, 1988). With the child's involvement in the intervention process, he or she may assimilate the system of skills without adult assistance in the future. The more commitments or obligations the youth meets, the more he or she maintains a self-perception of normalcy and confidence.

| **Technique** | **Limit Inappropriate Attention**

Counseling Intention: To reinforce behaviors that gain attention in positive ways

Description. Sometimes family relationships become co-dependent where individuals take responsibility for another's behavior and consequences. Members of the intervention team should not feel that they need to ask continually how the child is feeling. Response efforts should be focused on behaviors that gain attention in positive ways.

| **Technique** | **Teaching Coping and Change Skills**

Counseling Intention: To learn ways to avoid feelings or ideas that may provoke depression

Description. Clients can be taught to be aware of depressive feelings and thoughts when they occur. The client should be helped to develop a repertoire of activities to implement when feeling depressed such as (a) increasing their activity level, (b) redirecting thoughts to pleasant experiences, (c) using deliberate internal affirmations, (d) utilizing productive fantasies or daydreams, or (e) using biofeedback either to increase or to decrease their pulse rate to control their body. All strategies have one common denominator—they empower the client with strategies that put him or her in control to actualize change (Cantwell & Carlson, 1983; Downing, 1988).

Phototherapy: Light as a Therapeutic Agent

Bright artificial light has antidepressant effects on Seasonal Affective Disorders (SAD). The effectiveness of light in treating SAD was first shown by researchers at the National Institute of Mental Health in the early 1980s. Clients who are being treated for SAD typically receive two hours of phototherapy per day. The light source most frequently used has been full-spectrum fluorescent light (Vitalite®, Six Powertwist®). Eight regular 40–watt tubes inserted into a

---

Perspective for the Therapist: On turning darkness into light . . .

Whoever wishes to pursue the science of medicine in a direct manner must first investigate the seasons of the year and what occurs in them.

Hippocrates

---

rectangular metal fixture, approximately two by four feet, with a reflecting surface behind them, also may work. The light intensity should be 5 to 10 times brighter than ordinary room lighting. Clients simply sit close to the light box with lights on and eyes open.

How phototherapy improves SAD is unclear. Rosenthal, Carpenter, and James (1986) suggested that bright light might exert its antidepressant effects by the suppression of melatonin secretion. Lewy, Sack, and Miller (1987) have suggested that light exerts its antidepressant effects by means of its circadian phase-shifting properties, a theory that continues to be researched. In addition, it appears as though "certain individuals have a neurochemical vulnerability (perhaps genetically determined), which, in the absence of adequate environmental light exposure, produces the behavioral changes seen in SAD."

Bright light, probably acting via the eye and presumably via retino-hypothalamic projections, appears capable of reversing this biochemical abnormality if the light is of high enough intensity and is used regularly and for sufficient duration (Rosenthal, 1989, p. 3). Bright artificial light may be capable of shifting the timing of circadian rhythms in humans, which may be helpful in conditions of abnormal circadian rhythms, such as those created by jet lag, shift work, or chronic reactions as in *delayed sleep phase syndrome* and *seasonal affective disorders*. Scientists at the National Institute of Mental Health have demonstrated successful treatment using full spectrum florescent lights placed on the floor. Bright light relieves SAD symptoms through alterations in hormone production and body chemistry.

TECHNIQUES FOR MANAGING STRESS

Meditation Techniques

| Technique | Meditation

Counseling Intention: To reduce stress among clients; to empower them to gain control over self-defeating behaviors that manifest a chronic stress response; to evoke the relaxation technique with meditation

Description. Techniques like progressive muscle relaxation training (PMRT), biofeedback, self-hypnosis, rhythmic breathing, and exercise can elicit the relaxation response. Relaxation training can reduce physiological arousal and attenuate

---

Perspective for the Therapist: On turning inward . . .

When one turns his attention inward, he discovers a world of inner space which is as vast and as real as the external world. Through exploring this inner world, each of us potentially has access to vast realms of knowledge through his own mind, including secrets of the universe so far known only to a very few. And the deepest desire of man is to know himself and to experience his relationship to the universe about him.

George Harmon

---

the effects of chronic stress. There remains to be an interest in various meditative techniques for therapeutic purposes (Benson, 1974; Goldman, 1976; Goldman & Schwartz, 1976; Heider, 1985; Maharishi, 1972).

The practice of meditation can be categorized by the dimension of human experience: (a) intellectual as in trying to achieve a greater mental consciousness of reality; (b) emotional as in trying to expand to greater awareness of positive emotion; (c) physical as in trying to become completely absorbed in physical movement; and (d) action as in the practice of a particular skill or technique (LeShan, 1974). Weinhold (1987) listed the benefits of reaching an altered state of consciousness:

> to experience a state of ecstasy,
> to gain spiritual insights,
> to escape from pain and suffering,
> to obtain new creative ideas,
> to improve health or alleviate illness, and
> to increase sensory acuity. (p. 11)

Meditation takes on many forms. One simple method is to select a quiet place for a few minutes a day for prolonged reflective thought or contemplation and clear one's mind of all conscious thoughts and concentrating on a particular sound, image, object, or word. Some approaches to meditation emphasize restricting of consciousness, whereas others stress consciousness expansion. Experienced mediators are able to produce major changes in their physiological functioning such as reduced heart rate, slowed respiration, and changes in brain waves. Ultimately the outcome is to reach an inner harmony, a peace within one's self through the use of positive self-suggestions. Devi (1963) offered the following meditation instructions. The client uses a candle as a fixation point:

> Now keep your eyes upon the flame and don't let them wander.
> Start breathing rhythmically. Next close your eyes, and try to retain

---

Perspective for the Therapist: On overload . . .

No world has ever bombarded its occupants with more options, saturated them with more stress, or pitted them against each other in more relentless competition. . . . The options are endless. One person subscribes to twenty-two magazines, another gets eighty-three TV channels, another claims to have visited more than forty countries on discounted fares, still another has taken up a different new sport every year for fifteen years.

Linda Eyre
Richard Eyre

---

the impression of the flame. You can visualize it clearly, hold the picture, but if the light eludes you, open your eyes for another look at the light. Close them again and see if you are able to envision the flame this time. Repeat this until you are able to capture and hold the impression.

If you are still unsuccessful, try the same procedure again the following day, and continue trying until you have succeeded. Do not hurry or force anything—do not try too intensively. Not only will such an approach expedite matters, but it also may even retard everything. Remember that it is most important to remain inwardly relaxed and motionless. (p. 126)

Or one may try the Harvard Meditation Technique recommended by the Harvard Medical School (Benson, 1974).

Technique	*Harvard Meditation for Relaxation*

Counseling Intention: To evoke the relaxation response using the Harvard meditation technique

Description. Have the client do the following:

Select a quiet environment where you will not be distracted or disturbed.
Select two times during the day when you can afford 10 to 20 minutes of uninterrupted time. For some people a good time is before breakfast or before dinner. A particularly good time is when you are experiencing stress.
Find a comfortable chair, or sit in a position in which you feel at ease.

Loosen any tight clothing, take off your shoes or related clothing that may be uncomfortable.

Close your eyes.

Begin to relax by thinking of relaxing while successively thinking about your feet, legs, trunk, body, arms, neck, and head.

Breathe through your nose and become aware of your breathing.

Say a simple one- or two-syllable word to yourself as you breathe out. Almost any word will do. Words some people like are gohum, carim, shaim, sharin, sharing, one. A word without meaning works best.

Breathe easily and naturally. Ignore worries, ideas, or anxieties as you meditate. Keep repeating your word.

After you finished meditating, sit quietly for a minute with your eyes closed then with your eyes open.

| Technique | *Increasing Sensory Awareness*

Counseling Intention: To heighten sensory awareness

Description. Have the client do the following:

Go to a location where you feel comfortable, preferably outside.

Focus your eyes on an object—a tree, a rock, a picture—as if you never seen it before.

Become aware of its size, shape, color, and texture.

Now allow it to fade away and let the background come into focus.

Repeat this with other objects or, if you are calm, stay there and let your mind and senses rest.

Next, focus your attention on listening to the sounds around you.

Which sounds are constant? Which are intermittent?

Be aware of their intensity, pitch, and rhythm.

Try repeating these experiments every day for at least 10 minutes. Choose different settings and objects to contemplate. In addition to active observing and listening you can also become more aware of odors, tastes, and textures. Heightening your sensory awareness is a form of meditation that will not only help you to relax but will also allow you to appreciate more fully the world around you.

Perspective for the Therapist: On overload . . .

There is too much materialism, too much advertising, too much leisure, too much entertainment, too much passive time wasting (e.g. watching television), too many books with too many self-improvement ideas, too many vacation options, too many new car models, too much complexity, too much access to information, too much hustling, too many traffic jams, too many people, too many talk shows! The list itself is too much.

Linda Eyre
Richard Eyre

| Technique | *Evoking Relaxation Techniques Autogenically*

Counseling Intention: To evoke the relaxation technique autogenically

Description. With autogenic or self-directed relaxation techniques, the client is urged to relieve tension by saying that he or she feels calm, relaxed, or warm, etc. The client is guided to use his or her creative awareness and repeat self-statements as he or she feels and experiences deep relaxation.

The following outline of self-statements (at least two times each) are directed to the client's entire body beginning with legs and arms:

Slow breathing. "I take a slow deep breath."
Slight tension, then release. "I feel slight tension in my foot, and now I am completely relaxed."
Feeling warm and heavy. "My foot feels warm and heavy."
Flow of warmth. "Warmth flows from my arm to my chest."
Rate of heartbeat. "My heartbeat is calm and regular."
Quiet mind. "My mind is quiet and still."
Separation from surroundings. "I withdraw my mind from my environment. I feel calm, quiet, still. My thoughts are turned completely inward."
Peace and harmony. "My body and my mind are in perfect harmony."
Closing statement. "I am now calm, quiet, and renewed with energy."

Autogenic or self-directed relaxation can be used in mental training (Zilbergeld & Lazarus, 1987); for tension release leading to better sleep; in management of stress and increased efficiency (Carrington, 1977); in treatment of neurotic, compulsive, and depressive disorders (Romen, 1981); and in achieving a state of optimum health (Pelletier, 1980).

Perspective for the Therapist: On override . . .

The majority of us are required to live a life of constant, systemic duplicity.
Your health is bound to be affected if, day after day, you say the opposite of
what you feel, if you grovel before what you dislike and rejoice at what
brings you nothing but misfortune. Our nervous system isn't just a function,
it's a part of our physical body, and our soul exists in space and is inside us,
like the teeth in our mouth. It can't be forever violated with impunity.

Boris Pasternak

Biofeedback and Sensory Awareness Techniques

| Technique | *Self-management through Biofeedback*

Counseling Intention: To integrate self-management through biofeedback

Description. Biofeedback refers to a continuous aural or visual report of changes
in bodily reactions brought about by changes in thoughts and emotions (Marcer,
1986). By providing information about a bodily state frequently enough, the
client can learn to recognize the link between thoughts, feelings, and physical
reactions. Self-management is a technique developed to empower people to feel
better about themselves, by essentially changing destructive habits or inefficient
patterns of coping into positive behaviors.

It is essentially a step-by-step process for self-control and makes use of
many of the same techniques used by behavior therapists. Biofeedback involves
providing people with information about physiological process of which they are
normally aware. With the benefit of this information, people can learn to bring
under voluntary control physiological conditions that may be potentially harmful
to their health. Biofeedback training can be thought of as a three-step learning
process:

1.   developing increased awareness of body states,
2.   learning voluntary control over these states, and
3.   learning to use these new skills in everyday life.

The goal is for individuals to eventually learn to exercise this voluntary
control without the use of biofeedback instruments so that they can apply their
newly acquired skills to their daily lives in a manner which allows them to
control their stress responses. From this perspective, biofeedback is basically a
return of responsibility for one's health to the individual rather than to a caregiver.

Biofeedback and relaxation training techniques have found wide application and success in the treatment of anxiety states, diabetes, tension headaches, and migraine headaches. Biofeedback and relaxation techniques also are being applied in treating such varied conditions as hypertension, cardiac arrhythmia, stroke, epilepsy, asthma, psoriasis, chronic pain, and insomnia.

| Technique | *Progressive Muscle Relaxation Training (PMRT)*

Counseling Intention: To evoke the relaxation response through progressive muscle relaxation training (PMRT)

Description. Progressive muscle relaxation training (PMRT) is perhaps the most widely used of all cognitive-behavioral interventions. It is a procedure to enhance an individual's ability to learn to relax by becoming aware of the sensations of tensing and relaxing major muscle groups. Bernstein and Borkover (1973) provided the following directions for progressive relaxation. Steps for Progressive relaxation include the following:

Make sure that you will not be interrupted.

Lie down on a comfortable bed or couch, flat on your back, arms at your sides, and legs uncrossed.

Close your eyes gradually over a period of three to four minutes.

Spend only a few minutes at recognizing tensions in your muscles.

Never contract a muscle in order to relax it.

Do not shift your position, or try to hold still. Just let go.

If any step seems difficult, it is probably because you are holding a muscle under tension somewhere.

Sensations should seem to fall away if you are relaxing properly. Relaxing muscles often feel warm at first; later, possibly cool, tingly, or have no sensation.

Note: Straining and tensing your muscles before relaxing them is not progressive relaxation. Progressive relaxation starts by placing enough tension on a muscle so that the client can recognize and learn when you let go. Muscle relaxation is passive, a letting go of all tension.

| Technique | *Evoking Relaxation through Tension-Inattention*

Counseling Intention: To evoke the relaxation response through tension-inattention techniques

Description. Steps for Tension-Inattention Relaxation Technique were developed by White and Fadiman (1976). This technique can be learned in 3 to 4 practice sessions and assist in daily situations. The instructions are as follows:

Exercise 1

> Sit at the edge of your bed or floor.
> Close your eyes and keep them closed for all six exercises.
> Let your shoulders and neck be as loose as possible.
> Rotate your head slowly in a clockwise direction four times, making the muscles still more loose.
> Reverse direction and rotate your head in a counterclockwise direction four times.

Exercise 2

> Lie down and raise your right foot about 12 inches.
> Make your leg muscles as stiff and tense as possible.
> Visualize the muscles in your leg from toes to hip. Keep your attention on them and try to make them tight and tired.
> Hold your leg up as long as you can. Let it get tired that you can't hold it up anymore.
> Let your leg go completely limp and loose as you let it drop quickly.

Exercise 3

> Raise your left leg and divert all your attention to it.
> Now repeat all the steps for exercise two using your left leg.

Perspective for the Therapist: On stress . . .

The average American will spend 3 years sitting in meetings, 5 years waiting in lines, over 17,000 hours playing telephone tag, 4,000 hours stopped at a red light, and a lifetime trying to wind-down.

The more prevalent . . . and for all we know, most serious health problem of our time is stress. The war against microbes has been largely won, but the struggle for equanimity is being lost. It is not just the congestion outside us—a congestion of people, ideas and issues—but our inner congestion that is hurting us. Our experiences come at us in such profusion and from so many directions that they are never really sorted out, much less absorbed. The result is clutter and confusion. We gorge the senses and starve the sensitivities.

Norman Cousins

Exercise 4

> Raise your right arm, fist clenched in a salute position.
> Stiffen and tighten the muscles.
> Keep your thoughts on this arm only.
> Let your arm fall limp to your side when it is completely tired.

Exercise 5

> Immediately raise your left arm and repeat all steps as in exercise four.

Exercise 6

> Imagine a circle about four feet in diameter on the ceiling above you.
> Keeping your eyes closed, follow this circle with your eyes four times
>   in clockwise direction. Do this slowly.
> Reverse direction and follow the circle in a counterclockwise direction.
> Imagine a square instead of a circle.
> Go around the square four times in each direction.
> Lie for a few minutes and enjoy the relaxation.
> Divert your attention from your eyes by thinking of anything pleasant.

Enjoy the feeling of relaxation and arouse yourself gently and slowly. PMRT has demonstrated its effectiveness for treating insomnia, asthma, tension, headache, muscular tension, hypertension, increased heart rate, chronic anxiety, and phobias.

| Technique | *Evoking Relaxation through Yoga*

Counseling Intention: To evoke the relaxation response though basic yoga

Description. Yoga is a Hindu practice that can take any of four forms: (a) raja yoga, meditation through contemplation on universal truths; (b) jnana yoga, meditation on the nature of self; (c) karma yoga, active yoga in the service of others; and (d) bhaki yoga, meditation using prayer and chanting. In the Western world, hatha yoga is more often used as a form of exercise to promote good health, to alleviate stress, to energize and to relax the body and mind.

Maitland (1975) provided the following suggestions for basic yoga:

Let the movements compress or allow your lungs to expand.
Do one, two, or three repetitions of each movement.
Move in both directions, that is, clockwise and counter-clockwise.
Keep your attention on the muscles under tension.
Hold your position until your muscles are extended.
Maintain a continuous awareness of your body as you proceed through your
exercises.

| Technique | *Changing One's Awareness through Silva Mind Control* |

*Counseling Intention: To change one's awareness from everyday conscious-
ness via Silva Mind Control*

Description. Silva Mind Control is a process of changing one's present awakened
consciousness (beta) to a lower frequency consciousness (alpha) for better problem solving and increased memory, efficiency, and creativity. The technique "uses
the mind to mind itself: by first physical and mental relaxation, then affirmation,
visualization, and anchoring (Silva & Stone, 1983, p. 93). The relaxation method
consists of turning the eyes upward and counting back from 10 to 1. The anchor
is to put three fingers together.

The vision process consists of seeing the situation first as it is; then to see
the situation in the process of positive change, viewing the second image on the
left to activate the right brain; and finally to see the situation resolved (Silva &
Stone, 1983). This strategy has been used to accomplish personal goals, to
maintain energy and enthusiasm.

Perspective for the Therapist: On breaking points . . .

> *It's not the large*
> *things that*
> *send a man to the*
> *madhouse . . . no, it's the*
> *continuing series of*
> *small tragedies*
> *that send a man to the madhouse*
>
> *not the death of his love*
> *but a shoelace that snaps*
> *with no time left . . .*

Charles Bukowski

| Technique | *Creating Experiences through Visualization*

Counseling Intention: To use visualization to create experience in one or more sensory modes

Description. Visualization uses the imagination to create experience. Receptive visualization works to reduce the analytical activity of the brain allowing subconscious thoughts, emotions, ideas, or insights to emerge. A classic example of this type of visualization is having a solution to a complex problem emerge in a state of quiet. Active visualization works by giving form to thought (Gwain, 1982). An example of active visualization is creating an image of a new job or the successful transition through a stressful period. Repeated visualization works to change one's view of self. The most powerful visualizations are specific, tangible, repeated, and self-rewarding.

| Technique | *Enhancing One's Mind, Behavior, and Beliefs through Affirmations*

Counseling Intention: To direct one's mind, behavior, and beliefs through positive affirmations

Description. Inherently, beliefs present in one's mind create emotion, which influence actions, which in turn influence one's outlook on life, which fosters negative or positive self-talk. The intensity of the results or effects on one's life will be proportional to the depth of the belief and the intensity of the feeling (Helmstetter, 1986; Robbins, 1986). Changing negative beliefs and self-talk to positive beliefs and self-talk can change the circumstances of a client's life. A positive affirmation such as "I deserve this and much, much more" replaces "I'll never amount to anything."

Imagery Techniques

| Technique | *Enhancing One's Full Potential through Imagery*

Counseling Intention: To use imagery to enhance one's potential

Description. Using imagery as a counseling technique can be used as a primary psychological tool for assessment, intervention, and enhancement of human potential. Over the past two decades imagery has been cited as an effective treatment medium for a wide spectrum of psychological maladies such as uncovering emotional blocks or inhibiting them (Anderson, 1980); reducing anxiety, improving memory and achievement, increasing self-esteem (Lazarus, 1977; Sheikh & Sheikh, 1985); insomnia (Sheikh, 1976); depression (Schultz, 1978); obesity (Bornstein & Sipprelle, 1973); sexual malfunctioning; chronic pain (Jaffe & Bresler, 1980); and psychosomatic illness (Shorr, 1974; Lazarus, 1977; Simonton, Mathews-Simonton, & Creighton, 1978).

Currently, there is a renewed interest in imagery as a tool for counseling with the shifting paradigm away from strict adherence to schools of counseling and psychotherapy toward a more integrated cognitive-behavioral approach. Furthermore, contemporary developments in brain research and health psychology have legitimized nontraditional approaches (Korn & Johnson, 1983). Imagery is natural function of the human mind and does not have to be taught.

Witmer and Young (1985) outlined the areas in which imagery can be used to expand human possibilities:

> increasing awareness of self and others;
> future planning and career or life-style development;
> gaining control over undesirable behavior;
> treating illnesses;
> improving learning, skill development, and performance;
> reducing stress and enhancing health; and
> enhancing creativity and problem solving in everyday living.
>   (p. 187)

The clinical use of imagery as a tool for therapeutic intervention is outlined by Sheikh and Jordan (1983), for example:

Imagery can act as a source of motivation for future behavior; guided imagery can produce fresh data and new solutions; goals and solutions rehearsed through imagery during therapy can be applied more easily outside the therapeutic setting.

Imagery can facilitate the access to important events occurring early in one's life. Early recollections is a therapeutic component of a more Adlerian perspective to ascertain individual attitudes, beliefs, and motives.

Imagery provides a focus which can uncover very intense affective states or emotional reactions which fosters greater communication by moving the discussion to a more meaningful level, as well as facilitate the expression of more difficult feelings. Through imagery, empathy, and interpersonal relationship, skills can be developed.

Imagery can be used to resolve dilemmas by circumventing defenses or inhibitions that may occur in verbal blockage as well as produce therapeutic change in the absence of any interpretation by the therapist or intellectual insight by the client.

Witmer and Young (1985) also outline a number of prerequisites for imagery development that can increase the effectiveness such as

Readiness. A quiet environment with few distractions, a comfortable position and a mental device that functions as a point of focus such as a sound, word, phrase, or a spot at which to gaze. All imagery exercises should begin by creating a safe place in the client's imagery world (e.g. a warm beach, a special room, a quiet path). If images become too anxiety provoking or uncomfortable, the client can return to his or her safe place to process or work through threatening images.

Vividness. A certain degree of vividness is essential to creating images. The greatest effectiveness is reported when multiple sensory experiences are experienced (e.g., visual, sound, or emotional components).

Controllability. Imagery control insures therapeutic effectiveness. A technique that assists in controlling the imagery is cueing, that is, giving the person an instructional set to focus on either the desired outcome or the process. When the outcome image is established, the mind intuitively creates a script or scenario to achieve the imagined outcome.

Cautela and McCullough (1978) concluded that control can be improved further by emphasizing to clients that (a) the imagery is theirs—they create it and they are free to change it, (b) imagining the desired response inhibits an unwanted response, and (c) keeping a log of incidents and accompanying images that evoke tension will enable them to identify or modify subsequent images.

| Technique | *Increasing Self-knowledge*

Counseling Intention: To help the client gain a better knowledge of self

Description. Images from memory and fantasy can be used to increase self-knowledge through imaginary questions (Strauss, 1984). Ask the client questions such as the following:

You just received a medal or an award. Why was it given to you?
If you could change yourself into something else, what would it be?
You have found a key to a door. What kind of door would it open?

What would you find beyond the door?

Your hand has become a magic wand. You can change anything to whatever you want. What would you change? What would it become?

| Technique | *Wise Person Exercise (Witmer & Young, 1987)*

Counseling Intention: To enable the client to experience through imagination a conversation with a wise person

Description. The image that appears may be a stranger, a friend, or a spiritual being. Relax and let go of all tension and worrisome thoughts. Allow the face or figure of a very wise, loving person to appear. You may ask a question. Listen and be receptive to whatever comes. You may want to hold a conversation. The wise person may have a special message for you, something you did not ask.

If you are willing to receive this, tell the wise person and wait for a response. Allow yourself to see the situation as the wise person sees it. Now see how this fits or makes sense in your life. It is time to leave the wise person. You can return at any time and find guidance and strength (Witmer & Young, 1987, p. 8).

| Technique | *Visualization for Physical and Mental Relaxation (Witmer & Young, 1987)*

Counseling Intention: To enable the client to gain physical and mental relaxation through visualization

Description. Suggest the following to the client:

visualize your body relaxing by using a rag doll image;
visualize your favorite quiet place;
blow away bad feelings and thoughts like bubbles that break or float away;
imagine the light and warmth of sunlight entering your body and flowing to all parts, bringing relaxation;

Perspective for the Therapist: On the value of self . . .

One important element which helps people locked in their loneliness is the conviction that their real self . . . the inner self, the self that is hidden from others . . . is one which no one could love. It is easy enough to trace the origin of the feeling. The spontaneous feelings of a child, his real attitudes, have so often been disapproved of by parents and others that he has come to introject this same attitude himself, and to feel that his spontaneous reactions and the self he truly is, constitute a person whom no one could love.

Carl Rogers

---

visualize a trip and scenes from nature (e.g., mountains, beach, woods, field, or stream); or

use phases that elicit heaviness, warmth and an inner quietness. (Witmer & Young, 1987, p. 9)

| Technique | *Determining One's Sensory Modality*

Counseling Intention: To enable the client to explore his or her sensory imagery

Description. Mental images can be visual, auditory, proprioceptive (feelings and skin sensations), kinesthetic (body movements), or olfactory and gustatory (smell and taste). Although visual imagery is dominant for most people, many people respond more readily to auditory, kinesthetic, or olfactory images. Weinhold (1987) developed the following exercise to determine one's sensory modality:

1. **Visual**

    Close your eyes and imagine all the colors in a box of paints or crayons— pink, orange, yellow, purple, brown, white, red, and green.

    Close your eyes and imagine yourself walking or driving through a familiar street. Be aware of all the things that you see.

    Close your eyes an take a trip through your own house or apartment, see everything you can in each room.

2. **Proprioceptive**

    Close your eyes and imagine the feel of the water on your body as you take a bath or a shower.

    Imagine an egg breaking in your hand; feel the slipperiness of it.

Imagine holding a snowball in your bare hands, and imagine the wind nipping at your nose and ears.

3. Auditory

Close your eyes and imagine a church bell ringing.
Imagine an orchestra or group playing or singing a favorite tune.
Imagine the sound of an emergency siren.

4. Kinesthetic

Imagine yourself swinging on a playground swing or going in a circle on a merry-go-round.
Imagine yourself climbing a hill with a backpack on your back.
Imagine yourself dancing or playing some sport.

5. Olfactory and Gustatory

Imagine yourself ready to sit down to a Thanksgiving dinner.
Imagine tasting honey or bananas on your toothpaste.
Imagine smelling your favorite cologne or perfume (Weinhold, 1987, p. 9).

Guided imagery is most helpful in developing cognitive flexibility, imagination, and creativity. Zilbergeld and Lazarus (1987) found that their clients have experienced success in using visualization to deal with stressful situations and to accomplish their goals. It also can be used to rehearse mentally for events, to imagine alternative futures, to synthesize facts, and to visualize getting well.

| Technique | *Favorite Quiet Place*

Counseling Intention: To help learn how to relax through imagination

Description. Repeat to the client the following:

No matter where you are, you can always go to a special place in your mind. Picture a place, real or imagined, where you feel safe, calm, and happy. Close your eyes and go to that place. See yourself as free to do whatever you want. Notice everything around you. Hear the sounds. Feel what is happening to your body. Just enjoy this feeling. You can go to this place to rest, think, be alone, feel good, no matter where you are. Slowly return to the place where your body is. Gently open your eyes. The place will always be there for you to return.

| Technique | *Creative Problem Solving*

Counseling Intention: To develop problem solving strategies through visualization

Description. Repeat to the client the following:

Try to imagine your mind as a movie or television screen. You are the producer, actor, and viewer, all at the same time. You can allow pictures to appear spontaneously on this screen without consciously willing or controlling them.

Step 1: Relaxing. Begin to free your mind of distractions by closing your eyes or gazing at a spot in front of you. Relax your body from your head to your toes. Pay attention to your breathing, take a deep breath or two, and let go of your tension each time you breathe out. Your mind is calm and clear. You are ready to turn your attention to pictures on the screen of your mind.

Step 2: Spontaneous Imagery. Allow images or pictures to come to your mind. Let them come and go. Now picture a problem or situation that has been puzzling you. Do not force yourself to look for an answer. Just see a clear picture of the situation or problem. Open your mind to possible answers and solutions. Let them come and go. Keep picturing the problem and solution, then wait. You will know whether one of the pictures fits your question or situation. It will feel right and you will have a tingle of satisfaction. It may be an answer to a problem.

Step 3: Directed Imagery. Continue feeling relaxed and quiet. Now you are directing the pictures. You will take charge. Put the problem or situation on your screen. Explore in your mind's eye ways you might answer the question that appears on your screen. Notice how the story ends. Create another story with a different ending. You are trying different ways to reach a solution. You see yourself doing things to find out whether they work. Store these pictures in your memory for later use. If no ideas or answers appeared, be satisfied that you were able to picture the problem. The answer may come later. Write your ideas, draw them, or tell someone else so you will remember. When processing, sometimes answers come immediately, but other times they may need time to develop over a few days or months. All problems and questions must be explored however so that the mind van consider alternative and potential solutions. "Solutions to problems often are inhibited because of restrictive or convergent thinking that is emphasized in seeking the prescribed right-wrong, ready-made answer. Thinking about possibilities or divergent thought can be encouraged by picturing oneself trying a solution and considering all the possible consequences. (Reprinted from Witmer, J. M., & Young, M. E. (1987). Imagery in counseling. *Elementary School Guidance & Counseling, 22,* 11. © ACA. Reprinted with permission. No further reproduction authorized without written permission of the American Counseling Association.)

| Technique | *Stress Management—Quieting Response (QR)* |

Counseling Intention: To provide a systematic plan to eliminate or greatly reduce stressors

Description. Quieting response (QR) is a systematic, practical technique that can be used any time. It can empower a client to gain control of stress reaction within minutes of the event. Instruct the client to do the following.

1. Learn and practice the following steps:

   Recognize your stress symptoms (rapid breathing, heart palpitations, rapid heart beat, lump in throat, knot in stomach);
   breathe in slowly through the imaginary holes in the bottom of your feet (Byrum, 1989);
   begin to exhale, relax jaw, lower tongue, permit warm air to leave through the imaginary holes in your feet; and
   imagine warmth and heaviness simultaneously with the exhalation as warm air descends through your neck, shoulders, arms, and chest.

2. Process why QR is an effective stress reduction technique and how it can be used in their daily experiences.
3. Compare feelings of tension and relaxation in various muscle groups; use QR to initiate the relaxation state.

Writing as an Introspective Tool in Counseling

Writing is largely a process of choosing among alternatives from the images and thoughts of endless flow, and this choosing is a matter of making up one's mind, and this making up one's mind becomes, in effect, the making up of one's self.

John Miller

| Technique | *Writing for Introspection*

Counseling Intention: To help the client explore more deeply own thoughts and feelings through use of writing

Description. Writing can be a powerful therapeutic tool in counseling because it can generate a profound network of thoughts, feelings, emotions, and images. It also refines cognition. On an even deeper level, writing enhances awareness by (a) helping individuals organize their inner selves, (b) contributing to personal integration and self-validation, and (c) providing a cathartic emotional release (Brand, 1987, p. 266).

Expressive writing can be psychologically liberating, having intrinsic worth because of an entire range of inner satisfactions and deeper regions of personality development. Psychoanalytic, humanistic, and cognitive therapeutic models have made a significant impact on current therapeutic writing practices. Approaches to writing can be open-ended, loosely structured, expressive, or directed.

Brand (1987) maintained that although therapeutic writing practices are not necessarily organized around a particular psychological premise, they tend to be linked to certain theoretical biases (p. 267). Below is a compendium of descriptors of therapeutic writing practices:

Writing in Individual or Group Writing Sessions. A counselor may take notes during an individual counseling session for a client to review between sessions. As homework, the client can process insights gained during the counseling session, work on behavior change, and preface the next counseling session with significant learning or personal triumphs.

Double Dialogue Technique. After group counseling, a double dialogue technique (Powers & Hahn, 1977) can be used among group members to provide feedback to other members over issues discussed, or the counselor may have each member close the group experience by writing to the counselor using index cards about their group experience at that particular session. This allows the counselor to keep in touch with each individual group member about significant issues that may be affecting them.

Long-distance Writing. Long-distance writing may be used when counseling is interrupted by illness or professional obligations (Hofling, 1979; Oberkirch, 1983). "Internet" and electronic mail ("e-mail") are additional options as are bulletin boards and computer link-ups.

Structured Journal Logs.   Structured journal logs or journal keeping as described by Progoff (1975) and Hughes (1991) has particular value in the counseling process. Progoff introduced the structured journal that divides life experiences into several categories that guide personal, written responses. The intensive journal process enables all individuals regardless of age, social, or educational background to begin wherever they are and to draw their lives progressively into focus.

The client could begin with a "period log" placing oneself between the past and the future in particular situations that are issues in his or her life. The client is encouraged to feel the implications of the question, "Where am I now in my life?" "What is this present period in my life?" "What marks it off?" "How far does it reach?" "What have been the main characteristics of this recent period?" The exercise is intended for the client to position himself or herself in the moment of his or her life (e.g., "This period in my life has been like a . . ."). The goal of the intensive journal process is to teach clients how to make a more contact with themselves and gain deeper meaning from their life experiences.

Keeping a Daily Log.   Keeping a daily log reinforces the client to keep himself or herself in a dialogue with the ongoing relationships with whatever is taking place inside him or her (i.e., examining the strong-flowing stream of inner experience). The individual's entries must be a succinct reflection of his or her mental, emotional and imagery occurring within.

The Period Log.   Clients are encouraged to define a recent period in their lives, reflect on their experiences and life events during that period. They should record their feelings, impressions, and descriptions

Listing the Steppingstones of One's Life.   Please see Progoff (1975).

| Technique | *Creative Writing*

Counseling Intention: To encourage clients to project inner thoughts and feelings through writing

Description.   Creative writing is another written format through which clients can clarify projections and in which problems are explored and therapeutic dialogue interchanged. Troubling issues and concerns can have a therapeutic outlet especially among adolescents (Dehouske, 1979).

| Technique | Poetry

Counseling Intention: To have clients express themselves and reveal inner feelings through poetry

Description. Poetry is a popular form of written expression used in counseling (Blades & Girualt, 1982; Mazza, 1981). Developmental tasks and interpersonal struggles often project the angst of and universality of life's struggles. The following two poems are examples.

Winter Storms

Silently
    I watch the snow drift up into little piles
        on my office window.
    Suddenly winter storms, like anger,
        sometimes frighten me.
    Yet, with the wind and fury of outbursts,
        there is also a calm.
    Nature has a way of balancing.

In the midst of our session
    I wanted to quiet your rage,
        settle you down and send you home.

Instead, I waited.
Restlessly, your words came out
    falling on my ears like heavy snow.
I both absorbed the thoughts
    and helped you shape them into forms you could handle.
Carefully now, I walk down clear iced paths
    sliding occasionally, as I make my way
        toward the train to New Haven.
Spring is only two months away,
    but time, like adolescence,
        travels slowly in the process of change.

Samuel T. Gladding

Walking in the morning
he returns home
no longer confused
just battered
and
empty.

sent to school
and directed
to a room without windows
he waits.
the counselor
late in arriving
switches on a small lamp
and together
they begin
to take the light in slowly . . .

Nicholas Mazza

| Technique | *Structured Writing and Therapeutic Homework*

Counseling Intention: To encourage clients to keep records of their ideas and questions so that counseling time can become more structured

Description. Therapeutic homework originated from behavioral and cognitive models that traditionally have favored briefer forms of therapy. This method tends to reduce the need for repeated counseling and is applicable with both individuals and small groups. Clients who seek help for personal or academic problems may keep structured notebooks about their concerns and receive highly organized answers and instructions from counselors. They may complete inventory questionnaires, writing contracts, or document behavior modification procedures systematically (Klier, Fein, & Genero, 1984; Corbishley & Yost, 1985).

Chapter 14

LOSS, GRIEF, AND POSTTRAUMATIC LOSS DEBRIEFING

Nothing in life is perhaps more painful than experiencing the loss of a friend or a loved one. Even though most people experience varying degrees of loss, the grief cycle is not fully understood until it comes closer to the heart.

When sudden death comes with no time for anticipation, many additional feelings are involved in the grief process. The grief work normally will be longer, lonelier, and more debilitating to lasting emotional stability because of the intensity of the anguish experienced when one is taken suddenly or senselessly.

Grief work is not a set of symptoms but rather a process of suffering which marks a transition from an old lifestyle to a new one punctuated by numbness, denial, anger, depression and eventual recovery. Posttraumatic loss debriefing offers a therapeutic structure to "work through" the experience of traumatic loss and accompanying stress.

Talking about the death and related anxieties in a secure environment provides a means to "work through" the experience and serves to prevent destructive fantasy building. Because loss is so painful emotionally, however, our natural tendency (personally or professionally) is to avoid or to deny coming to terms with loss. Inherently, loss is a process that extends over time and more often than not has a lifelong impact.

TASKS OF MOURNING AND GRIEF COUNSELING

The tasks of mourning and grief counseling include the following:

To accept the reality of the loss and to confront the fact that the person is dead. Initial denial and avoidance becomes replaced by the realization of the loss;

To experience the pain of grief. It is essential to acknowledge and to work through this pain or it will manifest itself through self-defeating behavior(s).

To adjust to an environment in which the deceased is missing. The survivor(s) must face the loss of the many roles the deceased person filled in their life.

To withdraw emotional energy and reinvest it in another relationship. Initial grief reaction to loss may be to make a pact with oneself never to love again. One must become open to new relationships and opportunities.

To accept the pain of loss when dealing with the memory of the deceased.

To express sorrow, hostility, and guilt overtly, and to be able to mourn openly.

To understand the intense grief reactions associated with the loss, for example, to recognize that such symptoms as startle reactions, including restlessness, agitation, and anxiety may temporarily interfere with one's ability to initiate and maintain normal patterns of activity.

To come to terms with anger, which often is generated toward the one who has died, toward self, or toward others—to redirect the sense of responsibility that somehow one should have prevented the death.

STRATEGIES

The sudden, unexpected death by suicide or the sudden loss from an accidental death often produces a characteristic set of psychological and physiological responses among survivors. Persons exposed to traumatic events such as suicide or sudden loss often manifest the following stress reactions: irritability, sleep disturbances, anxiety, startle reactions, nausea, headaches, difficulty concentrating, confusion, fear, guilt, withdrawal, anger, and depression (Thompson, 1990, 1993).

Posttraumatic Stress Disorder (PTSD) can be grouped in three categories: (a) natural disasters like floods, fires, earthquakes, hurricanes, and tornados; (b) accidents such as a car crash, bombing, shootings; and (c) human actions such as rape, robbery, assault, abduction, or abuse.

Diminished responsiveness to one's immediate environment with "psychic numbing" or "emotional anesthesia" usually begins soon after the traumatic event. Sometimes the stress reactions, however, appear immediately after the traumatic event or a delayed reaction may occur weeks or months later. With acute posttraumatic stress, the counseling intention is to help the client return as rapidly as possible to full activity, especially to the setting or circumstances in which the trauma occurred.

Goldenson (1984) provided the following profile of stress disorder as an anxiety disorder produced by an uncommon, extremely stressful life event (e.g., assault, rape, military combat, flood, earthquake, hurricane, death camp, torture, car accident, or head trauma) and characterized by (1) reexperiencing the trauma in painful recollections or recurrent dreams or nightmares, (2) diminished responsiveness (emotional anesthesia or numbing) with disinterest in significant activities and with feelings of detachment and estrangement from others, and (3) such symptoms as heightened startle response, disturbed sleep, difficulty in concentrating or remembering, guilt about surviving when others did not, and avoidance of activities that call the traumatic event to mind (Goldenson, 1984, p. 573).

With chronic PTSD, anxiety and depression are also prevalent. The particular pattern of the emotional reaction and type of response will differ with each survivor depending on the relationship of the deceased, circumstances surrounding the death, and coping mechanisms of the survivors. Grinspoon (1991a, 1991b) provided 16 suggestions that counselors can utilize when dealing with a client who is experiencing PTSD:

provide a safe environment for confronting the traumatic event;
link events emotionally and intellectually to the symptoms;
restore identity and personality;
remain calm while listening to horrifying stories.
anticipate one's own feelings or responses and coping skills—dread, disgust, anger at clients or persons who had hurt them, guilt, anxiety about providing enough help;
avoid overcommitment and detachment;
avoid identifying with the client or seeing oneself as rescuer;
tell the client that change may take some time;
introduce the subject of trauma to ask about terrifying experiences and about specific symptoms;

moderate extremes of reliving and denial while the client works through
memories of trauma;

provide sympathy, encouragement, and reassurance;

try to limit external demands on the client;

during periods of client numbing and withdrawal, pay more attention to the
traumatic event itself;

help client bring memories to light by any means possible including dreams,
association, fantasies, photographs, and old medical records (for children,
play therapy, dolls, coloring books, and drawings);

employ special techniques, systematic desensitization, and implosion to eliminate conditioned fear of situations evoking memories and achieve catharsis; and

facilitate group therapy.

POSTTRAUMATIC LOSS DEBRIEFING

Posttraumatic loss debriefing is a structured approach to understand and to
manage physical and emotional responses of survivors and their loss experiences.
It creates a supportive environment to process blocked communication, which
often interferes with the expression of grief or feelings of guilt, and to correct
distorted attitudes toward the deceased as well as to discuss ways of coping with
the loss. The purpose of the debriefing is to reduce the trauma associated with
the sudden loss, to initiate an adaptive grief process, and to prevent further self-
destructive or self-defeating behavior. The goals are accomplished by allowing
for ventilation of feelings, exploration of symbols associated with the event, and
enabling mutual support.

Posttraumatic loss debriefing is composed of six stages: introductory stage,
fact stage, feeling stage, reaction stage, learning stage, and closure. Posttraumatic
loss debriefing is a structured approach to the management of the acute emotional
upset affecting one's ability to cope emotionally, cognitively or behaviorally to
the crisis situation. Successful resolution and psychological well-being is dependent upon interventions that prepare individuals for periods of stress and help
survivors return to their precrisis equilibrium.

A debriefing should be organized 24 to 72 hours after the death. Natural
feelings of denial and avoidance predominate during the first 24 hours. The
debriefing can be offered to all persons affected by the loss. The tone must be
positive, supportive, and understanding.

| Technique | *Posttraumatic Loss Debriefing (Thompson, 1990, 1993)*

Counseling Intention: To process loss and grief; to inform about typical stress response and implications for participants

Description of Introductory Stage. This stage includes brief introductions to the debriefing process and establishment of rules for the process.

Acting as caregiver-as-facilitator, define the nature, limits, roles, and goals within the debriefing process.

Clarify time limits, number of sessions, confidentiality, possibilities, and expectations to reduce unknowns and anxiety for survivors.

Encourage members to remain silent regarding details of the debriefing, especially details that could be associated with a particular individual.

Assure participants in a debriefing the open discussion of their feelings will, in no way, be utilized against them under any circumstances.

Give reassurances that the caregiver-as-facilitator will continue to maintain an attitude of unconditional positive regard. Reduce the survivors' initial anxieties to a level that permits them to begin talking.

Description of Fact Stage. This stage includes warm-up, gathering information, and recreating the event. During the fact phase, participants are asked to recreate the event for the therapist. The focus of this stage is facts, not feelings.

Encourage individuals to engage in a moderate level of self-disclosure statements such as, "I didn't know. . . . Could you tell me what that was for you?" encourages self-disclosure.

Try to achieve an accurate sensing of the survivor's world and communicate that understanding to him or her.

Be aware of the survivor's choices of topics regarding the death to gain insight into their priorities for the moment.

Help survivors see the many factors that contributed to the death to curtail self-blaming.

Ask group members to make a brief statement regarding their role, relationship with the deceased, how they heard about the death, and circumstances surrounding the event.

Have group members take turns adding in details to make the incident come to life again.

This low initial interaction is a non-threatening warm-up and naturally leads into a discussion of feelings in the next stage. It also provides a climate to share the details about the death and to intervene to prevent secrets or rumors that may divide survivors.

Description of Feeling Stage. This stage includes expression of feelings surrounding the event and exploration of symbols. At this stage, survivors should have the opportunity to share the burden of feelings that they are experiencing and to be able to do so in a nonjudgmental, supportive, and understanding environment. Survivors must be permitted to talk about themselves, to identify and to express feelings, to identify their own behavioral reactions, and to relate to the immediate present, that is, the "here and now."

An important aspect in this stage is for the caregiver-as-facilitator to communicate acceptance and understanding of the survivor's feelings. Acceptance of the person's feelings often helps him or her feel better immediately. It also can serve as a developmental transition to a healthier coping style in the future. Thoughtful clarification or reflection of feelings can lead to growth and change, rather than self-depreciation and self-pity.

> Each person in the group is offered an opportunity to answer these and a variety of other questions regarding their feelings. Often survivors will confront the emotion of anger and where the feeling is directed. It is important that survivors express thoughts of responsibility regarding the event and process the accompanying feelings of sadness.
>
> At this stage, care is to be taken to assure that no one gets left out of the discussion, and that no one dominates the discussion at the expense of others.

At times, the therapist has to do very little. Survivors have a tendency to start talking and the whole process goes along with only limited guidance from the therapist. People will most often discuss their fears, anxieties, concerns, feelings of guilt, frustration, anger, and ambivalence. All of their feelings—positive or negative, big or small—are important and need to be listened to and expressed. More important, however, this process allows survivors to see that subtle changes are occurring between what happened then and what is happening now.

Description of Reaction Phase. This stage includes explanation of cognitive and physical reactions and ramifications of the stress response. This stage explores the physical and cognitive reactions to the traumatic event. Acute reactions can last from a few days to a few weeks. Inherently, the survivor wants to move toward some form of resolution and articulates that need in terms such as "I can't go on like this anymore." "Something has got to give." "Please help me shake this feeling," or "I feel like I'm losing my mind." Typical anxiety reactions are a sense of dread, fear of losing control, or the inability to focus or to concentrate.

The caregiver-as-therapist asks such questions as "What reactions did you experience at the time of the incident or when you were informed of the death?" "What are you experiencing now?"

The caregiver-as-therapist encourages clients to discuss what is going on with them in their peer, school, work, and family relationships.

To help clarify reactions, the caregiver-as-therapist may provide a model for describing reactions, such as the focus of "ownership plus feeling word plus description of behavior." For example, "I am afraid to go to sleep at night since this has happened," or "I feel guilty about not seeing the signs that he was considering suicide."

Description of Learning Stage. This stage includes the understanding of posttraumatic stress reactions to loss. This stage is designed to assist survivors in learning new coping skills to deal with their grief reactions. It also is therapeutic to help survivors realize that others are having similar feelings and experiences.

The caregiver-as-therapist assumes the responsibility to teach the group something about their typical stress response reactions.

The emphasis is on describing how typical and natural it is for people to experience a wide variety of feelings, emotions, and physical reactions to any traumatic event. It is not unique but is a universally shared reaction.

Critical to this stage is to be alert to danger signals in order to prevent negative destructive outcomes from a crisis experience and to help survivors return to their precrisis equilibrium and interpersonal stability.

This stage also serves as a primary prevention component for future self-defeating or self-destructive behaviors by identifying the normal responses to a traumatic event in a secure, therapeutic environment with a caring, trusted adult.

Description of Closure. The closure stage includes Wrap-up of loose ends, questions and answers, final reassurances, action planning, referrals, and follow-up. Human crises that involve posttraumatic stress often, if debriefed appropriately, serve as catalysts for personal growth. This final stage seeks to wrap up loose ends and to answer outstanding questions.

PHASES OF RECOVERY

Peter and Straub (1992) classified the recovery process into four phases.

Emergency or Outcry Phase

The survivor experiences heightened "fight or flight" reactions to the life-threatening event. This phase lasts as long as the survivor believes it to last. Pulse, blood pressure, respiration, and muscle activity are all increased. Concomitant feelings of fear and helplessness predominate. Termination of the event itself is followed by relief and confusion. Preoccupation centers around questions about why the event happened and the long term consequences.

Emotional Numbing and Denial Phase

The survivor shelters psychic well-being by burying the traumatic experience in subconscious memory. By avoiding the experience, the victim temporarily reduces anxiety and stress responses. Many survivors may remain at this stage unless they receive professional intervention.

Intrusive-repetitive Phase

The survivor has nightmares, mood swings, intrusive images, and startle reactions. Overreliance on defense mechanisms (e.g., intellectualization, projection, or denial) or self-defeating behaviors (e.g., abuse of alcohol or other drugs) may be integrated into coping behaviors in an effort to repress the traumatic event. At this juncture, the delayed stress becomes so overwhelming that the survivor may either seek help or become so mired in the pathology of the situation that professional intervention becomes necessary.

Perspective for the Therapist: On loss and grief . . .

The only cure for grief is action.

George Henry Lewes

Reflective-transition Phase

The survivor is able to put the traumatic event into perspective. He or she begins to interact positively and constructively with a future orientation and exhibits a willingness to put the traumatic event behind him or her (Peter & Straub, 1992, pp. 246–247).

| Technique | *Clinical Interventions*

Counseling Intention: To help clients through phases of grief and loss

Description. Rando (1984) provides the following clinical interventions for caregivers when confronting grief, dying, and death:

Be present emotionally as well as physically to provide security and support.
Do not allow grievers to become socially isolated.
Make certain that grievers have appropriate medical evaluation and treatment available if symptoms warrant.
Encourage the verbalization of feelings and recollections of the deceased.
Help grievers identify any unfinished business with the deceased and look for appropriate ways to assist closure (one way that comes to mind is having the client write a letter to the deceased addressing the dialogue he or she wished he or she had).
Help grievers find a variety of new sources of personal satisfaction following the loss.
Encourage grievers to be patient and not set unrealistic expectations for themselves.
Help grievers to recognize that loss always brings about change and the need for new adjustments.
Assist grievers in getting and maintaining a proper perspective on what the resolution if grief will mean.
Encourage grievers, at the appropriate time, to find rewarding new things to do and people to invest in.

PART E
IMPROVING
RELATIONSHIPS
WITH OUR FAMILY

Chapter **15**

ECLECTIC TECHNIQUES FOR USE WITH FAMILIES

In the past two decades, family therapy from a systems perspective has gained momentum as an innovative force in counseling. It has profoundly influenced therapeutic interventions in the lives of client and their families (Schafer, Briesmeister, & Fitton, 1984; Stanton, 1984). Systems theory, for example, provides both a conceptual and practical framework for organizing diagnostic information and evaluating presenting problems.

Family systems theory is appropriate when evidence of family dysfunction exists. Fundamentally, the systems theoretical framework views the family as a self-regulating system joined together by unspoken rules whose purpose is to maintain itself. Psychological symptoms are perceived as manifestations of a dysfunctional family. The focus of treatment becomes the family system, not the problem or symptomatic family member. The goal of counseling and family therapy is to engender human and systematic growth.

Therapists always have understood that the problems they deal with arise largely in families and take their form from family relationships. A number of theoretical models have evolved with their respective counseling techniques. Many therapists, however, are eclectic and use the model and technique most appropriate for a particular family and treatment setting. A brief synopsis of eight models follows:

Psychodynamic—an object relations approach to family therapy pioneered by Ackerman (1958) and originally described by Fairbairn (1967) and

Klein (1959) and applied to marital relationships by Dicks (1967). It views dysfunction as the result of inappropriate behavioral attempts to work out issues of the past.

Generational—focuses on the importance of differentiation, relationships between generations, transgenerational dysfunctions (such as alcoholism), and triangulation (Bowen, 1978; Kerr, 1980). Therapists are directive, focusing as teachers and coaches.

Communications—describes pathology manifested in dysfunctional communication patterns (Bateson, 1972; Jackson & Weakland, 1961; Satir, 1967; Satir & Baldwin, 1983). Treatment focuses on changing interpersonal interaction patterns to promote growth and to increase self-esteem, conflict resolution, and new adaptive responses to dysfunctional communication.

Structural—views family dysfunction as a consequence of family structure (Haley, 1976, 1984; Minuchin, 1974; Taylor, 1984). Wisdom and insight come only after structural change.

Systems—emphasizes the influence of networks of relationships upon individuals. Relationships can be understood as any unit of interaction or communication between individuals.

Strategic Intervention—a brief treatment model of therapeutic change designed by the Akerman Institute, Haley (1976, 1984), and Selvini-Palazzoli (1978). Strategic intervention is aimed at changing the powerful family rules in families particularly resistant to change.

Transactional Analysis—created by Eric Berne (1961, 1964) and deals with aspects of the personality that other techniques may exclude: the behavioral, the interpersonal, and the intrapsychic. It is a contractual form of therapy that focuses on ego states of parent, adult, child, and aspects of rescripting for redecision and change.

Multiple-Family Group Therapy—proposed by Bahatti, Janakiramariah, and Channabasvanna (1982) and employs multiple family group therapy as a means for establishing support and help to a family. The family benefits through an extended family living experience. Mutual support and belongingness are common goals; the entire group serves as a resource for problem solving, generating alternatives, and developing action plans for change.

The typical family relationship has changed dramatically in the last two decades. Currently, 22% of children in America today were born out of wedlock. Family organizational structures include blended, common-law, single parent, communal, serial, polygamous, cohabitational, and homosexual (Goldenberg & Goldenberg, 1985). One of the latest family structures is that of skip generation parents—grandparents who are raising their children's children.

Taken in perspective, these kinds of family relationships are having a tremendous impact on schools, communities, childcare, health care, and the workforce. With changing demographics and the accompanying diversity, it becomes even more futile to rely on one model as an all inclusive intervention approach with families. As families journey through developmental stages, coping skills during important transitions may become impaired (Klimek & Anderson, 1988). Members of dysfunctional families can become fixated in self-perpetuating pathological patterns. Common characteristics of such families may include the following:

one or more symptomatic members;
blurred generational boundaries;
confused communication patterns;
overprotection;
enmeshment;
denial;
inability to resolve conflicts;
submerged tension;
scapegoating;
low tolerance for stress;
fragmented, disjointed, isolated individuals;
noncohesive, pseudo-closeness;
skewed relationships, for example, isolation of one member;
extreme positions by all members in an effort to differentiate; and/or
lack of respect for individual differences.

MAJOR FAMILY ISSUES

Walsh (1992) identified 20 major issues in remarriage or step families and placed them in four categories: (a) initial family issues, (b) developing family

---

Perspective for the Therapist: On familiarity and contempt . . .

Everything that irritates us about others can lead us to an understanding of ourselves.

Carl Jung

•

When we see men of a contrary character, we should turn inwards and examine ourselves.

Confucius

Perspective for the Therapist: On taking responsibility for our actions as parents . . .

We all carry our parents around inside us. Their presence is always felt, still nagging, praising, threatening, judging, advising. The extent that our parents were wise and loving, their presence is useful, as well as pleasant company. . . . When parents are unwise, insensitive, harsh, unloving, or misguided, their presence is detrimental.

Jack Lee Rosenberg
Majorie L. Rand

---

issues, (c) feelings about self and others, and (d) adult issues. These 20 major issues are significant contributors to family disharmony. Counselor sensitivity to these concerns may lead to more accurate assessments and more timely interventions (p. 714). The major issues identified were as follows:

Initial Family Issues

1. Name of the new parent. Issues of power and authority are concerns.
2. Affection for the new parent and absent parent. Issues of loyalty or allegiance are concerns.
3. Loss of natural parent. Issues of loss and grief.
4. Instant love of new family members. Issues of emotional bonding are concerns.
5. Fantasy about the old family structure. Issues of fantasy of parental reconciliation are concerns, especially for a child whose identification with the absent parent is strong.

Developing Family Issues

6. Discipline by the stepparent. Issues of being inattentive, disengaged or overly restrictive are concerns.
7. Confusion over family roles. Issues of role assignments involves cultural, personal, and legal spheres creating ambiguity.
8. Sibling conflict. Issues of stepsibling relationships are crucial to the success of step families.
9. Competition for time. Issues about contact with absent parent and increased competition of the custodial parent and jealously of the stepparent are concerns.
10. Extended kinship network. Issues of expectation, different views of values and lifestyles, and belongingness are concerns as well as issues of visitations during significant holidays.

Perspective for the Therapist: On growing old . . .

There is a fountain of youth: It is your mind, your talents, the creativity you bring in your life and the lives of people you love.

Sophia Loren

11. Sexual conflicts. Loosening of sexual boundaries are concerns.
12. Changes over time. Issues of remarriage, organization, and boundaries are concerns.
13. Exit and entry of children. Issues around children from their permanent home to the home of the noncustodial parent influence home, school, and peer relations.

Feelings about Self and Others

14. Society's acceptance of the remarriage family.
15. The connotation of step family.
16. Individual self concept and lower self esteem.

Adult Issues

17. Effects of parenting on the new marital relationship.
18. Financial concerns and obligations.
19. Continuing adult conflict from previous relationships and communication with children.
20. Competition of the noncustodial parent regarding child rearing and material possessions.

| Technique | *Counseling Techniques for Dysfunctional Families* |

Counseling Intention: To help family members demonstrate how they normally deal with situations

Description. Anderson (1988) capsulized several techniques that can be useful in assessing how families work together, their developmental stage and their real versus presenting problem.

Sequencing—ask questions such as who does what, when? When the kids are fighting, what is the mother/father doing?

Hypothetical Questions—who would be most likely to stay home if a child became ill? Which child can you visualize living at home as an adult?

Perspective for the Therapist: On extenuating circumstances . . .

The actuarial conditions that might have influenced her fate include such factors as what sex the child turns out to be, her place in the birth order of siblings (and how it relates to the parents' places in their own early families), the stage of the marriage at which she was born, the family's economic situation and so on. Her destiny did not have anything to do with what sort of child she really was.

Sheldon B. Kopp

Scaling Reports—on a scale of most-least, compare one another in terms of anger, power, neediness, happiness.

Family Map—organize information about the generational development of the family that reveals the transmission of family rules, roles, and myths (Bowen, 1978).

Tracking—how does the family deal with a problem. "What was it like for you when . . .? rather than "How did you feel when . . .? Such questions help keep the focus on the family rather than on the individual.

Sculpting—Create a still picture of the family that symbolizes relationships by having members position one another physically. This technique can be used to cut through defenses and helps nonverbal members express themselves.

Paradoxical Intervention—Instruct the family to do something they do not expect and to observe how the family then changes by rebellion or noncompliance. This is often most appropriate with highly resistant or rigid families.

SELF-DESTRUCTIVE BEHAVIOR

| Technique | *The Family Safety Watch*

Counseling Intention: To provide a family network for crisis intervention; to provide an intervention strategy for self-destructive behavior

Description. The Family Safety Watch (Stanton, 1984) is an intense intervention strategy to prevent self-destructive behavior of a family member (e.g., suicidal adolescent). The safety watch also can apply to such problems as child abuse, self-mutilation, eating disorders, and drug or alcohol abuse. The procedure is as follows:

Perspective for the Therapist: On suicide . . .

Those left behind are faced by a triple loss: that from death, rejection, and disillusionment. Suicide takes away self-worth. All these factors operate to increase the potential of hostility in the mourner and the danger of his turning it upon himself as the only available or most appropriate target.

Erich Lindeman

Ina May Greer

Family members conduct the watch. They select people to be involved in the watch from among their nuclear family, extended family, and network of family friends.

An around-the-clock shift schedule is established to determine what the adolescent is to do with his or her time over a 24–hour period, i.e., when he or she is to sleep, eat, attend class, do homework, play games, view a movie, etc. according to a structured planned agenda.

The intervention team leader consults with the family in (a) determining what the family resources and support systems are, (b) figuring out ways for involving these support systems in the effort (e.g., "How much time do you think Uncle Harry can give to watching your son/daughter?"), (c) designing a detailed plan for the safety watch, and (d) figuring out schedules and shifts so that someone is with the at-risk child 24 hours per day.

A back-up system also is established so that the person on watch can obtain support from others if he or she needs it. (A cardinal rule is that the child be within view of someone at all times, even while in the bathroom or when sleeping.)

The family is warned that the at-risk youth may try to manipulate situations to be alone (e.g., pretend to be fine) and that the first week will be the hardest.

A contractual agreement is established that if the watch is inadvertently slackened or compromised and the at-risk youth makes a suicide attempt or tries to challenge the program in some way, the regime consequently will be tightened. This is a therapeutic move that reduces the family's feeling of failure should a relapse occur during the year.

The primary goal of the watch is to mobilize the family to take care of their "own"; and feel competent in doing so. With tasks surrounding the watch, the family, adolescent, and helping professionals (as a team) collaborate in determining what the adolescent must do in order to relax and ultimately to terminate the watch. Task issues should focus around personal responsibility, age appropriate behavior, and handling of family and social relationships, such as the following:

> arise in the morning without prompting,
> complete chores on time,
> substitute courteous and friendly behavior for grumbling and sulking,
> talk to parents and siblings more openly, and
> watch less TV and spend more time with friends and significant others.

The decision to terminate the watch is made conjointly by the family and the therapeutic team. It is contingent upon the absence of self-destructive behavior as well as the achievement of an acceptable level of improvement in the other behavioral tasks assigned to the adolescent. If any member of the therapeutic team feels there is still a risk, the full safety watch is continued.

This approach appeals to families because it makes them feel potent and useful and reduces the expense of an extended hospital program. It also reestablishes the intergenerational boundary, opens up communication within the family, reconnects the nuclear and extended families, and makes the adolescent cared for and safe. In addition, it functions as a "compression" move that pushes the youth and family members closer together and holds them there and awaits the rebound or disengagement that almost inevitably follows. This rebound is often a necessary step in bringing about appropriate distance within enmeshed subsystems opening the way for a more viable family structure—a structure that does not require a member to exhibit suicidal or self-destructive behavior.

After-care Transition and Support Procedures

> Make contact with parent, student, and community mental health service with request for written permission for release of information from mental health community agency;
> ascertain the post-treatment plan for the individual and provide support with initial caregiver;
> provide feedback to support people and monitoring individuals; and
> provide feedback to others regarding adjustment concerns.

Perspective for the Therapist: On difficulties . . .

There are two ways of meeting difficulties: You alter the difficulties or you alter yourself meeting them.

Phyllis Bottome

A caveat: Assessment guides highlight the importance of patterns of signs or ideation and the use of clinical judgment along with a data base. No single rating scale or contract, however, ever should be used in isolation for evaluating suicidal risk.

OPENING COMMUNICATION

| Technique | *Airing Grievances Constructively*

Counseling Intention: To provide a constructive way to build a new relationship

Description. The following guidelines provided by Bach and Wyden (1968) are designed to provide a constructive way of rebuilding relationships between couples. It can be adapted for any two people with conflict or resentment toward each other. Make an appointment to confront each other. Many conflicts and accompanying dialogue are unproductive because only one individual is ready to confront the issues and the other may refuse to fight. Designating a time without distractions provides a more equitable advantage.

Take turns expressing resentments. Let one person talk for five minutes without interruption. Reciprocate the process.

When all issues are presented, have your partner repeat the concerns as your outlined them. Check for understanding. Reciprocate the process.

Clearly state your expectations of each other—the behavior you will not resent.

Determine together if your expectations are realistic, negotiable, or both. Then proceed with a mutually satisfactory agreement about the future. Be as specific as possible about compromises and expectations.

| Technique | *Exercises to Open Communication*

Counseling Intention: Satir (1967) provided a strategy for helping couples reach a deeper level of communication and understanding

---

Perspective for the Therapist: On conflict . . .

Difficulties are meant to rouse, not discourage. The human spirit is to grow strong by conflict.

William Ellery Channing

Perspective for the Therapist: On self-esteem . . .

I regard self-esteem as the single most powerful force in our existence. The way we feel about ourselves affects virtually every aspect of our existence: work, love, sex, interpersonal relationships of every kind.

Nathaniel Brandon

Description. Instruct couples to do the following:

First stand back to back and talk to each other. This frequently occurs when one wants to talk finances or schedules and the other is reading the newspaper, fixing dinner, or otherwise preoccupied.

Next stand face to face, and look at each other without talking. What do you think your partner is thinking and feeling? When discussing, check for the accuracy of your perception.

Now eyeball each other, and communicate without talking. See how much more communication gets through.

Close your eyes and communicate without talking.

Eyeball each other and talk without touching.

Finally, use all forms of communication (talk, touch, look at each other).

Most couples find it difficult to argue with each other without looking away or withdrawing physically. Touch and eye contact creates more intimacy.

| Technique | *Receiving Family Feedback*

Counseling Intention: To provide structured exercises for feedback from family members

Description. Lewis and Streitfeld (1970) provided the following strategies to solicit feedback from members of the family.

Stranger on a Train. Imagine that a stranger is coming to visit you. He has never met your family, and someone is to meet him at the train. How would each member of your family describe the others? Be specific, go beyond what they might be wearing to a personality or behavioral trait.

Biography. Imagine that somebody is writing a biography of each member

Perspective for the Therapist: On relationships . . .

For me, anything that gives new hope, new possibilities and new positive feelings about ourselves will make us more whole people and thus more human, real and loving in our relationships with others.

If enough of this happens, the world will become a better place for all of us. I matter. You matter. What goes on between us matters.

Since I always carry me with me, and I belong to me, I always have something to bring to you and me—new resources, new possibilities to cope differently and to create anew.

Virginia Satir

of your family. When interviewed, what would each member say about the other—likes/dislikes, turn-ons/turn-offs, values/goals, etc.

Self-portrait. After everyone has had a chance to describe everyone else, describe yourself. How would you tell someone to find you at the station? What would you tell your biographer? Then discuss the differences that turn up between self-impressions and family's impressions of you. What have you found out about yourself?

Family Adjectives. If you could choose just one adjective to describe each member in your family, what would it be? Check for discrepancies and congruencies among family members.

Sculpturing. Go up to each member of the family in turn, and arrange his or her body in a position that you feel characterizes him or her. Give the sculpture a title.

Family Classified. Write a classified ad for your ideal family (e.g.,"father wanted . . ." and "daughter wanted. . .") in which you describe, in 20 or 30 words, what you would like in a family member. Compose the ad in which you list your attributes. Describe the kind of relative you are and how you may improve. Examples are as follows:

Father Wanted
   "To be more involved with teenager. Be attentive, warm, and understanding. Let daughter be herself and trust her more. Listen without putting others down or without shouting."

Daughter Available
   "Warm and concerned about others when not hassled. Has made mistakes but is willing to learn. May be strong willed and assertive too much, but very honest."

Perspective for the Therapist: On relationships . . .

Many people prefer the initial rush of new relationships to the often less than exciting reality of long-term relationships. Although an attraction to each other may be spontaneous, a satisfying, self-esteem-enhancing relationship must require risk taking, hard work and acceptance of other people's flaws, and many people are not willing to do that kind of work.

Linda Tschirhart Sanford
Mary Ellen Donovan

Technique | *Time-limited Intercommunication*

Counseling Intention: To treat marital discord; to achieve more equitable levels of understanding and communication

Description. The couple is instructed to set aside at least three separate, hour-long appointments each week for prescribed communication. A timer is set for five minutes. During those five minutes the first speaker discusses any topic of choice. The listener may not interrupt. The listener may take notes in preparation for a rebuttal, but no verbal response may occur until the five minutes elapses and the timer sounds.

The timer is set for another five minutes and the other partner repeats the process under the same ground rules. Each partner has six 5-minute intervals in which to talk and six to attend to the other person's verbalizations. At the end of the hour, the couple is to embrace each other and to cease further communication on the issues until the next 1-hour appointment.

Technique | *The Simulated Family Game*

Counseling Intention: To explore family roles and gain insight into one's behavior and its effect on others

Description. The various family members simulate each other's behaviors; for example, the daughter plays the father, the father the stepson. The members may also be asked to pretend they are a different family. The therapist and family discuss how they differ from or identify with the roles they project.

| Technique | *Family Sayings* |

Counseling Intention: To encourage self awareness, expectations, and transgenerational belief systems

Description. Every family has its own favorite expressions, belief systems, slogans, warnings, or counsel. Have members list all the repetitive expressions they recall from their childhood. For example, "Fathers Knows Best" may be interpreted as you have no opinion of your own; "What will the neighbors think" may be interpreted as do not let anything tarnish our public facade; or "One man's trash is another man's treasure" may be warning not to discard anything!

Have members list all repetitive expressions that they can recall from childhood. Process: What were the underlying messages? What values do they represent? How do they influence growth or impede independence?

| Technique | *Family Sculpture* |

Counseling Intention: To assess communication and relationships

Description. Ask someone in the family to describe a typical family argument, then have them sculpt the argument by placing each family member in appropriate positions—complete with gestures, facial expressions, and touch. This can be followed by asking each of the other members how he or she would change it and letting each make the changes.

| Technique | *All Tied Up* |

Counseling Intention: To better understand the complexity of relationships and crossed transactions

Description. Each family member takes some long ropes, one for each of the other in the family, and ties all of them around his or her waist. Next, instruct them to tie one rope to each of the other family members. Process the resulting tension and mass of ropes to help members understand the complexity of its relationships and crossed transactions.

GENOGRAMS

•profession•values•coping style•parent-child relationships•traditions
•addictive behaviors•predispositions•education•career•obsessions
•identities•mediators•helplessness•politics•likes/dislikes•talents
•birth order•communication•pressures•power•depression•myths•abuse
•hobbies•incest•paternal•single status•armed services•disabilities•intimacy
•anxieties•tragedies•family secrets•maternal•married•interests•traits

The genogram is a format for constructing a family tree which can provide a structure as a diagnostic and treatment technique (Wachtel, 1982). It reflects the clinical perspective that the self originates within a family context. Systems models, self-psychology, and object relations theories all hold that personal identity is intricately intertwined with the intergenerational family—past, present, and future (Erlanger, 1990; Bowen, 1978; Kohut, 1971; Scharf & Scharf, 1987).

Murray Bowen (1978) developed the genogram in the late 1970's as a tool for analyzing family structures in his family systems for professional family assessment. Transgenerational issues play an important role in family dynamics. Families have different "scripts," and in any one family there can be several sets of directions and expectations.

| Technique | Genograms |

Counseling Intention: To recognize transgenerational issues, enmeshed boundaries, communication patterns, family rituals, and family dysfunctions

Description. The genogram provides an enormous amount of information in a relatively short period of time. There are three types of genograms (a) the basic genogram, (b) the distance genogram, and (c) the details genogram. The basic genogram focuses on individuals, gender, date of birth, career, marriage, divorce, remarriage, or death. The *distance genogram* focuses on interpersonal relationships within family systems. The *details genogram* provides a more comprehensive diagram of a family over three generations focusing on personality traits, unusual circumstances, family themes, family roles, traditions, belief systems, and interpersonal hierarchies.

Perspective for the Therapist: On women . . .

. . . [S]tudies of women have repeatedly shown disturbing patterns: lack of self-esteem, an inability to feel powerful or in control of one's life, a vulnerability to depression, a tendency to see oneself as less talented, less able than one really is. The myriad of studies that have been done over the years give the distinct impression of constriction, a crippling, a sense of being somehow not quite as good, not quite as able, not quite as bright, not quite as valuable as men. . . . When you leaf through the studies you can sense, floating in the air, ghosts of unborn dreams, unrealized hopes, undiscovered talents. The tragedies are the "might have beens," and they are the most poignant.

Caryl Rivers
Rosalind Barnett
Grace Baruch

A number of therapeutic aspects can occur when completing a genogram. First, the process of creating a genogram provides a focus for the interview while fostering an empathic relationship between the client and the counselor. Second, the genogram may take the focus off the identified client and subtly reframe the situation as a "family problem." Third, the genogram provides a natural framework for a life review presenting problems in wider context while identifying psychological resources that may link the past with the future. Another analysis could include a distance genogram to identify emotional links as well as generational lines. The counselor also may want to focus on a client's relationships or family "scripts." In any one family there may be several sets of directions.

INTERACTIVE APPROACHES

| Technique | *Interactive Techniques for Working with Children*

Counseling Intention: To build rapport and a relationship

Description. Interactive techniques with children can include

> therapeutic game play (Corder, 1986; Nickerson & O'Laughlin, 1982; Schaefer & Reid, 1986; Serok, 1986),
> stories and metaphors (Brooks, 1985; Brooks, 1987; Gardner, 1986), and
> role-play and simulation (Larrabee & Wilson, 1981; Renard & Sockol, 1987).

Description of Games. The use of games as a structured therapeutic tool in child therapy is beginning to gain momentum within professional circles. Many counselors are familiar with psychologically therapeutic games, such as the "Talking, Feeling, and Doing Game" (Gardner, 1986) and the "Ungame" (Parker Brothers). Checkers or chess also can be used either as a diagnostic or therapeutic tool. By observing how the child plays the game, the counselor can gain insight about the child's attitude, viewpoint, and behavior of self and others.

The counselor can use the interaction during the game as a means for making therapeutic comments and suggestions. The counselor also may use the context of the game to make interpretations about children's behavior, thought patterns, and feelings. For example, Gardner (1986) revealed that children who lack self-esteem may hesitate to play checkers because they are afraid they may lose. Rather than risk ineptitude, they may suggest a game of chance such as "black jack."

Kottman (1990) found that games can provide the counselor with a therapeutic tool for deepening the therapeutic relationship in a relatively short period of time. Playing games allows for a safe manner of expression for feelings, thoughts, and attitudes. It also offers a structured format for exploring children's concerns and interactional patterns. Games like checkers or chess also can be used to encourage children and to help them learn and assimilate new behaviors.

Description of Stories and Metaphors. Stories and metaphors can facilitate the expression of threatening emotions with a minimum of risk to the child.

One method that the counselor may find useful is the ***mutual storytelling technique*** (Gardner, 1986). Gardner developed this technique to communicate with children using their own language and to gain insight into their own behavior and interactions. In the mutual storytelling technique, the counselor tells the child that they are going to do a Make-Up-a-Story Television Program. To start this television program, the child must tell a story, with a beginning, a middle, and an end. The child invents the characters, the setting, the themes, and the plot of the story. The counselor listens to the story, attempting to grasp the symbolic meaning of the setting, the characters, and the plot. Then the counselor chooses one or two important ideas from the original story and tells a different story, using the same setting and characters. The characters in the counselor's story, however, should resolve their differences in a more mature, adaptive way then do the characters in the original story (Kottman, 1990).

In the ***creative characters technique***, Brooks (1987) uses stories to represent different aspects of a child's interpersonal life such as self-esteem, relationships, beliefs, values, feelings, learning style and coping style. The counselor audiotapes the beginning of the story before the counseling session. The counselor establishes characters, setting, and some general themes in the beginning story. Each story contains significant characters that represent the child and significant others in the child's life. The counselor takes on the active role of key character (such as "wise owl" or "super hero") to communicate to the child about the dynamics of problem situation and about possible alternative solutions to difficulties (Brooks, 1987). After the initial segment of the story in which the structure for the setting and characters is established, the child becomes the storyteller, responsible for the plot and themes from his or her point of view. Many times, simply by listening to the child describe various significant others, the counselor can generate metaphors that "will resonate with client's inner world and a significant level of understanding will be established" (Brooks, 1985, p.765). Kottman (1990) maintained that "communication through metaphors allows children to experience and express threatening emotions directly. This sanctioned distancing may help decrease some of the stress involved in the counseling process and convert resistance to cooperation" (Kottman, 1990, p. 142).

Description of Role-play and Simulation. Role-play and simulation provide a means for trying on new skills or creating self-awareness in a nonthreatening manner. Renard & Sockol (1987) have suggested that creative dramatics (role-playing and simulations) can be used by counselors to promote thinking, learning, and social skills by

> increasing one's ability to communicate feelings and thoughts;
> developing listening skills, concentration, and the ability to observe and discuss;
> fostering imagination, spontaneity, and visualization skills;
> encouraging increased originality, flexibility, and elaboration of thinking;
> creating an atmosphere in which children can begin to feel successful;

Perspective for the Therapist: On expressions of the heart . . .

What we say is important . . . for in most cases the mouth speaks what the heart is full of.

Jim Beggs

•

Everyone should carefully observe which way his heart draws him, and then choose that way with all his strength.

Hasidic Saying

---

sharpening abilities in cooperation, planning, decision making, and evaluating; and
having fun.

Using simulations and role-playing, the counselor frames an initial situation,
outlines any rules that have implications in the situation, and asks the child to
act out the particular situation. After the entire interaction is completed, the
counselor processes the experience with children focusing on reactions and observations. Simulations and role-plays have been successful for promoting peer
pressure refusal skills, communication, feeling-processing skills, decision-making
skills, moral dilemmas, skills for establishing positive behavior, assertiveness
skills, family relationship, or interpersonal skills.

Chapter **16**

PARADOXICAL STRATEGIES

Paradoxical interventions (techniques which seem self-contradictory or absurd, and yet explicable as expressing the truth) have been described as capable of effecting dramatic change in even the most difficult clients. The popularity and acceptance of these unorthodox methods seem to increase almost yearly, and approximately two-thirds of the burgeoning literature on the therapeutic paradox has appeared since the mid-1970s (Seltzer, 1986).

Paradoxical strategies have been effectively employed to deal with a full spectrum of dysfunctional behaviors. The literature reflects the following topics: academic problems, addictive behaviors, adolescent problems, aggression, agoraphobia, anorexia nervosa, anxiety, bulimia, compulsive behaviors, depression, insomnia, marital conflict, obsessive-compulsive disorders, phobias, psychosomatic symptoms, school problems, sexual problems and dysfunctions, and suicidal ideation.

Sometimes there is a value of utilizing seemingly irrational (paradoxical) strategies in psychotherapy. Currently, there is a rapidly growing interest in paradoxical techniques. From the theoretical perspectives of psychoanalysis, behavior therapy, humanistic psychotherapy, and interpersonal communications and systems theory, paradoxical interventions have been touted as capable of effecting dramatic change in even the most difficult clients. The initial introduction of paradox in psychotherapy is perhaps most accurately associated with systems-oriented therapists working primarily within a family context.

Stanton (1981) delineated an almost unlimited applicability of therapeutic paradox by cataloging the disorders successfully treated from a strategic view-

---

Perspective for the Therapist: On genuineness . . .

Today we come across an individual who behaves like an automaton, who does not know or understand himself, and the only person that he knows is the person that he is supposed to be, whose meaningless chatter has replaced communicative speech, whose synthetic smile has replaced genuine laughter, and whose sense of dull despair has taken the place of genuine pain. Two statements may be said concerning this individual. One is that he suffers from defects of spontaneity and individuality which may seem to be incurable. At the same time it may be said of him he does not differ essentially from the millions of the rest of us who walk upon this earth."

Erich Fromm

---

point. Stanton's categories include adolescent problems, aging, alcoholism, anorexia and eating disorders, anxiety, asthma, behavioral problems, delinquency, childhood "emotional" problems, crying, depression, dizziness, drug abuse and addiction, encopresis, enuresis, fire setting, homosexuality, hysterical blindness, identity crises, insomnia, leaving home, marital conflict, obesity, obsessive-compulsive behavior, obsessive thoughts, chronic pain, paranoia, phobias, postpartum depression and psychosis, public speaking anxiety, schizophrenia, school problems and truancy, sexual problems, sleep disturbances, stammering, suicidal gestures, excessive sweating, temper tantrums, thumb-sucking, tinnitus, vomiting and stomach aches, and work problems (pp. 368–369).

Strategic family therapists have been most identified with the use of paradoxical interventions. The basic tenet of strategic therapy is that therapeutic change comes about through the "interactional processes set off when a therapist intervenes actively and directly" in a family or marital system (Haley, 1973, p. 7). The goal is to change the dysfunctional sequence of behaviors manifested by couples and families. The therapist works to substitute new behavior patterns or sequences for the vicious, positive feedback circles already existing (Weakland, Fisch, Watzlawick, & Bodin, 1974).

The use of paradoxical intervention techniques have been described by a number of researchers (Anderson & Russell, 1982; Apante & Van Deusen, 1981; de Shazer, 1978, 1979; Frankl, 1960; Haley, 1967, 1973, 1976; Hare-Mustin, 1976; L'Abate & Weeks, 1978; Rimm & Masters, 1979; Seltzer, 1986; Watzlawick, Beavin, & Jackson, 1967; Weeks-L'Abate, 1982). Watzlawick, et. al (1967) defined paradox as a "contradiction that follows correct deduction from consistent premises" (p. 188).

Hare-Mustin (1976) further maintained that paradoxical interventions "those which appear absurd because they exhibit an apparently contradictory nature, such as requiring clients to do what in fact they have been doing, rather than requiring that they change, which is what everyone else is demanding" (p. 128). Rohrbaugh, Tennen, Press, and White (1981) more precisely described paradoxical interventions as "strategies and tactics in apparent opposition to the acknowledged goals of therapy, but actually designed to achieve them" (p. 454).

In comparison, Jacobson and Margolin (1979) described paradoxical interventions as "instructing clients to engage in the very behavior that has been identified as a target for elimination in therapy" (p. 150). Finally, Seltzer (1986) outlined a working definition of paradoxical intervention: "A paradoxical strategy refers to a therapist's directive or attitude that is perceived by the client, at least initially, as contrary to therapeutic goals, but which is yet rationally understandable and specifically devised by the therapist to achieve these goals" (p. 10).

Seltzer (1986) also outlined the employment of paradox by various schools: From the psychoanalytic perspective, which includes the work of paradigmatic psychotherapists, we have inherited the descriptors "antisuggestion," "going with the resistance," "joining the resistance," "reflecting (or mirroring) the resistance," "siding with resistance," "paradigmatic exaggeration," "supporting the defenses," "reduction act absurdum," "re-enacting an aspect of the psychosis," "mirroring the patient's distortions," "participating in the patient's fantasies," "outcrazing the patient," and "the use of the patient as consultant."

From the perspective of behavior therapy, paradoxical elements are in such procedures as "blow-up," "implosion," "flooding," "negative practice," "paradoxical intention," "stimulus satiation," and "symptom scheduling." Furthermore, from a systems' approach to therapy or strategic therapy especially applicable to family systems, the strategic paradoxical strategies include "the confusion technique," "declaring hopelessness," "exaggerating the position," "paradoxical injunction," "paradoxical instructions," "paradoxical rituals and tasks," "paradoxical written messages," "restraining (or "inhibiting") change," "predicting a relapse," "prescribing a relapse," "positive connotation," (or "interpretation"), "reframing," "redefinition," "relabeling," "symptom prescription" (or "prescribing the resistance, symptom, or system"), "therapeutic paradox," and the "therapeutic double bind" (Seltzer, 1986, p. 20).

| Technique | *Negative Practice*

Counseling Intention: To break a compulsive habit

Description. Negative practice is a corrective learning procedure defined as "the practice of a response for the purpose of breaking the habit of making the response" (Dunlap, 1942, p. 191). This approach could be applicable to such problems as habitual spelling and typing mistakes, muscular tensions, stage fright, obsessions, compulsions, hypochondria, social anxieties, chronic worry, tics, nailbiting, and stammering (Dunlap, 1946).

| Technique | *Stimulus Satiation*

Counseling Intention: To overdue a particular habit that is satisfying yet dangerous

Description. "Stimulus satiation refers to the repeated presentation of a positive stimulus to the satiety, in order to lessen or eliminate its abnormally high positive valence" (Seltzer, 1986, p. 50). This technique could be useful when dealing with difficult smoking or eating behaviors. For example, a client may need to chain smoke for extended periods of time in order to finally break the habit. It also could be used with an adolescent who begins to experiment with cigarettes by having the client smoke a pack until smoking becomes undesirable.

| Technique | *Implosion and Flooding or "Forced Reality Testing"*

Counseling Intention: To overcome habitual responses of avoidance

Description. Implosion or flooding focuses on the repeated presentation of an intense phobic stimuli to eradicate the problematic responses connected to them. The technique involves exposing individuals to increasingly intense phobic stimuli while preventing their habitual response of avoidance. Both implosion and flooding concentrate on the presentation of highly anxiety provoking scenes (arranged in a hierarchy).

The client is confronted with the stimulus (imagined or in vivo) without relaxation or pause so as to elicit the maximum sustained emotional response

---

Perspective for the Therapist: On family rules . . .

. . . the spoken and unspoken rules of many families in terms of the way the child is raised militate against successful separation/individuation."

David Klimek
Mary Anderson

---

possible and ultimately to "exhaust" the response. Seltzer (1986) pointed out that "overexposure to highly charged stimuli leads, at least theoretically, to an ever-decreasing emotional response, so that self-control is regained through the very process of the individual's agreeing to allow himself to be put "out of' control" (p. 52). This is most applicable to individuals with poor impulse control, stress, insomnia, fear of rejection, depression, grief, or guilt. It has also been used with such anxiety-provoking fears as speaking in public, receiving injections, being in an elevator, spiders, and snakes.

Marshall, Gauthier, Christie, Currie, and Gordon (1977) and Redd, Porterfield, and Anderson (1979) have suggested, however, that imaginal exposure to horrifying situations may, under certain conditions, strengthen a client's fear. The therapist should be very familiar with (a) identifying anxiety cues, (b) formulating highly anxiety-provoking scenes, and (c) alternative therapeutic approaches for individuals who have a very negative experience.

| *Technique* | *Paradoxical Intention*

Counseling Intention: To challenge and immerse clients in their symptomatic behavior

Description. Frankl (1960) introduced paradoxical intention as a logo therapeutic technique. Paradoxical intention advises clients to experience their symptoms freely, frequently, and to the extreme. Deliberately practicing the behaviors adamantly avoided opens them up to their anxiety directly.

| *Technique* | *Prescribing, Restraining, and Positioning*

Counseling Intention: To modify the problematic behavior

Description. "Prescribing" tactics encourage or direct clients to engage in the behavior targeted for elimination. "Restraining" methods discourage changes or suggest that change is not even possible. "Positioning" techniques involve altering a problematic stance by accepting and exaggerating it.

| *Technique* | *Reframing, Relabeling, and Redefinition*

Counseling Intention: To modify the problematic behavior

Perspective for the Therapist: On the family . . .

With increased incidence of divorce and remarriage it is not unusual for the initial family developmental cycle to be disrupted and split into several separate life cycles.

Adequate support is particularly difficult to come by in a new or reconstituted family that is trying to consolidate.

David Klimek
Mary Anderson

Description. "Reframing," relabeling, and redefinition are treated synonymously by Seltzer (1986). Treatment involves altering the meaning attributed to a situation by changing the cognitive or emotional context (the frame) in which the situation is experienced. Since the problem is the result of the prevailing cognitive-emotional situation, to modify that situation is inevitably to modify the problem as well (Seltzer, 1986, p. 106).

| *Technique* | *Positive Interpretation* |

Counseling Intention: To reframe the problem

Description. In this technique, the therapist ascribes positive motives to clients. The therapist might relabel "hostile" behavior as "concerned interest" (Weakland, Finch, Watzlawick, & Boden, 1974) or perhaps as a desire to "get the best care possible" for the identified client. Rationale: blaming, criticism, and negative terms tend to mobilize resistance, rendering the therapist as incapable.

| *Technique* | *Positive Connotation* |

Counseling Intention: To relabel the problem from a positive perspective

Description. Positive connotation is the hallmark of Selvini-Palazzoli, Boscolo, Cecchin, & Prata (1974) and associates in the Milano group. By describing relationships in a positive way, that is, positively addressing the homeostatic tendency of the family system rather than individual members, greater access to the family system is achieved. Selvini-Palazzoli et al. (1974) maintained that through positive connotation that

> We implicitly declare ourselves as allies of the family's striving for homeostasis, and we do this at the moment that the family feels

it is most threatened. By strengthening the homeostatic tendency, we gain influence over the ability to change. Total acceptance of the marital or family system by the therapists enable them to be accepted in the family game, a necessary step toward changing the game through paradox. (p. 441)

Dell (1981) perhaps capsulized the relationship that is fostered. He suggested that the therapist's stance is paradoxical in its being at once "benevolent" and "toxic": benevolent because of the loving and charitable motives it ascribes to the family and its symptom bearer (dysfunctional member), and toxic because it radically contradicts family members' perceptions as to what is actually happening in the family." In such a context, Dell perceived the family members as changing "in the process of trying to rid themselves of the toxic and stupefying reframing of their family game" (pp. 49–50).

| Technique | *Symptom Exaggeration* |

Counseling Intention: To magnify or enlarge the problem

Description. Symptom exaggeration is an amplification technique where the client is instructed to magnify or enlarge upon the problem. Again, the deliberate intensification of behavior previously regarded as involuntary serves to demonstrate to the client that he or she can control the behavior, hopefully in a more positive direction. Aponte and Van Deusen (1981) concluded that symptom exaggeration can increase the magnitude of the symptom beyond the point that it can continue to serve a compensatory function with the result that it must eventually be abandoned.

| Technique | *System Prescription* |

Counseling Intention: To make covert family rules more overt

Description. System prescription is another benchmark of Selvini-Palazzoli and associates. The very rules that have resulted in a symptomatic family member are prescribed. The therapist prescribes the various interpersonal components of problem-perpetuating behavior. This maneuver serves to make more overt the covert rules that control the family's interaction. Once members become aware of how the "roles" dictated by their self-defeating rules contribute to their problems, it becomes increasingly difficult to follow them.

| Technique | *Paradoxical Written Messages* |

Counseling Intention: To obtain greater client involvement by being ambiguous or obscure

Description. Paradoxical written messages are unexpected mail. L'Abate and his colleagues at the Family Study Center at Georgia State University are perhaps the major proponents of the paradoxical written message. Weeks and L'Abate (1982) found that paradoxical letters are almost always reacted to as "cryptic, obscure, confusing, perplexing, or noncommonsensical and it helps to secure the client's involvement, since the person or system receiving the letter must work on deciphering its meaning" (p. 156). To illustrate the paradoxical techniques of reframing and prescribing defeat, Seltzer (1986) provided the following:

> Reframing positively can be used in families when they are acting
> out to protect the parental relationship. The defeating pattern can
> be reframed in order to tie it to success, enjoyment, caring, protec-
> tiveness, closeness, or intimacy. (p. 36)

Below is a list of rules for this assignment followed by a typical letter, much like the ritualized prescriptions used by Selvini-Palazzoli et al. (1974).

Perspective for the Therapist: On ambiguity . . .

I know I'm better because I feel worse. The nicer you are, the harder it gets. The stronger I grow, the weaker I feel. You can't give it to me because I already have it. I can't be little because you are bigger. The more lost I become, the clearer it gets. I'm feeling confused, I must be in the right place.

I move the furthest when I'm stuck. The worst part is knowing that I can make it. The safest places are the most dangerous. The more I cry, the harder I laugh. The more I try, the harder you laugh. The more I love, the more I hate. The more I fight, the more friends I have.

I can't make you love me, you already do. I can't be special, everyone is. Given permission to rest, I work harder. When I rest you call it work; When I play, you call it work; When I work you call it work. I can't mess up.

Since I can't please or displease you, guess I'll just have to do what I want. I don't get to win but I don't have to lose. There is no winning or losing, but I get to keep what I have.

Marcia Dienelt

---

1. Father will read this letter to other members of the family.
2. The letter will be read after dinner on Monday, Wednesday, and Friday evenings.
3. Mother will remind father to read the letter.
4. Please do not discuss the content of this letter with anyone outside of counseling.

Dear _____,

We (the parents) are appreciative of your protecting us because as long as you act up neither Mother nor I will need to look at ourselves and deal with our middle age. You will also help your brother to stay the way he is.

Consequently, we will understand that anytime you blow up, it will be to protect us and your brother. We hope, therefore, that you will continue protecting us, because we need it.

| Technique | *Prescribing the Defeat*

Counseling Intention: To escalate the behavior that family members are using to defeat each other

Description. After reframing a behavior, the next step is to prescribe the behavior. Since the defeat is now a positive expression, it follows that the family should assist, continue, and even escalate and increase whatever they are doing to defeat each other. To make sure that the reframing and prescription are not going to be ignored or forgotten, it is helpful to put them in writing and to ritualize them (i.e., "Read this letter after supper on alternating days, either Monday, Wednesday, and Fridays, or Tuesdays, Thursdays, and Saturdays," as the Milano group recommends) (Selvini-Palazzoli, Boscolo, Cecchin, & Prata, 1978). This letter can be given to the child from the last example to read to his parents following these instructions:

1. To be read by son to other members of the family.
2. Please read on Mondays, Wednesdays, and Fridays after dinner.
3. Mother is to remind son to read and, if she forgets, father and daughter are to remind.
4. Do not discuss contents outside of counseling.

Dear _____,

I (the therapist) am impressed with the way in which you show how much you care about this family and especially your mother. I feel you need to be congratulated for having violent temper tantrums, because these tantrums serve as a safety valve for what your father and mother cannot do. I admire you for the way in which you show your loyalty to your mother.

If this is the way you want to protect your parents from each other and continue keeping them apart, you should continue to blow up, but do this on Monday, Wednesday, and Friday of each week. Be sure to break some inexpensive item in your home and continue these outbursts because if you stop, they might get back together.

The prescription of the behavior usually helps the child control the behavior that is problematic. This type of letter may help the parents see their part in the problem such that they begin to change spontaneously (Seltzer, 1986, pp. 266–267). The paradoxical written message has many advantages. First, it commands the attention of all parties involved. Second, communication that is in writing is much less likely to be ignored, repressed, distorted, or manipulated. Third, written communication has a bonding quality, which encourages repeated review outside the therapy session lending itself to a cumulative effect beyond even the most intense therapy session.

Technique | *Restraining Change*

Counseling Intention: To encourage therapeutic change

Description. The therapist actively discourages the individual, couple, or family from changing dysfunctional behavior by suggesting that such behavior change is futile. This paradoxical maneuver is particularly effective when therapeutic change is noticeably slow or at an impasse. This often is received as a challenge by recipients, empowering them to demonstrate that the therapist is incorrect in his or her observation.

Technique | *Relapse Prediction*

Counseling Intention: To empower the client to change

Description. Informing the client that he or she may experience a relapse—that the problem will reappear—creates a therapeutic double bind (Seltzer, 1986). If the symptoms recur as predicted by the therapist, it places the therapist in control. If it does not recur, it comes under the client's control, thus empowering his or her ability to change behavior—a fundamental therapeutic intention. Seltzer (1986) maintained that "when the client's relationship to the therapist is predominantly oppositional, the relapse prediction will be regarded as a challenge to continue to be asymptomatic, so as to deny the validity of (and external control implied by) the therapist's pessimistic forecast" (p. 125). Relapse prescription is a logical extension of relapse prediction. Watzlawick, Weakland, & Fisch (1974) concluded that prescribing a relapse is appropriate when a client has overcome a substantial obstacle making behavior change very fragile. Seltzer (1986) outlined the therapeutic double bind generated through prescription relapse:

> (1) should the client experience a relapse, such an event can be seen as proof that he now has sufficient control over his problem to produce it deliberately, and (2) should he fail to produce a relapse, such nonreoccurrence demonstrates that he now has sufficient control to avoid this problem deliberately. (p. 126)

Technique | *Declaring Helplessness*

Counseling Intention: To gain control during a power struggle between family and therapist

Description. When there are power struggles between the therapist and the individual or family, it is sometimes advantageous for the therapist to admit defeat. Paradoxically, the therapist must honestly and humbly admit inadequacy to effect changes. The family often moves in this direction of proving that treatment is indeed working. As the therapist proceeds to the door, he or she is invited back by the family and paradoxically gains even greater control in the therapeutic arena.

Technique | *Confusion Technique*

Counseling Intention: To overcome resistance and focus on the primary problem

Description. The confusion technique is another version of restraining change. The therapist accepts every topic or lists of problems a couple or family may present. He also identifies problem areas of his or her own, which may stimulate the need for change in other areas as a ploy to better understand their relationship.

The therapist continues with the confusion tactic until the couple becomes more explicit about their primary problem and goals so that therapy can begin and resistance can end. Essentially, the frustration of identifying so many problems sets the stage for the couple to rebel against what initially began as their own resistance toward articulating essential problems and using treatment productively.

PART F
TREATMENT PLANS, CONTRACTUAL FORMS, AND INVENTORIES

Chapter 17

DETAILED SESSION AND TREATMENT PLANS

The following sessions plans have been gleaned from the literature and focus on target behaviors and intervention. Their function is to provide a frame of reference for counseling intervention and is not limited to those included in this section. Counselors and therapists have conducted interventions from as little as eight hours for one session to as long as eight sessions over time.

GROUP TREATMENT PLAN INITIATIVES—
ON FAMILIES

Treatment Plan | *Marathon Family Counseling*

Description. Dinkmeyer (1988) outlined a form of family therapy from an Adlerian perspective and entitled it "marathon family counseling." Completed in an 8-hour day, marathon family counseling focuses on family constellation, mutual respect, encouragement, and taking responsibility for one's behavior. Dinkmeyer proposed the following four stages:

> **Stage I:** **Orientation and Organization.** Determine if marathon family counseling is appropriate for this family. Obtain family background. Arrange for family members to participate.
>
> **Stage II:** **Exploration.** Give overview and summary of Stage I. Obtain

overview of family's life circumstances. Explore problems in more depth.

Stage III: **Action.** Encourage family members to commit to doing something to improve the family situation. Confront family members who are reluctant to change. Encourage family members to take responsibility for their own behavior.

Stage IV: **Termination.** Have family members talk about their commitment to change and how they will accomplish their goals. Thank family members for participating in the session. Talk individually with family members who want more counseling.

| Treatment Plan | *Integrating Blended Families*

Description. Walsh (1992) identified 20 major issues in remarriage or step families and placed them in four categories: (a) initial family issues, (b) developing family issues, (c) feelings about self and others, and (d) adult issues. These 20 major issues are significant contributors to family disharmony. Counselor sensitivity to these concerns may lead to more accurate assessments and more timely interventions (p. 714). They are as follows:

Initial Family Issues

1. Name of the new parent. Issues of power and authority are concerns.
2. Affection for the new parent and absent parent. Issues of loyalty or allegiance are concerns.
3. Loss of natural parent. Issues of loss and grief need to be processed.
4. Instant love of new family members. Issues of emotional bonding are concerns.
5. Fantasy about the old family structure. Issues of fantasy of parental reconciliation are concerns, especially for a child whose identification with the absent parent is strong.

Developing Family Issues

6. Discipline by the stepparent. Issues of being inattentive, disengaged, or overly restrictive are concerns.
7. Confusion over family roles. Issues of role assignments involves cultural, personal, and legal spheres creating ambiguity.
8. Sibling conflict. Issues of stepsibling relationships are crucial to the success of step families.

9. Competition for time. Issues about contact with absent parent and increased competition of the custodial parent and jealously of the step-parent are concerns.
10. Extended kinship network. Issues of expectation, different views of values and lifestyles, and belongingness are concerns.
11. Sexual conflicts. Loosening of sexual boundaries are concerns.
12. Changes over time. Issues of remarriage, organization, and boundaries are concerns.
13. Exit and entry of children. Issues around children from their permanent home to the home of the noncustodial parent influence home, school, and peer relations.

Feelings about Self and Others

14. Society's acceptance of the remarriage family is a concern.
15. The connotation of step family needs to be processed.
16. Individual self-concept and lower self-esteem are concerns.

Adult Issues

17. Effects of parenting on the new marital relationship needs to be discussed.
18. Financial concerns and obligations need to be worked out.
19. Continuing adult conflict from previous relationships and communication with children may need clarification.
20. Competition of the noncustodial parent regarding child rearing and material possessions may need to be outlined.

Dinkmeyer (1988) provided another strategy for brief therapy from an Adlerian perspective that may extend over several sessions:

The counselor and couple discuss reasons why the couple is seeking counseling.
The counselor and couple discuss the couple's goals for counseling.
The counselor shares expectations.
The counselor draws a family constellation for each person and uses this and early recollections (ERs) to construct a lifestyle from each individual.
The couple works on the basic marriage skills of conflict resolution, communication, time management, work, and leisure pursuits.

The couple uses paradoxical strategies of practicing at home those things that annoy each partner.

The couple keeps daily journal entries of feelings, thoughts, and behaviors.

GROUP TREATMENT PLAN INITIATIVES— ON CONFLICT RESOLUTION

| *Treatment Plan* | *Conflict Resolution* |

Description. Dysinger (1993) outlined the following conflict resolution strategies to use with group members:

Session I: **Conflict and People.** Introduce the technique of separating people from problems so that in negotiating conflict, members can understand difference of personal interest, individual wants, and human rights versus personalities. Have members list examples of situations such as ganging up, forming alliances, or being left out. Encourage members to watch for those happenings in the coming week and how they felt and reacted.

Session II: **Conflicts, Feelings, and Reactions.** Ask for reports on feelings or reactions noted in the previous week. Listen for members' inclination to report reactions erroneously. Process how conflict resolution requires acceptance of the equal value of each person and that individuals must resolve problems differently because their feelings, wishes, wants, and reactions are different. Point out the value of considering options instead of reacting. Encourage members to be aware of problems, feelings, reactions, and consequences in the coming week.

Session III: **Discussing a Problem.** Introduce several roadblocks to communication such as labeling another person, listening to hearsay, and magnifying a situation. Encourage a discussion of a designated problem describing feelings, thoughts, and opinions of it.

Session IV: **Responding Versus Reacting.** Introduce specific responses useful in conflict situations, such as using "I" messages.

Session V: **Making Choices.** Have members practice learning from criticism and ask them to separate the harmful meanings from possible truth.

Session VI: **Consider Options.** Ask clients the following questions: "Have you noticed any changes in the frequency or intensity of conflict?" "If so, what do you believe you did to bring about changes?" "If not, what do you believe you need to do to cause positive changes?" Provide clients with a reminder bookmark of the strategies taught:

Problems can be defined and thought about carefully.
Problems are different among people and people's problems are different.
Roadblocks of communication and problem solving can be removed.
Specific skills can help resolve conflict: "I" messages, using helpful criticism, changing chain reactions, and choosing the best option are four of them.
Friendliness helps reduce conflict (Dysinger, 1993, p. 307).

Session VII: **Friendship.** Describe levels of friendship. Brainstorm relationship skills such as complementing sincerely, inviting, listening and responding, telling the truth, considering feelings, allowing differences, understanding mistakes, and supporting someone in need.

Session VIII: Plan a reunion in four to six weeks to check on progress.

GROUP TREATMENT PLAN INITIATIVES—
ON ADDICTIVE BEHAVIORS

Eating disorders are developmental dysfunctions that occur when one's self is sacrificed or abandoned (Woodman, 1985). When a clear perception of self is not developed, acute fears contribute toward developmental impasses. Dysfunctional coping mechanisms such as binge-purge behaviors, obsessions over thinness, fasting, or strict dieting are developed in response to fears, anxieties, and anger (Teusch, 1988).

Anorexia nervosa (self-starvation) and bulimia nervosa (binge-purge syndrome) have emerged as major psychological and wellness epidemics. Eating disorders occur most often among young, white, affluent (upper-middle to upper class) children and women (Anderson & Hay, 1985; Hsu, 1989; Taub & McLorg, 1989). Elements of gender-role orientations are associated with the development of eating disorders (Striegal-Moore, Silberstein, & Rodin, 1986). Concern with thinness has been related to perceived and preferred femininity.

In general, the more females diet and worry about their weight, the more traditionally feminine they are in their actual and ideal gender role orientations (Squires & Kagen, 1985). Not surprisingly, eating disorders have been reported in female populations where a lean body is valued, including ballet dancers (Brooks-Gunn, Burrow, & Warren, 1988; Szmukler, Eisler, Gillies, & Hayward, 1985), models (Garner & Garfinkel, 1980), cheerleaders (Lundholm & Littrell, 1986), and other athletes (Brooks-Gunn et al., 1988; Weight & Noakes, 1987).

| Treatment Plan | *Cognitive-Behavioral Group Treatment for Eating Disorders*

Description. Kettlewell, Mizes, & Wasylyshyn (1992) outlined the following cognitive-behavioral treatment plan for the group treatment of bulimia:

Session I.   Discussions focused on the medical and psychological consequences of bulimia. Counseling intention was to give accurate information about bulimia and to enhance motivation and commitment for change.

Sessions II & III.   The focus was on goal setting, that is, how to set behavioral goals that were specific, time-limited, realistic, individually tailored and measurable. For example, to avoid fasting, eat some food at breakfast each day; to develop plans for behaviors competing with purging take a walk with a friend; or to shower before breakfast rather than afterward to avoid vomiting in the shower. Members were taught how to revise and to reset goals.

Session IV.   A functional analysis of antecedent and consequent variables in the binge-purge cycle was discussed. The participants were helped in identifying the key components of this cycle such as (a) cognitions like "I must be thin"; (b) fasting, which leads to a preoccupation with food; (c) anxiety reduction immediately following a binge; (d) an increase in anxiety and guilt as delayed consequences of a binge; (e) anxiety reduction immediately following purging; (f) guilt and depression as delayed consequences of purging; and (g) the mistaken resolve to do a better job of fasting the next day. Participants were encouraged especially to consider different ways of breaking the cycle such as changing cognition from "I must be thin" to "I want to be physically fit."

Session V. Selecting an appropriate weight. Weight history, age, normative data, set point theory was reviewed. Each member selected an appropriate weight and shared that with the other group members.

Session VI. Additional coping strategies were reviewed, including reducing the availability of binge food, restructuring activities incompatible with bingeing such as exercise or relaxation, positive self-talk, and gradually reintroducing avoided foods into the diet.

Session VII. The idea of striving for thinness was reviewed including benefits and risks. Irrational cognitions about thinness were challenged again.

Session VIII. Ways to maintain progress and to avoid a relapse were reviewed. Specific strategies to take after a relapse, such as eating three meals the next day, were identified.

Participants can be instructed to keep a journal log of bingeing and purging during baseline, treatment, and for one week at each follow-up meeting. Weekly homework assignments were given such as selecting goals, identifying circumstances precipitating a binge, and selecting desired weight.

Family involvement is a prerequisite to the successful treatment of eating disorders. It is important to understand family dynamics and the accompanying feelings generated in order to construct new and healthier patterns. By assessing the patterns of family, the counselor can begin to change the patterns of responses of the eating disordered. From a family systems model, bulimia nervosa arises from and is maintained by dysfunctional family relationship problems that may be multigenerational. The client's changed responses will change the interaction within the family environment.

Ruth Weissberger, chair of the *Eating Disordered Special Interest Network for Mental Health Counselors,* outlined three predominant family patterns:

1. **The Perfect Family** (*Motto:* "A Job Worth Doing Is Worth Doing Well." *Messages:* "United we stand, divided we fall." "Don't rock the boat." "Hear no evil, see no evil, speak no evil.")

   • Emphasis on appearance, achievement, status, family reputation, and a positive family identity.

- Important to keep family members together and outsiders out. Family secrets are hidden and loyalty expected.
- Caring and love are expressed but are attached to performance. Tears of sadness and anger are unacceptable. Pain is not expressed and is discounted in this family.
- Decision-making is encouraged, but family members need to make the "correct" decision in the eyes of the parents. Conformity is expected.
- There are unresolved issues of grief and rigid rules around the appropriate time and manner of grieving a loss.

2. **The Chaotic Family** (*Motto:* "The Only One You Can Really Count On Is Yourself." *Messages:* "Don't ask questions." "Spare the rod, spoil the child." "You can't trust anyone.")

- Resembles an alcoholic family system. Inconsistency of rules, unavailability of one or both parents. Victimization experiences of family members. Destructive expressions of anger.
- Relationships are inconsistent. No protection from verbal, physical, or sexual abuse. All family members experience having no power or control and feel helpless. Protective mechanisms developed to shield members from the pain they experience.
- Personality changes frequent as environmental changes.
- Anger is explosive, pervasive, and unpredictable. Love and affection is based on performance. Sadness is not recognized or acknowledged.
- Many losses: divorce, incest, physical abuse, emotional or physical unavailability of parents.

3. **The Overprotective Family** (*Motto:* "All For One And One For All." *Messages:* "Don't trust anyone outside the family." "There is no place like home.")

- Impact of unresolved family of origin issues (typically, victimization experience of the mother). Obvious lack of confidence expressed toward the eating disordered member. Lack of rules for age appropriate behavior.
- Family members talk for each other, not for themselves. Intrusive quality to family interactions (e.g., listening in on telephone conversations).
- The "we" identity is nurtured versus individual identities.
- Decisions are often made for the child or teen, leaving him or her feeling incompetent, ineffective, and dependent.
- Sadness and anger are not allowed. One member's pain is everyone's

pain. (Source: Ruth Weissberger, with research by Patricia Fallow and Maria Root, 120 Linden Oaks, Rochester, NY 14625, 716–385–1950. Reprinted with permission.)

| Treatment Plan | *Using Fairy Tales for Treating Eating Disorders*

Description. Fairy tales are a therapeutic alternative to assist in the transitional problems and anxieties by serving as a mechanism upon which the eating disordered client can project his or her desired identity. Inherently, clients with eating disorders have highly developed defense mechanisms, and the use of fairy tales as treatment medium can indirectly address underlying problems (Yapko, 1986). Fairy tales stimulate imagination, clarify emotions, assist in coping, and suggest solutions to problems and anxieties in the process of personality integration (Bettelheim, 1976). The fairy tale takes existential anxieties and dilemmas, addressing the need to be loved and the fear that one is thought worthless, the love of life and the fear of death.

Hill (1992) outlined the treatment model for addressing eating disorders. The model has four phases: (1) identification of the fairy tale, (2) development of connections with the fairy tale, (3) introduction of conflict, and (4) problem resolution (p. 584).

1. **Identification of the Fairy Tale**

    Identifying the fairy tale can occur during the intake interview or during the therapeutic interaction. The client may select the fairy tale or the counselor may select one. When the client selects the fairy tale, it may serve as a projection of the self. Thiessen (1983) maintained that fairy tales are very often mirrors of ourselves. Hill (1992) found that Cinderella was the most frequently identified fairy tale among the eating disordered clients in her practice. For example, Hill found that Cinderella was her favorite fairy tale because

    Cinderella overcame her social status. Used as a projective tool this response would indicate that the client needed to overcome her sense of inferior status. She also stated that she liked how the animals helped Cinderella in the forest. From a Jungian perspective, the forest scene is representative of the unconscious, and the animals are a metaphorical representation of the unconscious instinct that knows how to obey one's inner when reason fails. (p. 585)

2. **Developing a Connection with the Fairy Tale**

    According to Hill (1992) the connection phase applies a universal theme in the psychology of women—attachment with mother and with the self. The eating disordered client's identity is enmeshed with significant others such as the mother. This creates anger that is often forced to be repressed resulting in a diagnosis of depression and low self-esteem (Johnson & Maddi, 1986). The fairy tale provides a mechanism for the client to reconnect with both. Hill elaborated further:

> Transference occurs in the eating-disordered client when unresolved self-control is directed at significant others. The fairy tale becomes a substitute object of transference. She can transfer her anger and fears onto the fairy tale. In the same way, through the fairy tale, she can develop understanding and the ability to cope by rearranging suitable story elements that are responses to unconscious pressures. (p. 585)

The counselor serves as catalyst to bring the fairy tale into the therapeutic process. The counselor listens for themes that the client identifies. Relaxation exercises and guided imagery may serve to bring the client into present awareness. This provides the client with the opportunity to verbalize his or her own issues about eating as he or she projects them onto the fairy tale character. Hill (1992) maintained that the more active the client is with the fairy tale, the greater the potential for increased connection and identification with the characters in the story.

3.   Introduction of Conflict

The counselor can use the fairy tale to introduce conflict analogous to the dysfunctional symptoms of the client. Conflicts can include binge-purge behaviors, unexpressed anger, or self-starvation. Hill (1992) stated

> Confrontation with underlying unresolved developmental problems begins when the counselor introduces the client's analogous life dynamics into the fairy tale. The fairy tale paradigm is reframed, shifted, and stretched into a once well-known story that now has many new chapters. It becomes an altered story with created scenes for the client to consider. It serves as a means to face unresolved developmental fears externally, creating an opportunity to work through one's own impasse. (p. 586)

4.   Problem Resolution

Problem resolution occurs in two parts: (a) the client's proposed resolution while in the fairy tale and (b) the counselor's behavioral assignment outside the counseling session, using the client's solutions. The fairy tale becomes the source for strategic behavioral assignments outside the counseling sessions based on the client's self-defined resolutions. The counselor merely serves as the catalyst for the client to shift her or his locus of control from the external structure of the fairy tale to an internal structure to the internal control of problem solving and decision making.

GROUP TREATMENT PLAN INITIATIVES—ON ANGER

| Treatment Plan | *Managing Anger*

Description. Johnson and Wilborn (1991) provided the following treatment plan for managing anger.

Session I. Ask members to describe an experience when they were angry and focus on the feeling connect ed with anger. Recall how parents expressed anger, and decide which parent they most resemble in their experience and expression of anger. For homework, be aware of their own anger and that of others during the following week.

Session II. Begin the group with members sharing their anger experiences of past week and their observations of other people's expression of anger. Explain Ellis's Rational Emotive ABC theory (Walen, DiGuiseppe, & Wessler, 1980). Process that many people have trouble with the "C," their emotion because of underlying beliefs about the emotion. Explain that all emotions are justified because they exist. Help group members distinguish between thoughts and feelings.

Session III. Relate an anger provoking incident and ask members to respond to it in terms of the degree of anger experienced and how they would feel and react in such a situation. Introduce

---

One of the main functions of anger is it allows one to say what he really thinks. He may take it back later when he cools down, but it's important to remember what he said and to deal with it, because that is where the heart of the feeling is.

Elvin Semrad

---

the "push-button technique" (Mosak, 1971). Group members are asked to close their eyes and to see themselves in a pleasant experience. They are asked to remember the experience, how they felt, and to feel the same feeling in their bodies. Then ask them to change and remember an unpleasant experience, to remember how they felt, who was there and so on. Remember the pleasant experience again. Rationale: To help participants experience the changing of feelings and their power to create the feeling they choose to create. Members are guided to see the control they have over events and experiences in their lives.

Session IV. Ask members to recall how anger was expressed in their families of origin and to discuss the differences between the male and female experience and expression of anger. Introduce reflective listening and "I" messages as tools to use in dealing with anger. Ask members to, during the week, observe anger expression by men and women with whom they associate and as portrayed on television to compare observations at the next meeting.

Session V. Members are asked what advice they would give their parents about helping their children deal with anger, and what general advice they would give to today's teenagers about expressing anger. Ask members to discuss the most stressful events in their lives and how they dealt with those events.

Session VI. Introduce the concept of anger experienced as a task and problem solving technique (Novaco, 1975). Summarize the content of the group discussion; provide opportunity for follow-up.

GROUP TREATMENT PLAN INITIATIVES—
ON LOSS, DEATH, AND GRIEF

| *Treatment Plan* | *Loss Group*

Description. The loss group assists individuals who have suffered the loss of a parent or other caregiver with understanding the stages of grief, with clarifying and accepting their feelings, and by providing a supportive place to share their personal experiences with death.

I reject the notion that human beings, as they die, are somehow marched in lock step through a series of stages of the dying process. On the contrary . . . the emotional states, the psychological mechanisms of defense, the needs and drives, are as variegated in the dying as they are in the nondying. . . . They include such reactions as stoicism, rage, guilt, terror, cringing, fear, surrender, heroism, dependency, ennui, need for control, fight for autonomy and dignity, and denial.

Edwin Shneidman

Session I: **Getting to Know You Exercise.** Clients will discover that they are not alone in their loss. They will become acquainted with group members. Provide a low-risk, get-acquainted exercise that focuses on similarities among group members.

Session II: **Explore the Causes of Death.** Clients will identify the many ways people die. Clients will write their ideas and share them with the group (e.g. accidents, murder, old age, illness, or suicide). Process how some causes of death are easier to accept than others. Each member shares his or her experience with the group.

Session III: **Stages of Grief.** Explain the stages of grief: denial, anger, bargaining, depression, and acceptance. Discuss the five stages of grief and the progression to each stage. Identify which stages clients felt "stuck" and took longer to move onto the next stage. Ask group members to determine what stage they are in now.

Session IV: **Concerns and Acceptance.** Determine group members' concerns about death that interfere with acceptance. Ask the members to draw a picture illustrating a dream they have had about their parent or caregiver since their death. Older group members may prefer just to describe their dream. Look for similarities in themes such as fear, feelings of loneliness, wishing for the parent to return, or other unfinished business. Discuss the importance of talking about their concerns with someone they trust to help them understand.

Session V: **Special Personal Achievement.** Ask members to write a letter to their late parent sharing something that they are especially proud of and wish they could tell their parent. Grieving people often miss the daily contact and enjoy the feeling of sharing a proud moment as they read their letters to the group. It is important to leave the group on a positive note. Briefly summarize the issues discussed. Process if the group would like to continue meeting as a support group.

GROUP TREATMENT PLAN INITIATIVES— ON VICTIMIZATION

Child maltreatment is one of the most critical problems in the United States today. Each year, tens of thousands of children are maltreated in ways that lead to serious developmental, psychological, or medical problems that sometimes culminate in death. At least 2,000 children die each year as a result of neglect or physical abuse.

More than 2.4 million incidents of child abuse and neglect were reported to child-protective-services agencies in 1990, a 10% increase over the previous year. One million adolescents run away from home every year. Most are victims of abuse and a majority of these adolescents become prostitutes or delinquents.

Researchers have concluded that 1 out of 3 girls and at least 1 out of 5 boys will be sexually abused before age 18, and 1 in 10 is a victim of incest. The majority of victims reach adulthood carrying their secret undetected.

| Treatment Plan | *Symbolic Confrontation for Childhood Sexual Victimization*

Description. Apolinsky and Wilcoxon (1991) concluded that the theoretical foundation for a victimization group should be multidimensional. Aspects of person-centered, psychoanalytic, Gestalt, transactional analysis, rational-emotive, and behavioral approaches were integrated into 10, two-hour sessions featuring both structured activities and group process experience. Global therapeutic issues included anger, trust, interpersonal relationships, sexuality and intimacy, self-esteem, and guilt as well as personal responsibility and empowerment (Apolinsky & Wilcoxon, (1991, p. 87). Each of the 10 sessions provided an opportunity for dialogue, personal reflection, and planning for homework between sessions.

Session I.   The victimization experience and its significance

Session II.   Secrecy and disclosure

Session III.   Guilt and depression

Session IV. Self-blaming beliefs, shame, and remorse

Session V. Negative self-image, damaged goods, self-esteem, and sadness

Session VI. Family boundaries and roles, isolation, loss, and compulsion

Session VII. Fear and anxiety, mistrust of men and sexuality

Session VIII. Hostility and rage, the offending and nonoffending parent

Session IX. Comparing developmental tasks, social assertiveness, and preparing for group closure

Session X. Self-mastery and control

GROUP TREATMENT PLAN INITIATIVES— ON INFERTILITY

As couples delay their childbearing years, some experience infertility and the accompanying by long-term feelings of frustration, anxiety, and loss. The counseling needs of infertile couples continue to be reflected in the literature (Cook, 1987; Mahlsted, 1985). The profound effects of medical investigations of infertility effect couples physically (Daniluk, 1988; Schinfeld, Elkins, & Strong, 1986), interpersonally (Link & Darling, 1986; Morse & Dennerstein, 1985), and emotionally (McEwan, Costello, & Taylor, 1987; Valentine, 1986). Collectively it represents a *biopsychosocial crisis* for the infertile couple. Often couples are unprepared for the invasive and exhausting experience of prolonged infertility.

| Treatment Plan | *Counseling for Infertile Couples*

Description. (The Daniluk material used in this section, either quoted or paraphrased, was reprinted or adapted from "Strategies for Counseling Infertile Couples," *Journal of Counseling and Development* [volume 69, 1991, March/April] pp. 317–320. Copyright ACA. Reprinted with permission. No further reproduction authorized without written permission of the American Counseling Association.) Daniluk (1991) outlined the goals of counseling as follows:

to negotiate the grieving process,
to relinquish and accept control where appropriate and realistic,
to heal their relationship(s),
to reassess their motivation and desire for parenting, and
to make decisions regarding their future parenting options.

Daniluk found that achievement of these goals will depend on the specific needs and values of the client and the stage at which the client enters treatment. Time-out from the intrusiveness of infertility evaluations will allow couples to refocus their attention on healing their relationship after loss and disappointment. To help clients negotiate the grieving process the counselor needs to facilitate the appropriate expression of anger, to acknowledge the injustice of the situation, and to validate the couple's feelings.

Avenues for the expression of affect could include the techniques of art therapy, body work, and journal writing. Forgiveness rituals may also be helpful in facilitating the process of self-vindication (Daniluk, 1991). Since many women have fantasies about the child they hope to have, visualization or guided imagery may facilitate making the child more real (name, sex, and physical characteristics).

> Having made the child more real, the couple then can be asked to write a letter to their child. The letter is used as a means of expressing the couple's dreams, hopes, and anticipations for their relationship with their son or daughter and their painful grief at never having the opportunity to share a life together. Couples may find this exercise facilitative in letting go of a large part of their grief and pain. Clients may then place the letter in an area of significant personal meaning, a place that comes to represent their memories of their lost child. (Daniluk, 1991, p. 318)

To help clients relinquish and take control, the counselor should encourage clients

to acknowledge that while they may not have control over their own fertility, they do have control over other life options and over their responses to decisions concerning their future;

to set time lines for infertility evaluations;

to access information regarding the availability and success of various medical procedures, common reactions to the infertility experience, and alternatives for parenthood;

to assume control over the pursuit of other life or career goals; and/or

to attend an infertility support group.

To begin healing relationships, the counselor must attend to the needs of both partners as well as the needs of the couple as a unit. There is a need to rework and separate sexuality, self-image, and self-esteem from childbearing. The counselor may encourage the couple to separate their intimate relationships from the rigors of the medical workup (e.g., performance anxiety);

to reintroduce play and romance into their relationship;

to enhance their communication and their understanding by reframing the man's reluctance to discuss their infertility as reflecting his frustration with being unable to help heal his partner's pain and by connoting the woman's need to discuss their infertility as reflecting her desire to share in and understand her partner's needs (Daniluk, 1991);

to express perceptions, thoughts, and feelings in verbal or written form; and/ or

to heal within their family and social networks and negotiate the social and familial contacts.

Counseling techniques for this dimension of the intervention may include role-playing, conflict resolution techniques, and assertiveness skill development to explore with couples various creative ways of dealing with insensitive comments and reactions (Daniluk, 1991).

To reassess the motivation for parenting, the counselor explores with the couple their reasons for abandoning or proceeding with their goal for parenthood. The counselor may facilitate this by (a) reviewing each partner's needs and values and (b) assessing the cognitive and affective aspects of the decision with such questions as "Why do you want to have children?" and "What would it mean to you not to have a child?" (Daniluk, 1991).

The counselor may facilitate an examination of the client's feelings, perceptions, and motivation by helping the clients separate the concept of pregnancy from parenting. If pregnancy is first and foremost, the couple needs to come to terms with this loss prior to considering other parenthood options (Salzer, 1986).

As the couple begins to consider decisions regarding future parenting options, the counselor may assist the clients to go on with their lives. Daniluk (1991) maintained that the goal of this stage is to invite clients to (a) confront possible child-free options, (b) begin to understand their degree of investment in the parenthood role, (c) begin to set realistic limits on their pursuit of parenthood, and (d) to begin planning together for their future.

This can be accomplished by having the couple do the following:

write a five-year plan with a child in their lives or a five-year plan with a child-free lifestyle;

seek accurate information regarding the contradictions of the various forms of treatment as well as accurate estimations of their likelihood for realizing a child as an outcome of treatment;

examine the medical, legal, ethical, and religious implications of these alternatives;

examine the possibilities of adoption;

join a support group; and

examine their options very carefully in light of their individual needs and aspirations within the context of their mutual five-year life plans and their goals as a couple.

GROUP TREATMENT PLAN INITIATIVES— ON DIVORCE

| Treatment Plan | *"Breaking Up Is Hard to Do"—Working through*
Parental Divorce

Description.   This treatment plan seeks to diminish the couple's feelings of guilt, helplessness, and inadequacy and to enhance the couple's self-esteem and locus of control orientation.

Session I: **Introduction and Group Rules.** Group members form pairs, and partners interview each other to determine likes, dislikes, hobbies, and interests. Partners are introduced to the group. Consensus for some rules for the group also are established.

Session II: **Non-divorce-related Self-disclosure.** Adjective checklist and pleasant and unpleasant feeling words are processed so that clients can feel more comfortable about self-disclosing and discussing feelings.

Session III: **Bibliography on Divorce and Discussion.** A story is read about parents getting a divorce. Participants discuss their feelings and thoughts about the characters' feelings and behaviors.

Session IV: **Divorce-related Self-disclosure.** Members draw a shield and divide it into four parts. They are asked to draw a picture of a good time they had with their families in one block, an unpleasant time in another block, why they think their parents got a divorce in the third block, and what they would like to happen to their families during the upcoming year in the fourth block. Members share their shields and discuss them with others in the group.

Session V: **Role-playing the Problems of Divorce.** Members brainstorm the problems of divorce. Then they are divided into groups. Each group selects one problem and role-plays the situation for three to five minutes.

Session VI: **Role-playing Continues.** Another problem is role-played, followed by an in-depth discussion.

Session VII: **Positive Aspects of Divorce.** Members discuss things that have turned out pleasant, or for the better, because of the divorce. Members complete a personal collage that reflects the pleasant experiences and shares them with the others. The session is processed.

Session VIII: **Building Self-esteem.** Members select adjectives that best describe them and members receive positive feedback (strength bombardment) from the other group members.

Session IX: **Coping with Parents' Divorce.** Ways of coping are introduced, including stress management, communication skills, and empathy.

Session X: **Wrap-up.** A summary of the sessions is conducted. Members express their feeling and feedback on what they have learned (Adapted from Omizo & Omizo, 1988, pp. 56–57).

Note: Omizo and Omizo (1988) found that adolescents who participated in the group sessions were significantly different from adolescents in a control group on posttest measures. The adolescents in the treatment group had higher levels of self-esteem and possessed a more internal perception of locus of control (p. 58).

GROUP TREATMENT PLAN INITIATIVES— ON DIVORCE AND THE DISTRIBUTION OF LOVE

The change in family structure precipitated by divorce, separation, death, and other parental absences often creates psychological, social, and economic problems for some individuals. The stages of personal reaction to loss of a significant other are denial, anger, bargaining, depression, and acceptance. Each of these stages is marked by specific identifiable behaviors, and the meaning of the stage and its associated behavior should be presented to group members. In this content intervention, students should be asked to investigate themselves on the five stages and discuss their placement. The stages are as follows:

Stage	Meaning
denial	refusing to think about or believe it; acting like all is the same; keeping the truth from friends; lying about it; pretending all is the same
anger	becoming very upset over the facts; feeling that I have been mistreated; slamming doors for little reason; hitting people; yelling; being rude to parent, brother, or sister; sassing teachers
bargaining	trying to get things back as they were; being bad so dad must come to help mom with me; missing a ride with Bill so dad must take me to mom's house; promising God I'll never do a bad thing if he gets mom and dad back together
depression	feeling like all is lost, like I can't laugh; sitting around my room; not going out with friends; crying often; not eating
acceptance	feeling like it's done, and I can go on laughing when I feel like it; getting along with friends and family as before; having fewer fights

INDIVIDUAL TREATMENT PLAN INITIATIVES— ON SUBSTANCE ABUSE AND ADDICTION

| Treatment Plan | *Changing Alcohol or Other Drug Use*

Counseling Intention: To help the client through cognitive restructuring to realize that he or she can be happy and fully functioning without using alcohol or other drugs

Description. After the client has identified the situations and has developed a plan to eliminate the problem behavior, he or she can be supported with the following visualizations, affirmations, and cognitive restructuring:

Visualizations

I picture myself looking healthy and relaxed.
I see myself removing big clamps that are keeping my arms and legs from

Addiction isn't the battle you are fighting. The battle is with your thoughts and the psychological needs the addiction meets.

Joel C. Robertson

•

We drink for joy and become miserable. We drink for sociability and become argumentative. We drink for sophistication and become obnoxious. We drink to help us sleep and awake exhausted. We drink for exhilaration and end up depressed.

We drink to gain confidence and become afraid. We drink to make conversation flow and become incoherent. We drink to diminish our problems and see them multiply.

Richard Blummer

moving as I want them to move. I see my arteries and veins filled with a sparkling red liquid that represents my blood, which is perfectly free of chemicals.

I see my brain as if it were the pistons in a fine-tuned automobile. Each piston fires in perfect timing, enabling me to think clearly.

I see myself feeling perfectly happy and at ease at a party without a drink in my hand.

Affirmations

I am getting healthier and healthier every day without alcohol or other drugs.
I like being able to function without any chemical interference to my body.
I am free of any desire to drink alcoholic beverages or to use drugs.
I enjoy being at parties without drinking or getting high.

Cognitive Restructuring

White-is-black thinking: I stop telling myself I can't quit or that I can't enjoy myself without alcohol or other drugs. I will predict success rather than failure in breaking my habits.

Fictional fantasies: I will remember that I can choose to do whatever I wish. Although I formerly used alcohol or other drugs to escape bad moods, I now choose to deal with them in more constructive ways, like running, biking, or working out.

Mistaken identity: I will remind myself that I have broken other bad habits, such as overeating or overworking. I will be able to break this one, too. I am worthy of success.

Acting As If

I will refuse offers of drinks or other drugs.

I will tell everyone I know that I have stopped using alcohol or other drugs.

I will do some advanced planning rather than depend on alcohol to have a good time at a party. I will plan ways to demonstrate my interest in others rather than worrying whether I am making a good impression.

I will record my achievements and review them often (Handley & Neff, 1985, pp. 211–212).

The techniques used in the above treatment plan use self-statements to change behavior. One of the first proponents to develop this approach was Meichenbaum with his cognitive behavior modification therapy, which is closely aligned with Beck's cognitive therapy. Meichenbaum (1977) added a behavior component to his theory. For behavior change to occur, the client must be taught three strategies:

1. self-observation—clients must listen to themselves and become sensitive to thoughts and how they reflect their feelings and behaviors (e.g., they are not victims of depression but rather are a contributing factor);
2. self-instruction—the client needs to start a new internal dialogue to combat automatic self-defeating thoughts; and
3. new coping skills—the client must also learn new coping skills in an individual or a group counseling setting.

INDIVIDUAL TREATMENT PLAN INITIATIVES— ON MULTIMODAL TREATMENT PLANS

In multimodal therapy, the therapist-client interaction focuses on seven modalities: Behavior, Affect, Sensation, Imagery, Cognition, Interpersonal relationships, and Drugs/Biology. These modalities make up the acronym BASIC ID. These modalities are interactive as well as interdependent as they relate to behavior change. The practice of multimodal therapy is based on the assumption that an effective way to understand clients and assess their problems is in terms of their various actions and interactions across the seven modalities of functioning. The multimodal therapy modal has been successful in treating depression, alcoholism, agoraphobia, obesity, anorexia, and procrastination. It provides a systematic and comprehensive assessment/treatment approach.

The trend in current counseling processes and psychotherapy is toward a multidimensional, multidisciplinary, and multifaceted approach that does not rigidly attempt to fit clients into a preconceived treatment plan (Lazarus, 1981). Human processes are multilayered because we are biological beings who move, feel, sense, imagine, think, and relate to one another.

Each of these dimensions requires our attention when problems emerge (Lazarus, 1967, 1971, 1976, 1977, 1981, 1985, 1993). The great depth and detail in the multimodal's examination of the sensor, cognitive, and interpersonal constituents and their interactive effects enable the counselor to transcend the confines of most cognitive-behavioral approaches.

Lazarus (1992) provided a brief description of the **BASIC ID** as follows:

Behavior refers mainly to the overt responses, actions, habits, gestures, and motor reactions that are observable and manageable.

Affect refers to emotions, moods, and feelings.

Sensation covers inputs from each of the five senses (clinically, we are usually required to address negative sensations—tension, dizziness, pain, etc.)

Imagery includes dreams, fantasies, and vivid memories; mental pictures, and the way people view themselves (self-image). Auditory images, recurring tunes or sounds also fall into this category.

Cognition refers to attitudes, values, opinions, ideas, and self-talk. (Clinically, in this modality, the main task is to identify and modify dysfunctional beliefs and replace them with views that enhance adaptive functioning).

Interpersonal relationships include all significant interactions with other people (relatives, lovers, friends, colleagues, co-workers, acquaintances, etc).

Drugs/biology includes drugs (self-medication or physician-prescribed medication) in addition to nutrition, hygiene, exercise, and all basic physiological and pathological inputs. It involves the panoply of neurophysiological-biochemical factors that influence temperament and personality.

Essentially, the multimodal treatment intervention embraces four principles:

1. Clients act and interact across the seven modalities of the BASIC ID.
2. These modalities are connected by complex chains of behavior and other psychophysiological events and exit in a state of reciprocal transaction.
3. Accurate evaluation (diagnosis) is served by the systematic assessment of each modality and its interaction with every other.
4. Comprehensive therapy calls for the specific correction of significant problems across the BASIC ID (Lazarus, 1992, p. 50).

Among the most frequently used group methods are *behavioral rehearsal and role playing, positive reinforcement, recording and self-monitoring, feeling identification, bibliotherapy, social skills, assertiveness training, anxiety management training, imagery, desensitization, modeling, and Gestalt techniques.* Multimodal therapy draws heavily from behavioral notions; however, it "presupposes no identification with any specific school of psychological thought, nor is it a separate school in itself" (Lazarus, 1976, p. 4). It is pragmatic and didactic in approach reflecting a "technical eclecticism" in constructing a modality profile for the client.

| Treatment Plan | *Multimodal Treatment of Depression* |

Description. Lazarus had the following to say about depression:

Depression—be it major or minor—will have an impact on a client's behaviors, affective processes, sensory inputs, images, cognitions, and interpersonal relations. The multimodal orientation is considerably more systematic and comprehensive than most cognitive and cognitive-behavioral approaches.

Arnold A. Lazarus

The following list displays symptoms and modality of depression and the interventions relevant and effective for each.

Modality and Referral Problems	Related Interventions
Behavior Reduced work performance Diminished activity Statements of self-denigration	Implement a "pleasant event schedules" (ascertain numerous behaviors, sensations, images, ideas, and people the client used to find rewarding) to ensure a daily sampling of personally pleasing activities
Affect Sadness, guilt, "heavy hearted" Intermittent anxiety and anger	Standard anxiety reduction methods (e.g., relaxation, meditation, calming self-statements combined with assertiveness training; a repertoire of self-assertive and uninhibited responses

Modality and Referral Problems	**Related Interventions**
Sensation Less pleasure from food Diminished libido Easily fatigued	A specific list of pleasant visual, auditory, tactile, olfactory, and gustatory stimuli is added to the "pleasant events schedule" to create a "sensate-focus" of enjoyable events (e.g., exercises to promote muscle tone, jogging, biking, going to a comedy club)
Imagery Visions of loneliness and failure Pictures himself being rejected by important people in his life	"Recall past successes" "Picture small but successful outcomes" "Apply coping imagery," the use of "time projection" (i.e., client pictures him or herself venturing step-by-step into a future characterized by positive affect and pleasurable activities)
Cognition Negative self-appraisal Exaggerates real or imagined shortcomings "I'm no good at anything." "Things will always be bad for me."	Employ Ellis's (1989) methods of cognitive disputation, challenges categorical imperatives, "should and oughts" and irrational beliefs Identify worthwhile qualities and recite them everyday
Interpersonal Decreased social participation	Clients are taught four skills: saying "No!" to unreasonable requests, asking for favors by expressing positive feelings, and volunteering criticism and "disputing with style" (i.e, the client learns to ask for what he or she wants, resists unwelcomed requests or exploitation from others, initiate conversations, and develop more interpersonal relationships) Family therapy also may be recommended to teach family members how to avoid reinforcing "depressive behavior" as well as how to encourage the client to engage in pleasurable activities
Drugs/Biology Appetite unimpaired but has intermittent insomnia	Issues pertaining to increased exercise, relaxation appropriate sleep patterns, and overall physical fitness are addressed Biological intervention such as antidepressants frequently are recommended in the case of bipolar disorders

---

| **Treatment Plan** | *Multimodal Profile for Gifted Adolescents* |

Description. The following displays referral problems and related interventions for working with gifted adolescents:

Modality and Referral Problems	Related Interventions
Behavior Low risk-taking behavior	Reduce inhibition and increase the risk-taking through teaching self-evaluation standards and replacing external evaluation criteria with self-evaluation (internal) standards Provide encouragement for effort (process) as opposed to outcome
High risk-taking behavior (e.g., drugs, counter-culture activities)	Provide accurate information about potentially self-hurtful risks; teacher's nonjudgmental attitude Valuing of self; self-talk; psychosocial stress management; enhance self-concept
Affect Loneliness	Grouping with other gifted students; social reinforcement for a talent or ability (e.g., soccer, chess) rather than a cognitive ability (e.g., math) Bibliotherapy
Affect overshadowed by cognition	Structured experience in effective development; adult mentors; helping relationships with younger children; peer counselors Bibliotherapy
Humor used to diffuse affect	Paradoxical intention; emotive imagery; self-disclosure Use humor to confront affective issues; education with regard to humor as a defense mechanism; bibliotherapy with regard to emotional vulnerability; media
Depression	Educational media approach, grief counseling, cognitive restructuring
Affiliation needs versus achievement needs	Teacher in-service; grouping with other gifted students Role models; self-awareness; participation in nonthreatening activities; role playing and projective activities; bibliotherapy

Modality and Referral Problems	Related Interventions
School Adaptation to Lazarus's Basic ID to children and adolescents	Systems consultation; staff development; enhance teacher self-concept
Motivational network	Seek source of underachievement; examine behavioral consequences of under-achievement; withhold the use of failure as punishment
Underachievement (e.g., Whitmore, 1980)	Communicate evaluation system; establish rigorous standards; reward creative work; reward logical, well thought-out solutions; vary grading standards; evaluate fairly and consistently Group students with similar abilities; improve questioning techniques; teacher as learner
Student motivation	Examine why student is unmotivated and the consequences of same Teacher consultation, reduce punishment for low motivation, develop intrinsic achievement motivation, use learning contracts, allow student choice of activities
Imagery Inadequate self-image	Strengthen the supportive nature of the teacher-pupil relationship, values clarification activities; bibliotherapy Imagery therapy; reduce the discrepancy between one's real and ideal self-image Positive imagery; role shift; fixed-role therapy; drama; behavioral rehearsal Explore their heroes (images they pattern themselves after); exposure to individuals with significant talents In-service training on the unique personal and social needs of gifted adolescents (e.g., self-image)
Cognition Faulty cognitive self-statements (e.g., "You're a hero or a zero")	Cognitive restructuring techniques; increasing unconditional acceptance and reducing conditional worth; encourage acceptance of the human condition (albeit imperfect)

Modality and Referral Problems	Related Interventions
Understanding their own giftedness	Define gifted with them; group with other gifted students; role models of excellence; bibliotherapy
Overreliance on cognition	Encourage discovery of noncognitive worlds of experience; counter-intuitive puzzles, games, and activities and paradoxical intention
Dichotomous thinking	Cognitive restructuring of the all-or-nothing judgmentalism; discussion of controversial issues; discuss dominant contemporary social values and traditional
	Increase tolerance of ambiguous experiences; discuss judgment issues involving error variance (e.g., Math/Science/Engineering Summer Program for Gifted Students, University of Maine)
Problems associated with global information processing style (e.g., increases social distance from peers; threatens teachers)	Improve educational programming; contact with other gifted students; education with regard to nature of giftedness
Interpersonal Relationships Inadequate peer relationships	Redefine the terms peers and friends to include developmental levels; provide mentors; encourage flexible classroom grouping
Differentiated interest patterns impact social relationships	Encourage self-expression and personal processing experiences; journal keeping and creative writing to validate the unique self
	Have students teach or engage others in interests; peer tutoring; lab monitors
	Interest clubs and societies; team problem solving; simulation activities
	Friendship training; facilitate the development of social skills

Modality and Referral Problems	Related Interventions
Achievement versus group acceptance	Encourage contributory roles in group problem solving; increase competition survival courses
	Structure helping relationships with younger students; Big Brother-Big Sister Program
	Same-sex role models; "share your person"
Drugs/Diet	Issues related to escape and curiosity leading to drug experimentation; health and wellness issues

Source: Edwards, S.S., & Kleine, P.A. (1986). Multimodal Consultation: A Model for Working with Gifted Adolescents. *Journal of Counseling and Development, 64,* 9. Reprinted with permission.

 Treatment Plan *Multimodal Plan for an Alcoholic or Substance Abuser*

Description. Referral problems and related interventions are identified below.

Modality	Problem	Intervention
Behavior	Excessive Drinking	Keep a diary to assess stimulus situations and accompanying responses
	Negative self-talk	Positive self-talk
	Drinks to excess on weekends	Develop more productive outlets and hobbies
Affect	Depression	Increase range of positive activities on a daily basis
	Anxious at work and career	Assertiveness training, positive imagery, positive self-talk Dispute irrational beliefs

Modality	Problem	Intervention
	Difficulties with anger	Anger management strategies, relaxation and breathing techniques
Sensation	Headaches and gastrointestinal difficulties	Time and stress management activities
Imagery	Vivid images of not meeting deadlines and of failing	Systematic desensitization techniques and positive imagery
Cognition	Cognitive dissonance regarding drug and long-term consequences	Cognitive restructuring, bibliotherapy
Interpersonal	Lack of support or network	Join a support network such as A.A.
Drugs/Biological	Using alcohol as a tranquilizer	Consult with doctor regarding need for anti-depressants
	Inadequate diet and exercise	Bibliotherapy on importance of good nutrition. Join recreation center for weight training and aerobics

INDIVIDUAL TREATMENT PLAN INITIATIVES— ON BURNOUT

Counselors and therapists are resourceful, creative, and a highly motivated population of helping professionals who use these same qualities to help the children, adults, and families they serve. Yet the emotional, physical, and social demands of being a helping professional can be overwhelming. Excessive demands experienced on a daily basis can produce burnout.

In approaching burnout, Gonzales, Jones, Whitely, and Whitely (1988) have described four stages of burnout: (a) enthusiasm, which is ". . . a tendency to be overly available and to over identify with clients"; (b) stagnation, in which ". . . expectations shrink to normal proportions and personal discontent begins to surface"; (c) frustration, wherein difficulties seem to multiply, the counselor becomes bored, less tolerant, and less sympathetic, and he or she copes by avoiding or withdrawing from relationships; and (d) apathy, which is characterized by depression and listlessness, the embodiment of the burnout experience.

| Treatment Plan | *Eliminating Counselor Burnout*

Description. Suggestions for assessment and treatment of burnout across modalities are presented below.

Modality and Referral Problem	Related Behavioral Intervention

Behavior
Stressed
Overwhelmed
Beleaguered
	Define goals
	Educate service populations about
	    services that counselors provide
	Assess and modify role obligations
	Prioritize counseling duties
	Plan leisure time
	Keep a daily log of stresses encountered,
	    coping style and success or failure
	Join a support group
	Delegate responsibilities

Affect Helplessness Loss of control Anger, guilt, anxiety Bored, irritable, depressed	Join a support group Find a safe place to express emotions Seek creative outlets with books, poetry, or meditation
Sensory Stress reactions; alarm reaction, fight or flight syndrome Exhaustion Aroused physiological state	Relaxation training Neuromuscular massage Massage therapy Music, art, and dance therapies Meditational exercises

Imagery
Internalizing a "helper persona"
Lost boundaries between personal
and professional selves
Faulty images
	Integrate right hemisphere activities of
	    imagination, perspective and intuition
	Practice positive imagery
	Detach from professional role by
	    developing a personal identity other
	    than counselor
	Educate others about the proper use of
	    counselor skills; take own advice

Modality and Referral Problem	Related Behavioral Intervention
Cognition	Acknowledge limits
Cognitive stress through self-criticism, pessimism, learned helplessness	Clarify values
	Set goals
	Find private time for self-regulation
Disorganized thinking	Cognitive restructuring
Defensiveness	"Decompression routines"
Perfectionism	Spiritual or philosophical development
Paranoia and suicidal ideation	
Interpersonal Relationships	Learn to receive help
Refuse help or assistance	Seek life balance
Unable to develop a support system	Develop social skills to create mature relationships
Withdrawal from friends, family and colleagues	Assertiveness training
Strained relationship with school personnel	Develop baseline support for role and school staff
	Create a peer support group
Drugs/Diet	Healthy diet
Poor nutrition	Adequate rest
Poor sleep patterns	Exercise in a noncompetitive fashion
Eating, drinking, smoking too much	Relaxation exercises

INDIVIDUAL TREATMENT PLAN INITIATIVES— ON COUNSELING CHILDREN

| Treatment Plan | *HELPING Children Change*

Description. Keat (1990) gradually changed the acronym BASIC ID to HELP-ING to meet the developmental needs of children. It is a pragmatic and technically eclectic way of helping children.

Mode	Rank	Concern Number	Concern	Intervention
Health	5	H1	Pain	Avoid/Relief
		H2	Sickness	Wellness
Emotions	2	E1	Anxiety	Stress Management
		E2	Anger	Madness Management
		E3	Feeling down	Fun Training

Mode	Rank	Concern Number	Concern	Intervention
Learning	5	L1	Deficiencies	Life skills
		L2	Failing	Study skills
		L3	Sensory shallowness	Music
Personal Relationships	1	P1	Getting along (adults)	Relationship Enhancement (RE)
		P2	Lacks friends	Friendship Training
Imagery	4	I1	Low self-worth	IALAC
		I2	Coping lacks	Heroes (cartoons)
Need to Know	7	N1	Despair	Hope Cognitive
		N2	Mistaken ideas	restructuring
		N3	Lack of information	Bibliotherapy
Guidance of Actions, Behaviors, and Consequences	3	G1	Behavior deficits	Modeling
		G2	Motivation	Contracts

| **Treatment Plan** | *Empowering Youth Who Have "Deadline Disorder"* |

Description. Youth who procrastinate usually have not acquired the skills or strategies to approach and complete a task or an assignment in an organized way. Incomplete assignments or frantic last minute efforts often leave a client with feelings of frustration, anxiety, failure, and low self-esteem.

Even though teaching the study skills of problem-solving, goal setting and time management are helpful, a more comprehensive intervention that addresses the fears and negative feelings that procrastinators experience may have more long-term implications. Focusing on the structured modalities of emotions, learning, interpersonal relationships, interests and guidance of actions in a group setting may be the pivotal link to behavior change. Morse (1987) provided the following referral problems and related interventions for procrastinators:

Multimodal Group Intervention

Mode	Group Activities	Procrastinator Characteristics
Health	Participated in relaxation exercises	Locus of control
Emotions	Brainstormed and discussed feeling words.	Fear of failure Fear of success
	Shared common fears.	Fear of failure Fear of success
	Discussed and shared feelings of frustration.	Perfection
	Discussed power and the power one feels.	Locus of control
Learning/School	Shared feelings about school, favorite subjects, performance levels	Self-concept
	Discussed problems in completing assignments	Rebellion against authority; fear of failure; fear of success
	Completed worksheet "Getting Work Done Survey"	Perfection; fear of failure
People/Personal Relationships	Shared feelings about family and friends	Rebellion against authority
	Discussed relationships with classmates and the ability to function in the classroom group	Rebellion against authority; locus of control
Imagery/Interests	Discussed strengths and weaknesses	Fear of failure; Self-concept
	Shared likes and dislikes	Self-concept
	Discussed self put-downs	Fear of failure; Self-concept

Multimodal Group Intervention

Mode	Group Activities	Procrastinator Characteristics
	Participated in guided imagery to develop positive self-image	Self-concept
Need to Know	Discussed differences between thoughts and feelings	Self-concept; Rebellion against authority
	Identified thoughts and feelings under positive or negative categories	Self-concept; Rebellion against authority
	Practiced positive self-talk	Self-concept
	Role-played positive and negative aspects of putdowns	Self-concept
	Discussed how choices are made	Lack of skill Locus of control
	Listed choices students make during their day	Locus of control
Guidance of Actions	Identified "putting-off" behaviors	Perfection; fear of failure; fear of success
	Discussed ways time is wasted and saved	Lack of skill
	Listed activities to be done in a day and time required to accomplish them	Lack of skill
	Set priorities for completing tasks	Lack of skill
	Wrote short-term goals and implementation strategies	Lack of skill
	Recorded progress toward goals	Lack of skill

Multimodal Group Intervention (Continued)

Mode	Group Activities	Procrastinator Characteristics
	Wrote long-term goals (1, 5, & 10 year) and implementation strategies	Lack of skill

Source: Morse, L.A. (1987). Working with Young Procrastinators: Elementary School Students Who Do Not Complete School Assignments. *Elementary School Guidance and Counseling, 21,* 3. Published by the American School Counselor Association. Reprinted with permission.

INDIVIDUAL TREATMENT PLAN INITIATIVES— ON ADLERIAN TECHNIQUES WITH CHILDREN, ADOLESCENTS, PARENTS, AND TEACHERS

Dreikurs maintained that as children grow and interact with their environment, they gradually develop methods for achieving their basic goals of belonging. Children who do not have a pattern of misbehavior have an immediate goal of cooperation and constructive collaboration. They feel good about themselves and their usual behavior is socially and personally effective. Conversely, the child who has a pattern of misbehavior is pursuing one or more of the mistaken goals such as attention in order to belong. To understand the goal for which a misbehaving child is striving helps put the behavior in perspective along with a basis for corrective action.

Frank Wickers, a psychologist with the Child Development Clinic in Danville, Virginia, developed the Misbehavior Reaction Checklist to serve as a strategy for teachers to assess their immediate reactions to a child's misbehavior. It is based on the Adlerian Model that outlines four mistaken goals of a child's misbehavior—attention, power, revenge, and inadequacy. Misbehavior Reaction Checklist for Teachers and Goals of Behavior Inventory for Students presented here are two alternatives for evaluating teacher reactions and student needs.

The checklist given to teachers contains descriptions of four basic reaction patterns to a child's misbehavior. The teacher is asked to (a) choose the one response to the child's misbehavior that is most frequent or prominent and (b) rank order the other three responses to gain some idea of possible differences in the dominance of each goal.

Misbehavior Reaction Checklist for Teachers

Child's Name: _____,

    Please check one of the following descriptions that best fits your "usual" feeling-reaction when this student misbehaves in your classroom. Check the "most" appropriate statement, that is, the one that best describes your "most frequent or typical" feeling-reaction when this child misbehaves.

☐ annoyed, irritated, bothered—"Why is she being such a pest?" "I wish he'd stop doing that!" or "Why do I have to keep reminding, coaxing, helping her with that?"

    The goal of misbehavior: feeling reaction—attention

☐ angry, mad, challenged, feel like showing her who's boss—"He can't get away with that!" "Stop that this instant!" or "You will not leave this room until you have finished."

    The goal of misbehavior: feeling reaction—power

☐ hurt mixed with anger, wounded, maybe a little saddened—"How could she do that to me?" "Why is he being so mean and nasty?"—perhaps a momentary, secret desire to get even, to hurt back

    The goal of misbehavior: feeling reaction—revenge

☐ helplessness, despair, feel like giving up—"He'll just never learn to do that." "What's the use?" "I give up."—a sense of failure, inadequacy as a teacher

    The goal of misbehavior: feeling reaction—inadequacy

Caveat: Human behavior is rarely absolute or easy to categorize. This is particularly true when we are trying to determine the motivation behind another person's feelings or emotions. As a result, you may have experienced some difficulty selecting only one typical reaction about a child. If that is the case, please rank order the remaining three reactions-feelings in terms of their frequency. Place the numbers 2, 3, and 4 on the remaining blank lines of the original checklist.

Goals of Behavior Inventory for Students

Name: _____,

In life, as it is in school, people want different things. Please mark with a check mark (✓) any of the following sentences that are "true" for you:

☐ 1. I want to be in charge.
☐ 2. I want people to feel sorry for me.
☐ 3. I want people to see what it is like to be hurt.
☐ 4. I want people to stop telling me what to do.
☐ 5. I think that I have been treated unfairly.
☐ 6. I know I'll mess up so there's no point in trying.
☐ 7. I want people to feel sorry for what they have done.
☐ 8. I want people to notice me.
☐ 9. I want to be left alone. I can't do things right anyway.
☐ 10. I want some attention.
☐ 11. I want people to do more for me.
☐ 12. I want to get even.
☐ 13. I want people to do what I want to do.
☐ 14. I want people to stop asking me to do things.
☐ 15. I want power.
☐ 16. I want to be special.

Key: Attention = #8, 10, 11, 16
       Power = #1, 4, 13, 15
       Revenge = #3, 5, 7, 12
       Inadequacy = #2, 6, 9, 14

Note: The Misbehavior Reaction Checklist for Teachers can be modified for use with parents. The checklist is particularly useful in helping parents gain an understanding of their children's misbehavior. After being taught more effective responses to misbehavior, parents join educators in providing life skills to empower youth to self-efficacy.

PARTNERSHIPS WITH PARENTS
IN MANAGING THEIR CHILD'S MISBEHAVIOR

Students' misbehavior is often a recapitulation of their family system. Problems occur in an interpersonal context rather than in isolation. A change in one member's behavior effects change in the whole family as a system. Empowering students and their families to promote a positive change in behavior extends into the classroom and other interpersonal relationships.

Currently, on the market are numerous parenting programs that are systematically packaged for easy delivery to parents. *Active Parenting, Pride Parent Training,* and MegaSkills Parent Effectiveness Training represent a growing cornucopia of programs for parents.

Parent training and educational approaches are aimed at assisting parents to help their children by providing the parents with (a) practical information and parenting skills, (b) an understanding of the principles of learning and behavior modification, and (c) life-skill development such as communication, decision-making skills or problem-solving skills. Parent training and educational approaches have undergone extensive research to examine and critique their effectiveness, maintenance, and generalization of effects (McMahon & Forehand, 1984). Behavior parent training programs have

1. resulted in positive changes that have been maintained up to 4 1/2 years following the termination of formal treatment,
2. shown that parents are capable of generalizing their newly acquired therapeutic skills to untreated children in the family, and
3. been generalized to behaviors other than those initially targeted (Schaefer & Briesmeister, 1989). In addition, parents can be trained to identify and modify their child's dysfunctional behavior.

Christiansen, Johnson, Phillips, and Glassgow (1980) researched the differential effectiveness of three modes of parent training: (a) individual parent training, (b) parent training in groups, and (c) the use of independently motivated bibliotherapy. The comparison revealed that all three approaches enhanced the improvements in the child's targeted behavior with individual and group approaches being the most effective.

Within the last decade, there is a growing endorsement of the training as cotherapists. Milne (1986) examined the potential of training parents to be therapists and declared the efficacy of several training methodologies and formats. The rationale for training parents as cotherapists is pragmatic and cost effective. Parents are central figures in the child's microcosm with a clearly defined role that impacts the child in direct or subtle ways in an extensive array of situations.

Parents welcome and respond to pragmatic and accessible strategies or methods that empower them as child managers. Schaefer and Briesmeister (1989) maintained that parents accept the cotherapist collaborative partnership and usually view it as a natural extension of their parental roles, and one of their functions as parental-authority figures within the family composite.

Involving parents in the task of modifying school-related misbehavior can be a collaborative venture between family therapist and school counselor. Gaushell and Lawson (1989) proposed using a simple behavioral checksheet to provide information to parents concerning a child who is demonstrating disruptive or inappropriate behavior. The checksheet can be used as a means for directly involving parents in the change process.

Gaushell and Lawson (1989) found that by approaching common types of misbehavior from a family perspective, the counselor gains a powerful tool for effecting positive behavioral change, not only with the child but also within the parent-child relationship (p. 208). Parents are encouraged first to collect data that reflect the frequency and nature of the child's misbehavior. A single page checksheet is used to identify the frequency and specific nature of the child's misbehavior.

The following specific instructions are given to the parents:

Notify the child's teacher about the plan for the checksheet. The basic responsibility of initiating and following through with checksheet process is with the child.

At home, both parents introduce the checksheet and the responsibilities to their child—the child must deliver and retrieve the completed checksheet from the teacher and bring it home for the parent(s) to review at home.

Parents are to accept "no excuses" for the child's failure to bring the checklist home (i.e., block all excuses given and take whatever action is necessary to see that the child fulfills his or her responsibility). The parents also are instructed to confront the child if the checklist is not offered as soon as he or she arrives home.

The counselor processes any problems that the parent(s) foresees in using the checksheet and helps the parents rehearse their responses to the child's potential resistance to the plan.

During the first week, the focus is on successful action on the part of the child on bringing the checksheet home. Parents are instructed not to review or to act on the checksheet. Change will occur with successful approximation to the desired behavior change. A follow-up session can be scheduled for trouble shooting the failure to bring the checksheet home.

After a successful week of bringing home the checksheet, the focus of counseling moves to specific means of dealing with school misbehavior (Gaushell & Lawson, 1989 p. 211).

Parents should be prepared to respond to resistance, relapse, and testing of their firmness on the part of their offspring. Preparation in these issues improves cooperation and increases the parent's sense of control. Parents should be encouraged to maintain the use of the checksheet. Behavior change takes tenacity and time. Finally, parents should expect another series of misbehavior by the child within several weeks as a further test of the parent(s) firmness in maintaining the new behavior. "Only when the child has 4 to 5 weeks of reports of no misbehavior is it recommended that the parents reduce the frequency of bringing home the checksheet (e.g., two times per week—Tuesday and Friday)" (Gaushell & Lawson, 1989, p. 211).

Chapter **18**

SELECTED INVENTORIES, CHECKLISTS, AND CONTRACTS

This final chapter consists of a number of inventories, checklists, contracts, and forms to assist counselors and therapists in gathering information, monitoring interventions, and evaluating progress. The intention is to provide a small sampling of resources that can be enhanced and developed by the practitioner through professional experiences and therapeutic interactions. Contracting provides both the therapist and the client with a written record of what was agreed upon and an opportunity to evaluate progress or boundaries and limitations in the counseling relationship. Contracts in behavioral change programs help the client (a) initiate specific actions, (b) establish specific criteria for achievement, and (c) clarify consequences and rewards. In addition, contracts between client and therapist outline boundaries to issues such as confidentiality.

ANOREXIA NERVOSA/BULIMIA NERVOSA

Anorexia: An Introductory Questionnaire

Age: _____

Sex: _____

Martial Status: _____

Occupation: _____

Estimated yearly income: _____ Self

_____ Family

Estimated daily calorie intake: _____

Family Food Patterns

Please respond True or False to the following statements:

_____ I like to cook.

_____ I like to watch people enjoy my cooking.

_____ My family has "good" eating habits.

_____ I was taught to clean my plate.

_____ I have family members who are overweight.

_____ I have family members who are very thin.

Self-image

Please respond True or False to the following statements:

_____ I think I am neat.

_____ I think I am organized.

_____ I think I am pretty.

_____ I think I am intelligent.

_____ I think I am fat.

_____ I think I am skinny.

_____ I think I am healthy.

_____ I think I am fit.

_____ I think I am average looking.

_____ I think I am ugly.

Please check the methods of weight loss you have tried:

_____ Diet pills

_____ Vomiting

_____ Exercise

_____ Starvation

_____ Other _____

Please check the areas of your body that you are concerned with or the areas that you feel need to be thinner:

_____ Face

_____ Arms

_____ Chest
_____ Stomach
_____ Buttocks
_____ Thighs
_____ Legs
_____ Other _____

Your Relationship with Your Mother Figure

Please respond True or False to the following statements:

_____ My mother was my primary caretaker.
_____ My mother had the most significant influence on my development.
_____ My mother fulfilled my basic needs for food, security, and shelter.
_____ I trust my mother more than any other individual.
_____ I am confident of my mother's love regardless of my actions.
_____ My mother is significantly overweight and/or consistently overeats.
_____ My mother is significantly underweight and/or is consistently on diets.
_____ I seek my mother's approval over my own.

Your Relationship with Your Father Figure

Please respond True or False to the following statements:

_____ My father was my primary caretaker.
_____ My father had the most significant influence on my development.
_____ My father fulfilled my basic needs for food, security, and shelter.
_____ I trust my father more than any other individual.
_____ I am confident of my father's love regardless of my actions.
_____ My father is significantly overweight and/or consistently overeats.
_____ My father is significantly underweight and/or is consistently on diets.
_____ I seek my father's approval over my own.

Your Relationship with Siblings or Significant Others

Please respond True or False to the following statements:

_____ I am easily deterred by others' disapproval.
_____ I am often a victim of circumstances.
_____ I am confident in making my life decisions.
_____ I trust the advice of others more than my own opinions.
_____ I am confident of the love of others, regardless of my actions.

_____ I seek the approval of others over my own.
_____ I worry about new situations.
_____ I am less competent or successful than most people my age.

Your Relationship with Peers

Please respond True or False to the following statements:

_____ I frequently lead others or influence them.
_____ I have a definite plan for my future career.
_____ I am confident of meeting my own goals.
_____ I have a feeling of knowing who I am and where I am going.
_____ Others recognize that I am going to meet my career goals.
_____ I am a unique individual and others recognize my uniqueness.
_____ I am in total control of my own actions.
_____ I am troubled and confused about my future role in life.

Source: Akeroyd-Guillory, D. (1988). A Developmental View of Anorexia Nervosa. *The School Counselor, 36,* 27-32. Published by the American School Counselor Association. Reprinted with permission.

ASSERTIVENESS

Assertiveness Inventory

Directions: Below you will find a list of situations that involve social interactions. Work through all the questions twice. Record the first response that comes to mind. First, we would like you to indicate in the columns **preceding** each of the situations (items) how nervous or tense you would feel if you behaved in the way described. It is possible to answer in any one of the following ways:

1	2	3	4	5
not at all	*somewhat*	*often*	*very*	*extremely*

For example, if you feel tense when you start a conversation with a stranger, indicate this by putting a mark in the *third* column in the following way:

1	2	3	4	5
		×		

1. Starting a conversation with a stranger.

After you have worked through the items once, go through them again and indicate in the columns **following** the situations how often you behave in the way described. For this, use one of the following possibilities.

1	2	3	4	5
never	*rarely*	*sometimes*	*usually*	*always*

For example, if, when you find yourself with a stranger, you *usually* start a conversation indicate this by putting a mark in the *fourth* column in the following way:

	1	2	3	4	5
1. Starting a conversation with a stranger.				×	

To help you concentrate, cover up your answers to the first part while you are completing the second.

1	2	3	4	5	Questions	1	2	3	4	5
					1. Starting a conversation with a stranger.					
					2. Telling someone who interrupts you that you find this annoying.					
					3. Telling a group of people about something you have experienced.					
					4. Asking someone to explain something you have not understood.					
					5. Offering an opinion that differs from that of the person with whom you are talking.					
					6. Acknowledging a compliment about your personal appearance.					
					7. Telling a friend or an acquaintance that he or she is doing something that annoys you.					
					8. Telling someone that you like him or her.					
					9. Refusing a request made by a person in authority.					
					10. Asking people to make allowance for the fact that you are afraid of something.					

1	2	3	4	5	Questions	1	2	3	4	5
					11. Maintaining your opinion in the face of a good friend who disagrees with you.					
					12. Admitting that you are wrong.					
					13. Looking at the person to whom you are talking.					
					14. Inviting an acquaintance to join you at a social event (for instance a social evening or party).					
					15. Telling someone that you think he or she treated you unfairly.					
					16. Telling someone that you are fond of him or her.					
					17. Declining a drink, especially if it is offered to you repeatedly.					
					18. Telling someone who has justly criticized you that he or she is right.					
					19. Acknowledging a compliment on something you have done.					
					20. Accepting someone's invitation to join him or her at a social event.					
					21. Starting a conversation with a man or woman you find attractive.					
					22. Refusing a request made by someone of whom you are fond.					
					23. Discussing someone's criticism of something you have done.					
					24. Saying that you enjoy the experience of being told that you are liked.					
					25. Asking an acquaintance to help you with a job.					
					26. Putting forward your opinion during a conversation with strangers.					
					27. Joining in the conversation of a group of people.					

1	2	3	4	5	Questions	1	2	3	4	5
					28. Asking people to return things they have borrowed.					
					29. Inviting an acquaintance for a drink.					
					30. Accepting an offer of help.					
					31. Refusing to donate money to charities.					
					32. Maintaining your own opinion against a person who has a very pronounced opinion.					
					33. Asking a person to stop doing something that annoys you (e.g., on a subway, in a restaurant, or a movie theater).					
					34. Protesting when someone jumps in front of you while in a line.					
					35. Offering your opinion to someone who knows more about the subject than you do.					
					36. Asking someone whether you have hurt him or her.					
					37. Saying that you enjoy people telling you that they are very fond of you.					
					38. Giving your opinion to a person in authority.					
					39. Refusing unsatisfactory goods or services (e.g., in a store or in a restaurant).					
					40. Telling someone who did something for you how pleased you are.					
					41. Discussing with someone your impression that they are trying to avoid you.					
					42. Saying that you are sorry when you have made a mistake.					
					43. Telling someone that you are very pleased with something you have done.					

1	2	3	4	5	Questions	1	2	3	4	5
					44. Explaining your philosophy of life.					
					45. Going up to someone in order to make their acquaintance.					
					46. Asking someone for directions.					
					47. Asking someone to critique something you have made.					
					48. Refusing to lend something to a friend.					
					49. Admitting that you know little about a particular subject.					
					50. Insisting that someone does his or her share in a joint task.					

Scoring: Item Nos. 2, 7, 9, 10, 15, 22, 25, 28, 31, 33, 34, 39, 41, 48, and 50 define the **Display of Negative Feelings** subscale; Nos. 4, 11, 12, 13, 17, 18, 23, 30, 36, 40, 42, 46, 47, and 49 are included in the **Expression of and Dealing with Personal Limitations** subscale; Nos. 1, 3, 5, 26, 27, 32, 38, 44, and 45 are contained in the **Initiating Assertiveness** subscale; items 6, 8, 16, 19, 21, 24, 37, and 43 define the **Positive Assertion** subscale. The questionnaire contains four unscaled items: 14, 20, 29, and 35. The **General Assertiveness** scale score is obtained by summation of item scores on all 50 items.

Source: Arrindell, W. A., Sanderman, W. J., Hogeman, J. H., Pickersgill, M. G., Kwee, G. T., Van der Molen, H. T., & Lingsma, M. M. (1990). Correlates of Assertiveness. *Advances in Behavior Research and Therapy, 12,* 153-182, Elsevier Science Ltd., Pergamon Imprint, Oxford, England. Reprinted with permission.

BEHAVIOR

Behavior Checksheet

Name: _____

Instructions: Teachers, please check blanks and sign.

Monday		
Yes	**No**	
		Prepared with pencil, paper, boots, etc.?
		On time?
		Completed the assigned classwork?
		Disturbed the class?
		Behind in homework?
		Homework tonight?
Teacher's Signature		

Study Skills Progress Report

Student: _____   Teacher: _____

Dates covered by this report: _____   Subject: _____

Your help is requested in assessing the study habits and skills of this student. Please record your observation below and return to the guidance office by _____.

	5 Excellent	4 Good	3 Average	2 Fair	1 Poor
Use of study time					
Assignments in on time					
Attendance					
Necessary materials					
Classroom behavior					
Classroom attitude					
Scholastic progress					

Grade to date (if applicable) _____

Comments: _____

Behavior and Learning Contract

Behaviors	Points
1. Attending class on time	10
2. Bringing books, paper, pen, pencil	5
3. Giving correct answer	5
4. Working during assigned times	10
5. Assignments completed (6)	10 each
6. Unit tests (2)	50 each
7. Extra credit: projects, reports, presentations	10

Student _____ Teacher _____

Sample Bottom-Line Contract

For _____(name)   Week of _____(date) through _____(date)

Behavior/Task	Possible Points	S	M	T	W	Th	F	S	Total
Keep curfews Stay home after 6 p.m. on week nights	10	X	X	X	X	X			/50
Stay home after 12 a.m. on weekend nights	10						X	X	/20
No drunk or high behavior (stumbling, staggering, swearing, slurring) or drug paraphernalia	10	X	X	X	X	X	X	X	/70
No violence (physical or verbal)	10	X	X	X	X	X	X	X	/70
School attendance (all classes)	10		X	X	X	X	X		/50
Chores at home (dishes M, W, F and garbage T, Th, Sat)	5		X	X	X	X	X	X	/30
2nd-phase intervention group attendance	10			X					/10
See probation officer	10						X		/10
See outpatient counselor	10		X						/10
					Total points possible				320
					Total points earned				

Signed _____   Date _____
(Teenager)

_____   Date _____
(Parent)

_____   Date _____
(Witness—Probation Officer or Counselor)

Renegotiation Date _____

Source: Schaefer, D. (1987). *Choices and Consequences: What to Do When a Teenager Uses Alcohol and Drugs.* Minneapolis: Johnson Institute. Reprinted with permission.

COMMUNICATION

Personal Report of Communication Apprehension (PRCA)

This instrument is composed of 24 statements concerning feelings about communicating with other people. Indicate the degree to which each statement applies to you, using the following scale.

> 1 = *strongly disagree*
> 2 = *disagree*
> 3 = *undecided*
> 4 = *agree*
> 5 = *strongly agree*

1. I dislike participating in group discussions.
2. Generally, I am comfortable while participating in a group discussion.
3. I am tense and nervous while participating in group discussions.
4. I like to get involved in group discussions.
5. Engaging in a group discussion with new people makes me tense and nervous.
6. I am calm and relaxed while participating in group discussions.
7. Generally, I am nervous when I have to participate in a meeting.
8. Usually, I am calm and relaxed while participating in meetings.
9. I am very calm and relaxed when I am called on to express an opinion at a meeting.
10. I am afraid to express myself at meetings.
11. Communication at meetings usually makes me uncomfortable.
12. I am very relaxed when answering questions at a meeting.
13. While participating in a conversation with a new acquaintance, I feel very nervous.
14. I have no fear of speaking up in conversations.
15. Ordinarily, I am very tense and nervous in conversations.
16. Ordinarily, I am very calm and relaxed in conversations.
17. While conversing with a new acquaintance, I feel very relaxed.
18. I am afraid to speak up in conversations.
19. I have no fear of giving a speech.
20. Certain parts of my body feel very tense and rigid when I am giving a speech.
21. I feel relaxed while giving a speech.
22. My thoughts become confused and jumbled when I am giving a speech.

23. I face the prospect of giving a speech with confidence.
24. While giving a speech, I get so nervous that I forget facts I really know.

Calculation Formula for the PRCA

A = 18 + (Items 2 + 4 + 6) - (Items 1 + 3 + 5)
B = 18 + (Items 8 + 9 + 12) - (Items 7 + 10 + 11)
C = 18 + (Items 14 + 16 + 17) - (Items 13 + 15 + 18)
D = 18 + (Items 19 + 21 + 23) - (Items 20 + 22 + 24)

PRCA = A + B + C + D

PRCA Norms

1. *Low apprehensive* (25-59): An individual with low apprehension feels less anxiety in social situations than the normal or average person.
2. *Moderate apprehensive* (67-88): An individual with moderate apprehension is 'Typical' of most people.
3. *High apprehensive* (89-125): An individual in the high apprehensive range experiences a greater level of anxiety than the norm.

Source: Monroe, C., Borzi, M.G., & Burrell, R.D. (1992). Communication Apprehension among High School Dropouts. *The School Counselor, 39*(4), 273-280. Reprinted with permission.

SUICIDE

Suicide Warning Signs

Warning signs can be organized around the word *FACT*

Feelings

Hopelessness—*"It will never get any better." "There's nothing anyone can do." "I'll always feel this way."*
Fear of losing control, going crazy, harming self or others.
Helpless, worthless—*"Nobody cares." "Everyone would be better off without me."*
Overwhelming guilt, shame, self-hatred
Pervasive sadness
Persistent anxiety or anger

Action or Events:

Drug or alcohol abuse
Themes of death or destruction in talk or written materials
Nightmares
Recent loss—through death, divorce, separation, broken relationships, or loss of job, money, status, self-esteem
Loss of religious faith
Agitation, restlessness
Aggression, recklessness

Change:

In personality—more withdrawn, tired, apathetic, indecisive, or more boisterous, talkative, outgoing
In behavior—can't concentrate on school, work, routine tasks
In sleep pattern—oversleeping or insomnia, sometimes with early waking
In eating habits—loss of appetite and weight or overeating
Loss of interest in friends, hobbies, personal grooming, sex, or other activities previously enjoyed
Sudden improvement after a period of being down or withdrawn

Threats

Statements, for example, *"How long does it take to bleed to death?"*

Threats, for example, *"I won't be around much longer."*
Plans, for example, putting affairs in order, giving away
favorite things, studying drug effects, obtaining a weapon
Gestures or attempts, for example, overdosing, wrist
cutting

Source: Kalafat, J. (1990). Adolescent Suicide and the Implications for School Response
Programs. *The School Counselor, 37,* 5. Reprinted with permission.

Suicidal Tendencies Scale

Directions: Read each statement. Assess your client in each of the following categories. Place the appropriate score in the blank to the right of each statement. The statement applies if any of the conditions are met. If the question does not apply, consider it a zero (0). Add all the scores. Is your client at moderate, high, or very high suicide risk?

Question	Low 0	Moderate 1	High 2	SCORE
A. External behaviors	No change in communication, academic performance, dress, etc.	Moderate change	Significant change	
B. Self-Esteem	Intact	Low self-esteem, disheveled appearance and/or poor hygiene	Very low self-esteem, self-destructive or self-mutilating behaviors	
C. Support system	Intact	Alienated from some family or friends	Socially unresponsive; alienated from most family or friends	
D. Significant relationships	Healthy relationships	Moderate relationship problems	Broken relationships	
E. Significant loss and/or change	None	Recent death of a friend or pet; health, job, or financial problems	Unresolved loss or death of loved one; loss of job; financial disaster; terminal illness	
F. Depression	Not evident	Moderate, low in energy; not coping well	Severe, apathetic and withdrawn or sudden rise in energy—a "happy depression"	

G. Will to live	Has purpose/meaning for living	Questions life, afraid of losing control; beginning to feel helpless or hopeless	Consistent thoughts and feelings of helplessness and hopelessness	
H. Substance abuse; alcohol, drugs, food, etc.	None known	Alcohol/drug use moderate; social use; overeats or undereats	Alcohol/drug use heavy; addiction; bulimic, anorexic	
I. Family suicides, friends, or others	None	Distant family member; not known well	Immediate family member; loved one	
J. Frequency of suicidal thoughts	No thoughts of suicide	Isolated, with periods of persistence; has had prior thoughts but did not attempt	Constant and persistent	
K. Prior attempts	None known	One attempt	Wished it had been successful	
L. Method of suicide	No method considered	Considering methods	Has decided on a method and/or has access to a method	
M. Development of plan	No plans	Thoughts just beginning to develop	Thoughts becoming specific; giving away possessions	
Score: 3-6: Moderate risk; Further assessment recommended	7-10: High risk; Begin intervention procedures	10+ Very high risk; Crisis situation; immediate intervention necessary		**Total Score**

Source: Stefanowski-Harding, S. (1990). Suicide and the School Counselor. *The School Counselor, 37,* 5. Reprinted with permission.

BIBLIOGRAPHY

Arieti, S., & Bemporad, J. (1978). *Severe and mild depression*. New York: Basic Books.

Benson, H. (1984). *Beyond the relaxation response*. New York: Harper & Row.

Brown, N.W. (1986). Guided imagery for counselors. *Virginia Counselors Journal, 15*, 1.

Budman, S.H., & Gurman, A. (1983). The practice of brief therapy. *Professional Psychology: Research and Practice, 14*, 277–292.

Corsini, R.J. (Ed.). (1981). *Handbook of innovative psychotherapies*. New York: Wiley.

Davanloo, H. (Ed.). (1980). *Short-term dynamic psychotherapy*. New York: Jason Aronson.

de Shazer, S. (1979). Brief therapy with families. *American Journal of Family Therapy, 7*, 83–95.

de Shazer, S. (1980). Brief family therapy: A metaphorical task. *Journal of Marital and Family Therapy, 6*, 471–476.

Dinkmeyer, D. (1991). Mental health counseling: A psychoeducational approach. *Journal of Mental Health Counseling, 13*, 1.

Dinkmeyer, D., & Carlson, J. (1984). *Time for a better marriage.* Circle Pines, MN: American Guidance Service.

Dinkmeyer, D., & Carlson, J. (1989). *Taking time for love: How to stay happily married.* Englewood Cliffs, NJ: Prentice Hall.

Dryden, W. (1984). Rational emotive therapy and cognitive therapy: A comparison. In M.A. Reda & M.T. Mahoney (Eds.), *Cognitive psychotherapies: Recent developments in theory, research and practice* (pp. 81–99). Cambridge, MA: Ballinger.

Ellis, A. (1962). *Reason and emotion in psychotherapy.* New York: Lyle Stuart.

Ellis, A. (1987). Integrative developments in rational-emotive therapy (RET). *Journal of Integrative and Eclectic Psychotherapy, 6,* 470–479.

Ellis, A. (1989). Rational-emotive therapy. In R.J. Corsini & D. Wedding (Eds.), *Cognitive psychotherapies* (pp. 197–240). Itasca, IL: Peacock.

Frank, J.D. (1971). Therapeutic factors in psychotherapy. *American Journal of Psychotherapy, 25,* 350–361.

Gasman, D.H. (1992). Double-exposure therapy: Videotape homework as a psychotherapeutic adjunct. *American Journal of Psychotherapy, XLVI*(1).

George, R.L., & Cristiani, T.S. (1981). *Theory, methods, and processes of counseling and psychotherapy.* NJ: Prentice Hall.

Gladding, S.T. (1979). The creative use of poetry in the counseling process. *Personnel and Guidance Journal, 57,* 285–287.

Glass, G., & Kliegl, R. (1983). An apology for research integration in the study of psychotherapy. *Journal of Consulting and Clinical Psychology, 51,* 28–41.

Gordon, R.A. (1990). *Anorexia and bulimia: Anatomy of a social epidemic.* Cambridge, MA: Basil Blackwell.

Greenwald, H. (1984). *Active psychotherapy.* New York: Jason Aronson.

Haddock, B.D. (1989). Scenario writing: A therapeutic application. *Journal of Mental Health Counseling, 11,* 234–243.

Harper, R. (1959). *Psychoanalysis and psychotherapy: Thirty-six systems*. Englewood Cliffs, NJ: Prentice Hall.

Harris, G.A. (1991). Eclecticism, again. *Journal of Mental Health Counseling, 13*(4), 427–431.

Hart, J.T. (1983). *Modern eclectic therapy: A fundamental orientation*. New York: Plenum.

Hill, C.E. (1990). Is individual therapy process really different from group therapy process? The jury is still out. *The Counseling Psychologist, 18*(1), 126–130.

Hynes, A.M., & Hynes-Berry, M. (1986). *Bibliotherapy, the interactive process: A handbook*. Boulder, CO: Westview.

Hynes, A.M., & Wedl, L.C. (1990). Bibliotherapy: An interactive process in counseling older persons. *Journal of Mental Health Counseling, 12*, 3.

Kazdin, A.E., Siegel, T.C., & Bass, D. (1992). Cognitive problem-solving skills training and parent management training in the treatment of antisocial behavior in children. *Journal of Consulting and Clinical Psychology, 60*, 733–747.

Kesler, K.D. (1990). Burnout: A multimodal approach to assessment and resolution. *Elementary School Guidance and Counseling, 24*, 4.

Kirschenbaum, D.S., Fitzgibbon, M.L., Martino, S., Conviser, J.H., Rosendahl, M., & Latsch, L. (1992). Stages of change in successful weight control: A clinically derived model. *Behavior Therapy, 23*, 4.

Kutash, I.L., & Schlesinger, L.B. (1980). *Handbook on stress and anxiety*. San Francisco: Jossey-Bass.

Lasko, C.A. (1986). Childhood depression: Questions and answers. *Elementary School Guidance and Counseling, 20*, 283–289.

Luborsky, L., Singer, B., & Luborsky, L. (1975). Comparitive studies of psychotherapies: Is it true that "everyone has one and all must have prizes?" *Archives of General Psychiatry, 32*, 995–1008.

Marlin, E. (1989). *Genograms: The new tool for exploring personality, career, and love patterns you inherit*. New York: Contemporary Books.

Matthews, W.J., & Dardeck, K.L. (1985). Construction of metaphor in the counseling process. *American Mental Health Counselors Association Journal, 7,* 11–23.

Maultsby, M.C. (1986). Teaching rational self-counseling to middle graders. *The School Counselor, 33,* 3.

Mills, J.C., & Crowley, R.J. (1986). *Therapeutic metaphors for children and the child within.* New York: Brunner/Mazel.

Perls, F.S. (1976). *The Gestalt approaches and eye witnesses to therapy.* New York: Bantam Books.

Pietrofesa, J., Hoffman, A., & Splete, H. (1884). *Counseling: An introduction* (2nd ed.). Boston, MA: Houghton Mifflin.

Polster, E., & Polster, M. (1973). *Gestalt therapy integrated.* New York: Random House.

Ponzo, Z. (1976). Integrating techniques from five counseling theories. *Personnel and Guidance Journal, 54,* 415–419.

Prochaska, J.O., & DiClemente, C.C. (1982). Transtheoretical therapy: Toward a more integrated model of change. *Psychotherapy: Theory and Practice, 19,* 2766–288.

Rimm, D.C. (1973). Thought-stopping and covert assertion in the treatment of phobias. *Journal of Consulting and Clinical Psychology, 41,* 466–67.

Riordan, R.J. (1992). The use of mirror image therapy in substance abuse groups. *Journal of Counseling and Development, 71,* 1.

Rogers, C.R. (1961). *On becoming a person.* Boston: Houghton Mifflin.

Rogers, C.R. (1965). The therapeutic relationship: Recent theory and research. *Australian Journal of Psychology, 17*(2), 116–121.

Rogers, C.R. (1967). The condition of change from a client-centered viewpoint. In B. Berenson & R. Carkhuff (Eds.), *Sources of gain in counseling and psychotherapy* (pp. 92–201). New York: Holt, Rinehart & Winston.

Rogers, C.R. (1980). *A way of being.* Boston, MA: Houghton Mifflin.

Rossiter, C., & Brown, R. (1988). An evaluation of interactive bibliotherapy in a clinical setting. *Journal of Poetry Therapy, 1*, 157–168.

Sacco, W.P., & Graves, D.J. (1984). Childhood depression, interpersonal problem solving, and self-ratings of performance. *Journal of Clinical Child Psychology, 13*, 10–15.

Safran, J.D. (1990). Towards a refinement of cognitive therapy in light of interpersonal theory: I Theory. *Clinical Psychology Review, 10*, 87–105.

Schultz, D. (1978). Imagery and the control of depression. In J.L. Singer & K.S. Pope (Eds.), *The power of human imagination* (pp. 281–307). New York: Plenum.

Seibel, M.M., & Taymor, M.L. (1992). Emotional aspects of infertility. *Fertility and Sterility, 37*, 2.

Sheikh, A.A., & Shaffer, J.T. (Eds.). (1979). *The potential of fantasy and imagination.* New York: Brandon House.

Simon, S.B., Howe, L.W., & Kirschenbaum, H. (1972). *Values clarification: A handbook of practical strategies for teachers and students.* New York: Hart Publishing.

Smith, M.L. & Glass, G.V. (1977). Meta-analysis of psychotherapy outcome studies. *American Psychologist, 32*, 752–760.

Smith, M.L., Glass, G., & Miller, T. (1980). *The benefits of psychotherapy.* Baltimore, MD: Johns Hopkins University Press.

Soper, P.H., & L'Abate, L. (1977). Paradox as a therapeutic technique: A review. *International Journal of Family Counseling, 5*, 10–21.

Stanton, M.D. (1980). Family therapy: System approaches. In G.P. Sholevar, R.M. Benson, & B.J. Blinder (Eds.), *Emotional disorders in children and adolescents: Medical and psychological approaches to treatment* (pp. 167–192). Jamaica, NY: S. P. Medical and Scientific Books.

Stiles, W., Shapiro, D., & Elliot, R. (1986). Are all psychotherapies equivalent? *American Psychologist, 14*, 142–149.

Strober, M., McCracken, J., & Hanna, G. (1989). Affective disorders. In

L.K.G. Hsu & M. Hersen (Eds.), *Handbook of child psychiatric diagnosis* (pp. 299–316). New York: Wiley.

Thorne, F.C. (1961). *Personality: A clinical eclectic viewpoint.* Brandon, VT: Clinical Psychology Publishing.

Wenz, K.M., & McWhirter, J.J. (1990). Enhancing the group experience: Creative writng exercises. *Journal for Specialists in Group Work, 15*(1), 37–42.

White, J., Keenan, M., & Brooks, N. (1992). Stress control: A controlled comparitive investigation of large group therapy for generalized anxiety disorder. *Behavioral Psychology, 20,* 97–114.

REFERENCES

Ackerman, N. (1958). *The psychodynamics of family life*. New York: Basic Books.

Akeroyd-Guillory, D. (1988). A developmental view of anorexia nervosa. *The School Counselor, 36,* 24–33.

Albee, G.W. (1982). Preventing psychopathology and promoting human potential. *American Psychologist, 37,* 1043–1050.

Alberti, R.E., & Emmons, M.L. (1986). *Your perfect right: A guide to assertive living*. San Luis Obispo, CA: Impact Publishers.

Allen, D.M. (1988). *Unifying individual and family therapies*. San Francisco: Jossey-Bass.

American Psychiatric Association. (1994). *Diagnostic and statistical manual of mental disorders* (4th ed.). Washington, DC: Author.

Anderson, M. (1988). *Counseling families from a system perpective*. Ann Arbor, MI: ERIC/CAPS Digest.

Anderson, R.F. (1980). Using guided fantasy with children. *Elementary School Guidance & Counseling, 15,* 39–47.

Anderson, A.E., & Hay, A. (1985). Racial and socioeconomic influences in anorexia nervosa and bulimia. *International Journal of Eating Disorders, 4,* 479–487.

Anderson, S.A., & Russell, C.S. (1982). Utilizing process and content in designing paradoxical interventions. *American Journal of Family Therapy, 10*, 48–60.

Andrews, J.D.W. (1989). Integrating visions of reality: Interpersonal diagnosis and the existential vision. *American Psychologist, 44*, 5.

Apolinsky, S.R., & Wilcoxon, S.A. (1991). Symbolic confrontation with women survivors of childhood sexual victimization. *The Journal of Specialists in Group Work, 16*, 2.

Aponte, H.J., & Van Deusen, J.M. (1981). Structural family therapy. In A.S. Gurman & D.P. Kniskern (Eds.), *Handbook of family therapy* (pp. 116–134). New York: Brunner/Mazel.

Arrindell, W.A., Sanderman, W.J., Hogeman, J.H., Pickersgill, M.G., Kwee, G.T., Van der Molen, H.T., & Lingsma, M.M. (1990). Correlates of assertiveness. *Advances in Behavior Research and Therapy, 12*, 153–182.

Attneave, G.S. (1990). A network model for helping. *Journal of Mental Health Counseling, 12*, 1, 24–30.

Babensee, B.A., & Pequette, J.R. (1982). *Perspectives on loss: A manual for educators*, P. O. Box 1352, Evergreen, CO 80301.

Bach, G.R., & Wyden, P. (1968). *The intimate enemy*. New York: William Morrow.

Bahatti, R.S., Janakiramariah, N., & Channabasvanna, S. (1982). Group interaction as a method of family therapy. *International Journal of Group Psychotherapy, 32*, 103–113.

Barker, P. (1985). *Using metaphors in psychotherapy*. New York: Brunner/Mazel.

Bateson, G. (1972). *Steps to an ecology of mind*. New York: Random House.

Beck, A.T. (1976). *Cognitive therapy and emotional disorders*. New York: International Universities Press.

Beck, A.T., & Emery, G. (1985). *Anxiety disorders and phobias: A cognitive perspective*. New York: Basic Books.

Bednar, R.L., & Kaul, T. (1978). Experiential group research. In S.L. Garfield

& A.E. Bergin (Eds.), *Handbook of psychotherapy and behavior change* (2nd ed.) (pp. 66–82). New York: Wiley.

Bedrosian, R.C., & Beck, A.T. (1980). Principles of cognitive therapy. In M. J. Mahoney (Ed.), *Psychotherapy process* (pp. 115–135). New York: Plenum.

Belkin, G.S. (1988). *Contemporary psychotherapies* (2nd. ed.) Monterey, CA: Brooks/Cole.

Bellack, A.S., & Hersen, M. (1988). *Behavioral assessment: A practical handbook* (3rd ed.). New York: Pergamon.

Benson, H. (1974). Your innate asset for combating stress. *Harvard Business Review, 52,* 49–60.

Bent, R.J., Putman, D.G., Kiesler, D.J., & Nowicki, S., Jr. (1976). Correlates of successful psychotherapy. *Journal of Counseling and Clinical Psychology, 44,* 149.

Bergin, A.E., & Lambert, M.J. (1978). The evaluation of therapeutic outcomes. In S.L. Garfield & A.E. Bergin (Eds.), *Handbook of psychotherapy and behavior change: An empirical analysis* (2nd ed.) (pp. 139–190). New York: Wiley.

Bergman, J.S. (1985). *Fishing for barracuda.* New York: Norton.

Berne, E. (1961). *Transactional analysis in psychotherapy.* New York: Grove Press.

Berne, E. (1964). *Games people play.* New York: Grove Press.

Bernstein, D.A., & Borkover, T.D. (1973). *Progress relaxation training: A manual for the helping professionals.* Champaign, IL: Research Press.

Bettelheim, B. (1976). *The uses of enchantment.* New York: Knopf.

Beutler, L.E., Crago, M., & Arizmendi, T.G. (1986). Research on therapist variables in psychotherapy. In S.L. Garfield & A.E. Berginh (Ed.), *Handbook of psychotherapy and behavior change* (3rd ed.) (pp. 257–310). New York: Wiley.

Blades, S., & Girualt, E. (1982). *The use of poetry therapy as a projective technique in counseling and psychotherapy.* Paper presented at the meeting of the

California Personnel and Guidance Association, San Francisco (Eric Document Reproduction Service No. ED 213 040).

Bloch, S., & Crouch, E. (1985). *Therapeutic factors in group psychotherapy.* Oxford: Oxford University Press.

Blocher, D.H. (1974). *Developmental counseling* (2nd ed.). New York: Ronald.

Blocher, D.H. (1987). On the uses and misuses of the term theory. *Journal of Counseling and Development, 66,* 67–68.

Blocher, D.H. (1989). The interactional view: Family therapy approaches of the mental research institute. In A.S. Gurman & D.P. Kriskerr (Eds.), *Handbook of family therapy* (pp. 267–309). New York: Brunner/Mazel.

Bloom, B.L. (1981). Focused single-session therapy: Initial development and evaluation. In S.H. Budman (Ed.), *Forms of brief therapy* (pp. 66–82). New York: Guilford Press.

Bornstein, P.H., & Sipprelle, C.N. (1973, April 6). *Clinical applications of induced anxiety in the treatment of obesity.* Paper presented at the Southeastern Psychological Association Meeting, Atlanta, Georgia.

Boscolo, L., Cecchin, G., Hoffman, L., & Penn, P. (1987). *Milan systemic family therapy: Conversations in theory and practice.* New York: Basic Books.

Bowen, M. (1978). *Family therapy in clinical practice.* New York: Jason Aronson.

Bower, S.A., & Bower, G.H. (1976). *Asserting yourself: A practical guide for positive change.* New York: Addison-Wesley.

Boy, A.V., & Pine, G.J. (1983). Counseling: Fundamentals of theoretical renewal. *Counseling and Values, 27,* 248–255.

Brabeck, M.M., & Welfel, E.R. (1985). Counseling theory: Understanding the trend toward eclecticism from a developmental perspective. *Journal of Counseling and Development, 63,* 6, 343–348.

Brammer, L.M., & Shostrum, E.L. (1968). *Therapeutic psychology: Fundamentals of actualization counseling and psychotherapy.* Englewood Cliffs, NJ: Prentice Hall.

Brammer, L.M., & Shostrum. E.L. (1977). *Therapeutic psychology: Fundamentals of counseling and psychotherapy* (3rd ed.). Englewood Cliffs, NJ: Prentice Hall.

Brammer, L.M., & Shostrum, E.L. (1982). *Therapeutic psychology: Fundamentals of counseling and psychotherapy* (4th ed.). Englewood Cliffs, NJ: Prentice Hall.

Brand, A.G. (1987). Writing as counseling. *Elementary School Guidance and Counseling, 21*, 4.

Brigman, G., & Earley, B. (1990). *Peer helping: A training guide.* Portland, MA: J. Weston Walch.

Brooks, R. (1985). The beginning sessions of child therapy: Of messages and metaphors. *Psychotherapy, 22,* 761–769.

Brooks, R. (1987). Storytelling and the therapeutic process for children with learning disabilities. *Journal of Learning Disablities, 20,* 546–550.

Brooks-Gunn, J., Burrow, C., & Warren, M.P. (1988). Attitudes toward eating and body weight in different groups of female athletes. *International Journal of Eating Disorders, 7,* 749–757.

Budman, S.H. (Ed.). (1981). *Forms of brief therapy.* New York: Guilford Press.

Burlingame, G.M., & Fuhriman, A. (1987). Conceptualizing short-term treatment: A comparitive review. Counseling Psychologist, 15, 4, 557–595.

Burns, D.D. (1989). *The feeling good handbook.* New York: William Morrow.

Byrum, B. (1989). New age training technologies: The best and the safest. In J.W. Pfeiffer (Ed.), *The 1989 Annual: Developing human resources* (pp. 79–89). San Diego, CA: University Associates.

Cantwell, D.P., & Carlson, G.A. (1983). *Affective disorders in childhood and adolescence.* New York: Spectrum Publications Medical and Scientific Books.

Caple, R.B. (1985). Counseling and the self-organization paradigm. *Journal of Counseling and Development, 64,* 173–178.

Carkhuff, R.R., & Berenson, B.G. (1967). *Beyond counseling and psychotherapy.* New York: Holt, Rinehart & Winston.

Carrington, P. (1977). *Freedom in meditation.* Kendall Park, NJ: Pace Educational Systems.

Carroll, M.R., & Wiggins, J. (1990). *Elements of group counseling: Back to the basics.* Denver: Love Publishing.

Cautela, J., & McCullough, L. (1978). Covert conditioning: A learning-theory perspective on imagery. In J.L. Singer & K.S. Pope (Eds.), *The power of human imagination* (pp. 227–254). New York: Plenum.

Cavanagh, M.E. (1982). *The counseling experience.* Monterey, CA: Brooks/Cole.

Christiansen, A., Johnson, S.M., Phillips, S., & Glassgow, R.E. (1980). Cost efficiency in family behavior therapy. *Behavior Therapy, 11,* 208–226.

Cook, E.P. (1987). Characteristics of the biopsychosocial crisis of infertility. *Journal of Counseling and Development, 65,* 465–470.

Corbishly, M.A., & Yost, E.B. (1985). Therapeutic homework assignments. *The School Counselor, 33,* 1.

Corder, B. (1986). Therapeutic games in group therapy with adolescence. In C.E. Schaefer & S.E. Reid (Eds.), *Game play: Therapeutic use of childhood games* (pp. 279–290). New York: Wiley.

Corey, G. (1986). *Theory and practice of counseling and psychotherapy.* Monterey, CA: Brooks/Cole.

Corsini, R.J. (1989). Introduction. In R.J. Corsini & D. Wedding (Eds.), *Current psychotherapies* (4th ed.) (pp. 1–16). Itasca, IL: Peacock.

Corsini, R.J., & Wedding, D. (1989). *Current psychotherapies* (4th ed.). Itasca, IL: F.E. Peacock.

Crawford, T., & Ellis, A. (1989). A dictionary of rational-emotive feelings and behaviors. *Journal of Rational-Emotive and Cognitive Therapy, 7,* 3–28.

Crose, R. (1990). Reviewing the past in the here and now: Using Gestalt therapy techniques with life review. *Journal of Mental Health Counseling, 12,* 3.

Daniluk, J.D. (1988). Infertility: Intrapersonal and interpersonal impact. *Fertility and Sterility, 49,* 6.

Daniluk, J.D. (1991, March/April). Strategies for counseling infertile couples. *Journal of Counseling and Development, 69*(4), 317–320.

Davis, J.M. (1985). Suicidal crises in schools. *School Psychology Review, 14*(3), 313–322.

Dehouske, E.J. (1979). Original writing: A therapeutic tool in working with disturbed adolescents. *Teaching Exceptional Children, 11,* 66–70.

Dell, P.F. (1981). Some irreverent thoughts on paradox. *Family Process, 20,* 37–42.

de Shazer, S. (1978). Brief therapy with couples. *International Journal of Family Counseling, 6,* 17–30.

de Shazer, S. (1979). The confusion technique. *American Journal of Family Therapy, 7,* 23–30.

de Shazer, S. (1982). *Patterns of brief family therapy.* New York: Guilford.

de Shazer, S. (1985). *Keys to solutions in brief therapy.* New York: Norton.

de Shazer, S. (1988). *Clues: Investigating solutions in brief therapy.* New York: Norton.

de Shazer, S. (1991). *Putting difference to work.* New York: Norton.

Devi, I. (1963). *Renew your life through yoga.* New York: Prentice Hall.

DeVito, J.A., & Hecht, M.L. (1990). *The nonverbal communication reader.* Prospect Heights, IL: Waveland Press.

Dicks, H. (1967). *Marital tensions.* New York: Basic Books.

Dies, R.R. (1983). Clinical implications of research on leadership and in short-term group psychotherapy. In R.R. Dies & K.R. Mackenzie (Eds.), *Advances in group psychotherapy* (pp. 27–78). New York: International Universities Press.

Dinkmeyer, D. (1988). Marathon family counseling. *Individual Psychology: Journal of Adlerian Theory, Research, and Practice, 44*, 210–215.

Dinkmeyer, D.C., & Losoncy, L.E. (1980). *The encouragement book: Becoming a positive person.* Englewood Cliffs, NJ: Prentice Hall.

Dinkmeyer, D.C., Pew, W.L., & Dinkmeyer, D.C., Jr. (1979). *Adlerian counseling and psychotherapy.* Monterey, CA: Brooks/Cole.

Dohrenwend, B.S., & Dohrenwend, B.P. (1985). Life stress and psychopathology. In H. Goldman & S.I. Goldston (Eds.), *Preventing stress related psychiatric disorders* (DHHS Pub. No., ADM 85–1366) (pp. 37–51). Rockville, MD: NIMH.

Downing, J. (1988). Counseling interventions with depressed children. *Elementary School Counselor, 22*, 3.

Dunlap, K. (1946). The technique of negative practice. *American Journal of Psychology, 55*, 270–273.

Duttweiler, P.C. (1984). The internal control index: A newly developed measure of locus of control. *Educational and Psychological Measurement, 36*(2), 209–226.

Dyer, W.W., & Vriend, J. (1977). *Counseling techniques that work.* New York: Funk & Wagnall.

Dysinger, B.J. (1993). Conflict resolution for intermediate children. *The School Counselor, 40*(4), 113–118.

Edwards, S.S., & Kleine, P.A. (1986). Multimodal consultation: A model for working with gifted adolescents. *Journal of Counseling and Development, 64*, 9.

Egan, G. (1975). The skilled helper: A systematic approach to effective helping. Pacific Grove, CA: Brooks/Cole.

Egan, G. (1990). *The skilled helper: A systematic approach to effective helping.* Pacific Grove, CA: Brooks/Cole.

Eisenberg, G.M. (1981). Midtherapy training: Extending the resent system of pretherapy training. *Dissertation Abstracts International, 41*, 2754B.

Elias, M.J. (1989). Schools as sources of stress to children: An analysis of causal and ameliorative influences. *Journal of School Psychology, 27*, 393–407.

Ellis, A. (1973). Humanistic psychotherapy: The rational-emotive approach. New York: McGraw-Hill.

Ellis, A. (1975). *How to live with a neurotic.* North Hollywood, CA: Wilshire Books.

Ellis, A. (1979). The theory of rational-emotive therapy. In A. Ellis & J.M. Whiteley (Eds.), *Theoretical and empirical foundations of rational-emotive therapy* (pp. 33–60). Monterey, CA: Brooks/Cole.

Ellis, A. (1985). Expanding the ABCs of rational-motive therapy. In M.J. Mahoney & A. Freeman (Eds.), *Cognition and psychotherapy* (pp. 313–323). New York: Plenum.

Ellis, A. (1989). Comments on my critics. In M.E. Bernard & R. DiGiuseppe (Eds.), *Inside rational-emotive therapy: A critical appraisal of the theory and therapy of Albert Ellis* (pp. 199–260). San Diego, CA: Academic Press.

Ellis, A. (1990). How can psychological treatment aim to be briefer and better? The rational-emotive approach to brief therapy. In J.K. Zeig & S.G. Gilligan (Eds.), *Brief therapy: Myths, methods, and metaphors* (pp. 291–302). New York: Brunner/Mazel.

Ellis, A., & Dryden, W. (1990). The basic practice of RET. In W. Dryden (Ed.), *The essential Albert Ellis* (pp. 145–183). New York: Springer.

Ellis, A., & Harper, R.A. (1975). *A new guide to rational living.* Hollywood, CA: Wilshire Book Company.

Ellis, A., Sichel, J., Yeager, R., DiMattia, D., & DiGiuseppe, R. (Eds.). (1989). *Rational-emotive couples therapy.* New York: Pergamon.

Emery, G. (1981). *A new beginning: How you can change your life through cognitive therapy.* New York: Simon & Schuster.

Emery, G., & Campbell, J. (1986). *Rapid relief from emotional distress.* New York: Fawcett Columbine.

English, H.B., English, A.C. (1958). *A comprehensive dictionary of psychoanalytic terms.* New York: McKay.

Erickson, M. (1954). Special techniques on brief hypnotherapy. *Journal of Clinical and Experimental Hypnosis,* 2, 109–129.

Erlanger, M.A. (1990). Using the genorgram with the older client. *Journal of Mental Health Counseling, 12(3),* 321–336.

Fagan, J., & Shepherd, I.L. (1970). *Gestalt therapy now: Theory, techniques, applications.* New York: Harper & Row.

Fairbairn, W.R.D. (1967). *An object relations theory of personality.* New York: Basic Books.

Falvey, E. (1989). Passion and professionalism: Critical rapprochements for mental health research. *Journal of Mental Health Counseling, 11,* 86–105.

Fisch, R., Weakland, J.H., & Segal, L. (1983). *The tactics of change: Doing brief therapy.* San Francisco: Jossey-Bass.

Fluegelman, A. (Ed.). (1976). *The new games book.* Garden City, NY: Doubleday.

Foa, E.B., Stekette, G.S., & Ascher, L.M. (1980). Systematic desensitization. In A. Goldstein & E.B. Foa (Eds.), *Handbook of behavioral interventions: A clinical guide* (pp. 46–63). New York: Wiley.

Fodor, I.G. (1987). Cognitive behavior therapy: Evaluation of theory and practice for addressing women's issues. In M.A. Douglas & L.E. Walker (Eds.), *Feminist therapies: Integration of therapeutic and feminist systems* (pp. 91–117). Norwood, NJ: Ablex.

Frankl, V. (1960). Paradoxical intention. *American Journal of Psychotherapy, 14,* 520–535.

Frayn, D.H. (1992). Assessment factors associated with premature psychotherapy termination. *American Journal of Psychotherapy, XLVI(2).*

Freeman, A., & DeWolf, R. (1989). *Woulda, coulda, shoulda.* New York: Silver Arrow Books.

Friedlander, M.L. (1981). The effects of delayed role induction on counseling process and outcome. *Dissertation Abstracts International, 43*, 3887–3888B.

Fuhriman, A., & Burlingame, G.M. (1990). Consistency of matter: A comparative Analysis of individual and group process variables. *The Counseling Psychologist, 19*(1), 6–62.

Fuhriman, A., Paul, S.C., & Burlingame, J.C. (1986). Electic time-limited therapy. In J.C. Norcross (Ed.), *Handbook of eclectic psychotherapy* (pp. 48–62). New York: Brunner/Mazel.

Gardner, R. (1986). The game of checkers in child therapy. In C.E. Schaefer & S.E. Reid (Eds.), *Game play: Therapeutic use of childhood games* (pp. 215–232). New York: Wiley.

Garfield, S.L. (1980). *Psychotherapy: An eclectic approach.* New York: Wiley.

Garfield, S.L., & Bergin, A.E. (Eds.). (1986). *Handbook of psychotherapy and behavior change* (3rd ed.). New York: Wiley.

Garner, D.M., & Garfinkle, P.E. (1980). Socio-cultural factors in the development of anorexia nervosa. *Psychological Medicine, 10*, 647–656.

Gaston, L., Marmar, C.R., & Thompson, L. (1988). Relation of patient pretreatment characteristics to the therapeutic alliance in diverse psychotherapies. *Journal of Counsulting and Clinical Psychology, 56*, 483–89.

Gaushell, W.H., & Lawson, D.M. (1989). Using a checksheet with misbehaviors in school: Parent involvement. *The School Counselor, 36*, 6.

Gelso, C.J., & Carter, J.A. (1985). The relationship in counseling and psychotherapy: Consequences, componenets, and theoretical antecedents. *The Counseling Psychologist, 13*, 155–243.

Gentner, D.S. (1991). A brief model for mental health counseling. *Journal of Mental Health Counseling, 13* (1), 58–68.

Gill, S.J., & Barry, R.A. (1982). Group focused counseling: Classifying the essential skills. *The Personnel and Guidance Journal, 60*, 5.

Ginter, E.J. (1988). Stagnation in eclecticism: The need to recommit to a journey. *Journal of Mental Health Counseling, 10*, 3–8.

Ginter, E.J. (1989). Slayers of monster watermelons found in the mental health patch. *Journal of Mental Health Counseling, 11*, 77–85.

Glasser, W. (1985). *Control theory.* New York: Harper & Row.

Gleick, J. (1988). *Chaos: Making a new science.* New York: Penguin Books.

Goldenberg, I., & Goldenberg, H. (1985). *Family therapy: An overview.* Monterey, CA: Brooks/Cole.

Goldenson, R.M. (1984). *Post-traumatic stress disorder. Longman dictionary of psychology and psychiatry.* New York: Longman.

Goldfriend, M.R. (1982). Toward the delineation of therapeutic change principles. *American Pychologist, 35*, 991–999.

Goldman, D.J. (1976). Meditation helps break the stress spiral. *Psychology Today, 9*(9), 82.

Goldman, D.J., & Schwartz, G.E. (1976). Meditation as an intervention in stress reactivity. *Journal of Consulting and Clinical Psychology, 44*, 456–466.

Gonzales, M., Jones, D., Whitely, R.M., & Whitely, J.M. (1988). *The AACD stress management manual.* Alexandria, Virginia: American Counseling Association.

Goodman, J. (1985). *Turning points: New developments in values clarification* (vol. 1). Saratoga Springs, NY: Creative Resource Press.

Greenberg, L.S., & Safran, T.D. (1987). *Emotion in psychotherapy.* New York: Guilford Press.

Grieger, R. (1986). *A client's guide to rational-emotive therapy.* Charlottesville, VA: University Press.

Grinspoon, L. (Ed.). (1991a, February). Post-traumatic stress: Part I. *Harvard Mental Health Letter, 7*(8), 1–4.

Grinspoon, L. (Ed.). (1991b, March). Post-traumatic stress: Part II. *Harvard Mental Health Letter, 7*(9), 1–4.

Guidano, V.F., & Liotti, G. (1983). *Cognitive processes and emotional disorders.* New York: Guilford Press.

Gwain, G. (1982). Active visualization: Creating what you want. *Professional Psychology: Research and Practice, 13*, 211–216

Haley, J. (1963). *Strategies of psychotherapy.* New York: Grune & Stratton.

Haley, J. (Ed.). (1967). *Advanced techniques of hypnosis and therapy: Selected papers of Milton H. Erickson.* New York: Grune & Stratton.

Haley, J. (1973). *Uncommon therapy.* New York: W.W. Norton.

Haley, J. (1976). *Problem solving therapy.* San Francisco: Jossey-Bass.

Haley, J. (1984). *Ordeal therapy: Unusual ways to change behavior.* San Francisco: Jossey-Bass.

Handly, R., & Neff, P. (1985). *Anxiety and panic attacks: Their cause and cure.* New York: Ballantine Books.

Hansen, J., Stevic, R., & Warner, R. (1986). *Counseling: Theory and process* (4th ed.). Boston: Allyn & Bacon.

Hansen, J.C., Warner, R.W., & Smith, E.J. (1980). *Group counseling: Theory and practice* (2nd ed.). Chicago: Rand McNally.

Hare-Mustin, R. (1976). Paradoxical tasks in family therapy: Who can resist? *Psychotherapy: Theory, Research, & Practice, 13*, 128–130.

Hellman, C.A., Morrison, B.K., & Abramowitz, L.M. (1986). The stress if therapeutic work. *Journal of Mental Health Counseling, 8*, 36–40.

Helmstetter, S. (1986). *What to say when you talk to yourself.* New York: Pocket Books.

Henry, W.P., Schacht, T.E., & Strupp, H.H. (1986). Structural analysis of social behavior: Application to a study of interpersonal process in differential psychotherapeutic outcome. *Journal of Counseling and Clinical Psychology, 54*, 27–31.

Herr, E.L. (1989). *Counseling in a dynamic society: Opportunities and challenges.* Alexandria, VA: American Association of Counseling and Development.

Hershenson, D.B., Power, P.W., & Seligman, L. (1989a). Mental health counseling theory: Present status and future prospects. *Journal of Mental Health Counseling, 11*, 44–69.

Hershenson, D.B., Power, P.W., & Seligman, L. (1989b). Counseling theory as a prejective test. *Journal of Mental Health Counseling, 11*, 273–279.

Hill, C.E., Helms, J.E., Spiegal, S.B., & Tichenor, V. (1988). Development of a system for categorizing client reactions to therapist interventions. *Journal of Counseling Psychology, 35*, 257–306.

Hill, C.E., & O'Grady, K. (1985). List of therapeutic intentions illustrated in a case study with therapists of varying theoretical orientations. *Journal of Counseling Psychology, 32*, 3–22.

Hill, H. (1992). Fairy tales: Visions for problem resolution in eating disorders. *Journal of Counseling and Development, 70*, 584–587.

Hofling, C.K. (1979). An instance of psychotherapy continued by correspondence. *Bulletin of the Menninger Clinic, 43*, 393–412.

Hollis, J.W., & Wantz, R.A. (1986). *Counselor preparation 1986–1989: Programs, personnel, trends* (6th ed.). Muncie, IN: Accelerated Development.

Howard, M., Nance, D.W., & Myers, C. (1986). *Adaptive counseling and therapy: A systematic approach to selecting effective treatments.* San Francisco: Jossey-Bass.

Hsu, L.K.G. (1989). The gender gap in eating disorders: Why are eating disorders more common among women? *Clinical Psychology Review, 9*, 393–407.

Hughes, E.F. (1991). *Writing from the inner self.* New York: Harper Collins.

Ivey, A.E. (1973). Demystifying the group process: Adapting microcounseling procedures to counseling groups. *Educational Technology, 13*, 27–31.

Ivey, A.E. (1986). *Developmental therapy: Theory into practice.* San Francisco: Jossey-Bass.

Ivey, A.E. (1989). Mental health counseling: A developmental process and profession. *Journal of Mental Health Counseling, 11*, 26–35.

Ivey, A.E. (1990). *Developmental strategies for helpers: Individual, family, and network interventions.* Pacific Grove, CA.: Brooks/Cole.

Ivey, A.E., & Goncalves, O.F. (1988). Developmental therapy: Integrating developmental processes into clinical practice. *Journal of Counseling and Development, 66,* 406–413.

Ivey, A.E., & Rigazio-DiGilio, S.A. (1991). Toward a developmental practice of mental health counseling: Strategies for training, practice, and political unity. *Journal of Mental Health Counseling, 13*(1), 21–36.

Ivey, A.E., & Simek-Downing, L. (1980). *Counseling and psychotherapy: Skills, theories, and practice.* Englewood Cliffs, NJ: Prentice Hall.

Jacobson, N.S., & Margolin, G. (1979). *Marital therapy: Strategies based on social learning and behavior exchange principles.* New York: Brunner/Mazel.

Jackson, D.P., & Weakland, J.H. (1961). Conjoint family therapy: Some considerations on theory, technique, and results. *Psychiatry, 24,* 30–45.

Jaffe, D.T., & Bresler, D.E. (1980). Guided imagery: Healing through the mind's eye. In J.E. Shorr, G.E. Sobel, P. Robin, & J.A. Connella (Eds.), *Imagery: Its many dimensions and applications* (pp. 253–266). New York: Plenum.

Jakubowski, R., & Lange, A.J. (1978). *The assertive option: Your right and responsibilities.* Champaign, IL: Research Press Company.

Johnson, C., & Maddi, K. (1986). The etiology of bulimia: Biopsychosocial perspectives. In S. Feinstein (Ed.), *Adolescent psychiatry, developmental and clinical issues* (Vol. 13) (pp. 253–273). Chicago: University of Chicago Press.

Johnson, W.Y., & Wilborn, B. (1991). Group counseling as an intervention in anger expression and depression in older adults. *The Journal of Specialists in Group Work, 16,* 3.

Kalafat, J. (1990). Adolescent suicide and the implications for school response programs. *The School Counselor, 37,* 5.

Keat, D.B. (1985). Child-adolescent multimodal therapy: Bud the boss. *Journal of Humanistic Education and Development, 23,* 183–192.

Keat, D.B. (1990). Change in child multimodal counseling. *Elementary School Guidance and Counseling, 24*, 4.

Kelly, K.R. (1988). Defending eclectism: The utility of informed choice. *Journal of Mental Health Counseling, 10*, 210–213.

Kelly, K.R. (1991). Theoretical integration is the future for mental health counseling. *Journal of Mental Health Counseling, 13*(1), 106–111.

Kerr, M. (1980). Emotional factors in physical illness: A multigenerational perspective. In R.R. Sagar (Ed.), *Georgetown family symposia: Volume IV* (1977–78) (pp. 47–63). Washington, DC: Georgetown University.

Kerr, M., & Bowen, M. (1988). *Family evaluation: An approach based on Bowen theory*. New York: Norton.

Kettlewell, P.W., Mizes, J.S., & Wasylsyshyn, N.A. (1992). A cognitive-behavioral group treatment of bulimia. *Behavior Therapy, 23*, 4.

Klein, M. (1959). *Our adult world and its roots in infancy*. London: Tavistock.

Klerman, G., & Weissman, M. (1985). Affective responses to stressful life events. In H. Goldman & S. Goldston (Eds.), *Preventing stress-related psychiatric disorders* (DHHS Pub. No. ADM 85–1366 (pp. 55–76). Rockville, MD: NIMH.

Klier, J., Fein, E., & Genero, C. (1984). Are written or verbal contacts more effective in family therapy? *Social Work, 29*, 298–299.

Klimek, D., & Anderson, M. (1988). *Inner world, outer world: Understanding the struggles of adolescence*. Ann Arbor, MI: The University of Michigan, ERIC Clearinghouse on Counseling and Personnel Services (ED 290 118).

Kohut, H. (1971). *The analysis of self*. New York: International Universities Press.

Kolb, D.L., Beutler, L.E., Davis, C.S., Crago, M., & Shanfield, S. (1985). Patient and therapist process variables relating to dropout and change in psychotherapy. *Psychotherapy: Theory, Research, and Practice, 22*, 702–710.

Korn, E.R., & Johnson, K. (1983). *Visualization: The use of imagery in the health professions*. Homewood, IL: Dow-Jones-Irwin.

Kottman, T. (1990). Counseling middle school students: Techniques that work. *Elementary School Guidance and Counseling, 25,* 2.

Kranzow, K. (1973). Deliberate psychological education. *The Personnel and Guidance Journal, 48*(6), 72–78.

Krumboltz, J.D., & Thoresen, C.E. (1976). *Counseling methods.* New York: Holt, Rinehart, & Winston.

L'Abate, L., & Weeks, G.A. (1978). A bibliography of paradoxical methods in psychotherapy of family systems. *Family Practice, 17,* 95–98.

Lambert, M.J. (1989). The individual therapist's contribution to psychotherapy process and outcome. *Clinical Psychology Review, 9,* 469–485.

Lambert, M.J., Shapiro, D.A., & Bergin, A.E. (1986). The effectiveness of psychotherapy. In S.L. Garfield & A.E. Bergin (Eds.), *Handbook of psychotherapy and behavior change* (pp.111–141). New York: Wiley.

Larrabee, M., & Wilson, B. (1981). Teaching teenagers to cope through family-life simulations. *The School Counselor, 28,* 117–123.

Lazarus, A.A. (1967). In support of technical eclecticism. *Psychological Reports, 21,* 415–416.

Lazarus, A.A. (1971). *Behavior therapy and beyond.* New York: McGraw-Hill.

Lazarus, A.A. (1976). *Multimodal behavior therapy.* New York: Springer.

Lazarus, A.A. (1977). *In the mind's eye: The power of imagery for personal enrichment.* New York: Rawson.

Lazarus, A.A. (1981). *The practice of multimodal therapy.* New York: McGraw-Hill.

Lazarus, A.A. (1985). *Casebook of multimodal therapy.* New York: Guilford Press.

Lazarus, A.A. (1992). The multimodal approach to the treatment of minor depression. *American Journal of Psychotherapy, 86*(1), 50–56.

Lazarus, A.A. (1993). *The practice of multimodal therapy.* Baltimore, MD: The Johns Hopkins University Press.

Lazarus, A.A., & Mayne, T.I. (1990). Relaxation: Some limitations, side effects, and proposed solutions. *Psychotherapy, 27*(2), 261–266.

Lazarus, R.S., & Folkman, S. (1984). Coping and adaptation. In W.D. Gentry (Ed.), *The handbook of behavioral medicine* (pp. 378–384). Chicago: Science Research Associates.

LeShan, L. (1974). *How to meditate.* New York: Bantam Books.

Levitsky, A., & Perls, F.S. (1973). The rules and games of gestalt therapy. In J. Fagan & I.L. Shephard (Eds.), *Gestalt therapy now* (pp.140–149). Palo Alto, CA: Science and Behavior Books.

Lewis, H.R., & Streitfeld, H.S. (1970). *Growth games: How to tune in yourself, your family, your friends.* New York, NY: Bantam Books.

Lewy, A.J., Sack, R.L., & Miller, L.S. (1987). Antidepressant and circadian phase-shifting effects of light. *Science, 235*, 352–354.

Lieberman, M., Yalom, I., & Miles, M. (1973). *Encounter groups: First facts.* New York: Basic Books.

Linden, W., & Wen, F.K. (1990). Therapy outcome research, health care policy, and the continuing lack of accumulated knowledge. *Professional Psychology: Research & Practice, 21*, 482–488.

Link, P.W., & Darling, C.A. (1986). Couples undergoing treatment for infertility: Dimensions of life satisfaction. *Journal of Sex and Marital Therapy, 12*, 1.

Luborsky, L., Cruts-Cristoph, P., Mintz, J., & Auerbach, A. (1988). *Who will benefit from psychotherapy": Predicting therapeutic outcomes.* New York: Basic Books.

Lundholm, J.K., & Littrell, J.M. (1986). Desire for thinness among high school cheerleaders: Relationship to disordered eating and weight control behaviors. *Adolescence, 21*, 573–579.

Madanes, C. (1981). *Strategic family therapy.* San Francisco: Jossey-Bass.

Maharishi, M.Y. (1972). *The science of living and the art of being.* New York: Signet Books.

Mahlsted, P.P. (1985). The psychological component of infertility. *Fertility and Sterility, 43*, 3.

Mahoney, M.J. (1977). Reflections on the cognitive learning trend in psychotherapy. *American Psychologist, 32*, 5–13.

Mahoney, M.J., & Gabriel, T.J. (1987). Psychotherapy and the cognitive sciences: An evolving alliance. *Journal of Cognitive Psychotherapy: An International Quarterly, 1*, 39–59.

Main, A.P., & Roark, A.E. (1975). A consensus method to reduce conflict. *Personnel and Guidance Journal, 53*, 754–759.

Maitland, R. (1975). *Essentials of meditation.* Lakemont, GA: CSA Press.

Malan, D. (1975). Psychodynamic changes in untreated neurotic patients. *British Journal of Psychiatry, 32*, 110–126.

Maltz, M. (1960). *Psychocybernetics.* Englewood Cliffs, NJ: Prentice Hall.

Manley, L. (1986). Goals of misbehavior inventory. *Elementary School Guidance and Counseling, 21*, 160–162.

Mann, J. (1973). *Time-limited psychotherapy.* Cambridge, MA: Harvard University Press.

Mann, J. (1981). The core of time-limited psychotherapy: Time and the central issue. In S.H. Budman (Eds.), *Forms of brief therapy* (pp. 25–42). New York: Guilford Press.

Marcer, D. (1986). *Biofeedback and related therapies in clinical practice.* Rockville, MD: Aspen Publishers.

Marquis, J., Morgan, W., & Piaget, G. (1973). *A guidebook for systematic desensitization* (3rd ed.). Palo Alto, CA: Veterans Workshop.

Marshall, W.L., Gauthier, J., Christie, M.M., Currie, D.W., & Gordon, A. (1977). Flooding therapy effectiveness, stimulus characteristics, and the value of brief in vivo exposure. *Behavior Research and Therapy, 15*, 79–87.

Maultsby, M.C. (1975). *Help yourself to happiness.* New York: Institute for Rational Living.

Mazza, N. (1981). The use of poetry in treating the troubled adolescent. *Adolescence, 16*, 403–408.

McBride, M.C., & Martin, G.E. (1990). A framework or eclectiasm: The importance of theory to mental health counseling. *Journal of Mental Health Counseling, 12*, 495–505.

McEwan, K.L., Costello, C.G., & Taylor, P.J. (1987). Adjustment to infertility. *Journal of Abnormal Psychology, 96*, 2.

McKay, M., Davis, M., & Fanning, P. (1983). *Messages: The communication skills book.* Oakland, CA: Harbinger Publications.

McMahon, R.J., & Forehand, R. (1984). Parent training for the noncompliant child: Treatment, outcome, generalization,and adjunctive therapy procedures. In R.F. Dangel & R.A. Polster (Eds.), *Parent training: Foundations of research and practice* (pp. 47–67). New York: Guilford Press.

McMullin, R. (1986). *Handbook of cognitive therapy techniques.* New York: Norton Press.

McMullin, R., & Giles, T. (1981). *Cognitive behavior therapy: A restructuring approach.* New York: Grune & Stratton.

Mehrabian, A. (1971). *Silent messages.* Belmont, CA: Wadsworth.

Meichenbaum, D. (1977). *Cognitive behavior modification: An integrated approach.* New York: Plenum Press.

Meichenbaum, D., & Meichenbaum, A. (1974). *Cognitive behavior modification.* Morristown, NJ: General Learning Press.

Messor, S.B., & Boals, G.F. (1981). Psychotherapy outcome in a university-based psychology training clinic. *Professional Psychology, 12*(6), 785–793.

Milne, D. (1986). *Training behavior therapists: Methods, evaluation and implementation with parents, nurses, and teachers.* Cambridge, MA: Brookline Books.

Minuchin, S. (1974). *Families and family therapy.* Cambridge, MA: Harvard University Press.

Monroe, C., Borzi, M.G., & Burrell, R.D. (1992). Communication apprehension among high school dropouts. *The School Counselor, 39*(4), 273–280.

Morris, R., & Kratochwill, T. (1983). *Treating children's fears and phobias: A behavioral approach.* New York: Pergamon Press.

Morse, L.A. (1987). Working with young procrastinators: Elementary school students who do not complete assignments. *Elementary School Guidance and Counseling, 21*, 3.

Morse, C., & Dennerstein, L. (1985). Infertile couples entering an in vitro fertilization program: A preliminary survey. *Journal of Psychosomatic Obstetrics and Gynecology, 4*, 207–209.

Mosak, H.H. (1971). Lifestyle. In A.G. Kelly (Ed.), *Techniques for behavior change* (pp. 74–84). Springfield, IL: Thomas.

Nance, D.W., & Associates. (1995). *How therapists ACT.* Muncie, IN: Taylor & Francis.

Nance, D.W., & Myers, P. (1991). Continuing the eclectic journey. *Journal of Mental Health Counseling, 13*(1), 119–130.

Nicholson, R.A., & Berman, J.S. (1983). Is follow-up necessary in evaluating psychotherapy? *Psychological Bulletin, 93*, 261–278.

Nickerson, E., & O'Laughlin, K. (1982). The therapeutic use of games. In C.E. Schaefer & K.J. O'Conner (Eds.), *Handbook of play therapy* (pp. 174–187). New York: Wiley.

Norcross, J.C. (Ed.). (1986). *Handbook of eclectic therapy.* New York: Brunner/ Mazel.

Norcross, J.D., & Prochaska, J.O. (1983). Clinician's theoretical orientations: Selection, utilization and efficacy. *Professional Psychology: Research and Practice, 14*, 197–208.

Novaco, R.W. (1975). *Anger control: The development and evaluation of an experimental treatment.* Lexington, MA: Lexington Books/DC Heath.

Oberkirch, A. (1983). Personal writings in psychotherapy. *American Journal of Psychotherapy, 37*, 265–272.

O'Hanlon, W., & Weiner-Davis, M. (1989). *In search of solutions: A new direction in psychotherapy.* New York: Norton.

Ohlsen, M.M. (1977). *Group counseling.* New York: Holt, Rinehart, & Winston.

Ohlsen, M., Horne, A., & Lawe, C. (1988). *Group counseling* (3rd ed.). New York: Holt, Rinehart, & Winston.

Okum, B.F. (1990). *Seeking connections in psychotherapy.* San Francisco: Jossey-Bass.

O'Malley, S.S., Suh, C.S., & Strupp, H.H. (1983). The Vanderbilt Psychotherapy Process Scale: A report of the scale development and a process outcome study. *Journal of Consulting and Clinical Psychology, 51,* 581–586.

Omizo, M.M., & Omizo, S.A. (1988). The effects of participation in group counseling on self-esteem and locus of control among adolescents from divorced families. *The School Counselor, 36*(1), 54–58.

Orlinsky, D.E., Howard, K.I. (1986). Process and outcome in psychotherapy. In S.L. Garfield & A.E. Bergin (Eds.), *Handbook of psychotherapy and behavior change* (pp. 311–381). New York: Wiley.

Palmer, D., & Hampton, P.T. (1987). Reducing broken appointments at intake in a community mental health center. *Community Mental Health Journal, 23,* 76–78.

Patterson, C.H. (1986). *Theories of counseling and psychotherapy* (4th ed.). New York: Harper & Row.

Peiser, I. (1982). Similarity, liking, and missed sessions in relation to psychotherapy outcome. *Dissertation Abstracts International, 42,* 4587B.

Pelletier, K.R. (1980). *Holistic medicine.* New York: Delacorte Press.

Perls, F.S. (1969). *Gestalt therapy verbatim.* Lafayette, CA: Real People Press.

Peterson, S., & Straub, R.L. (1992). *School crisis survival guide: Management techniques and materials for counselors and administrators.* West Nyack, NY: The Center for Applied Research in Education.

Powers, R.L., & Hahn, J.M. (1977). Creativity in problem-solving: The double dialogue technique. *Individual Psychologist, 14*(1), 22–32.

Progoff, I. (1975). *At a journal workshop: The basic text and guide for using the intensive journal process.* New York: Dialogue House Library.

Purkey, W.W., & Schmidt, J.J. (1990). *Invitational learning for counseling amd development.* Ann Arbor, Michigan: An ERIC/CAPS Select Publication.

Rando, T.A. (1984). *Grief, dying, and death: Clinical interventions for caregivers.* Cambridge, IL: Research Press.

Rathus, S.A., & Nevid, J.S. (1977). *BT: Behavior therapy strategies for solving problems in living.* New York: Signet Books.

Redd, W.H., Porterfield, A.L., & Andersen, B.L. (1979). *Behavior modification.* New York: Random House.

Renard, S., & Sockol, K. (1987). *Creative drama: Enhancing self-concepts and learning.* Minneapolis: Educational Media.

Rimm, D., & Masters, J. (1979). *Behavior therapy: Techniques and empirical findings* (2nd ed.). New York: Academic Press.

Roark, A.E. (1978). Interpersonal conflict management. *Personnel and Guidance Journal, 57*, 400–402.

Roberts, C.G., & Guttormson, L. (1990). *You and stress: A survival guide for adolescence.* Minneapolis, MN: Free Spirit Press.

Robbins, A. (1986). *Unlimited power.* New York: Fawcett Columbine.

Rogers, C.R. (1986). Client-centered therapy. In I. Kutash & A. Wolf (Eds.), *Psychotherapist's casebook: Theory and techniques in the practice of modern therapies* (pp. 197–208). San Francisco: Jossey-Bass.

Rohrbaugh, M., Tennen, H., & Eron, J. (1982). Paradoxical interventions. In J.H. Masserman (Ed.), *Current psychiatric therapies* (vol. 21) (pp. 89–124). New York: Grune & Stratton.

Romen, A. (1981). *Self-suggestion and its influence on the human organism.* Armonk, NY: M. E. Sharpe.

Rosenthal, N.E. (1989). *Light therapy: Treatment of psychiatric disorders, Vol. 3.* Washington, DC: American Psychiatric Association, task force on treatment of psychiatric disorders.

Rosenthal, N.E., Carpenter, J.P., & James, S.P. (1986). Seasonal affective disorders in children and adolescence. *American Journal of Psychiatry, 143,* 356–358.

Rosenthal, N.E., Sack, D.A., Gillin, J.C., Lewy, A.J., Goodwin, F.K., Davenport, Y., Mueller, P.S., Newsome, D.A., & Wehr, T.A. (1984). Seasonal affective disorder: A discription of the syndrome and preliminary findings for light therapy. *Archives General Psychiatry, 41,* 72–80.

Rosenthal, N.E., & Wehr, T.A. (1987). Seasonal affective disorders. *Psychiatric Annals, 17,* 10.

Rychlak, J.F. (1985). Eclecticism in psychological theorizing: Good and bad. *Journal of Counseling and Development, 63*(6), 351–353.

Sabatino, J.A., & Smith, L.M. (1990). Rational self-analysis. *Journal of Counseling and Development, 69,* 167–172.

Salzer, L. (1986). *Infertility: How couples can cope.* New York: G. K. Hall.

Satir, V. (1967). *Conjoint family therapy.* Palo Alto, CA: Science and Behavioral Books.

Satir, V., & Baldwin, M. (1983). *Step by step.* Palo Alto, CA: Science and Behavior Books.

Schaefer, C.E., & Briesmeister, J.M. (Eds.). (1989). *Handbook of parent training: Parents as co-therapists for children's behavior problems.* New York: Wiley.

Schaefer, C.E., Briesmeister, J.M., & Fitton, M.E. (1984). *Family therapy techniques for problem behavior of children and teenagers.* San Francisco: Jossey-Bass.

Schaefer, C., & Reid, S. (Eds.). (1986). *Game play: Therapeutic use of childhood games.* New York: Wiley.

Schaefer, D. (1987). *Choices and consequences: What to do when a teenager uses alcohol and drugs.* Minneapolis: Johnson Institute Books.

Scharf, D., & Scharf, J.S. (1987). *Object relations family therapy.* Northvale, NJ: Jason Aronson.

Schinfeld, J.S., Elkins, T.E., & Strong, C.M. (1986). Ethical considerations in the management of infertility. *Journal of Reproductive Medicine, 31,* 11.

Schriner, C. (1990). *Feel better now: 30 ways to handle frustration in three minutes or less.* Rolling Hills Estates, CA: Jalmar Press.

Seltzer, L.F. (1986). *Paradoxical strategies in psychotherapy: A comprehensive overview and guidebook.* New York: John Wiley & Sons.

Selvini-Palazzoli, M. (1978). *Paradox and counterparadox.* New York: Jason Aronson.

Selvini-Palazzoli, M., Boscolo, L., Cecchin, G., & Prata, G. (1974). The treatment of children through brief therapy of their parents. *Family Process, 13,* 429–442.

Selvini-Palazzoli, M., Boscolo, L., Cecchin, G., & Prata, G. (1978). *Paradox and counterparadox: A new model in the therapy of the family in schizophrenic transaction.* New York: Aronson.

Serok, S. (1986). Therapeutic implications of games with juvenile delinquents. In C.E. Schaefer & S.E. Reid (Eds.), *Game play: Therapeutic use of childhood games* (pp. 311–329). New York: Wiley.

Sexton, T.L., & Whiston, S.C. (1991). Review of the empirical basis for counseling: Implications for practice and training. *Counselor Education and Supervision, 30,* 6.

Shapiro, D., & Shapiro, D. (1982). Meta-analysis of comparitive therapy outcome studies: A replication of refinement. *Psychological Bulletin, 92,* 581–604.

Sheikh, A.A. (1976). Treatment of insomnia through eidetic imagery: A new technique. *Perceptual and Motor Skills, 43,* 994.

Sheikh, A.A., & Jordan, C.S. (1983). Clinical uses of mental imagery. In A.A. Sheikh (Ed.), *Imagery: Current theory, research, and application* (pp. 391–435). New York: Wiley.

Sheikh, A.A., & Sheikh, D.S. (Eds.). (1985). *Imagery in education.* Farmingdale, NY: Baywood Publishing.

Shorr, J.E. (1974). *Psychotherapy through imagery.* New York: Intercontinental Medical Book Corporation.

Sifenos, S.P. (1979). *Short-term dynamic psychotherapy: Evaluation and technique.* New York: Plenum Press.

Sifenos, S.P. (1981). Short-term anxiety-provoking psychotherapy: Its history, technique, outcome, and instruction. In S.H. Budman (Ed.), *Forms of brief therapy* (pp. 45–80). New York: Guilford Press.

Silva, J., & Stone, R.B. (1983). *The Silva mind control method for business managers.* Englewood Cliffs, NJ: Prentice Hall.

Simkin, J., & Yontef, G.M. (1984). Gestalt therapy. In R. Corsini (Ed.), *Current psychotherapies* (3rd ed.) (pp.61–82). Itasca, IL: Peacock.

Simon, G.M. (1989). An alternative defense of eclecticism: Responding to Kelly and Ginter. *Journal of Mental Health Counseling, 11,* 280–288.

Simon, G.M. (1991). Theoretical eclecticism: A goal we are obligated to pursue. *Journal of Mental Health Counseling, 13,* 1.

Simonton, O.C., Mathews-Simonton, S., & Creighton, J.S. (1978). *Getting well again.* Los Angeles: Tarcher.

Slaveney, P.R., & McHugh, P.R. (1987). *Psychiatric polarities: Methodology and practice.* Baltimore, MD: Johns Hopkins University Press.

Smith, D. (1982). Trends in counseling and psychotherapy. *American Psychologist, 37,* 802–809.

Spitzer, R.L., Endicott, J., & Robins, E. (1978). Research diagnostic criteria: Rationale and reliablity. *Archives of General Psychiatry, 35,* 773–782.

Squires, R.L., & Kagen, D.M. (1985). Sex-role and eating behaviors among college women. *International Journal of Eating Disorders, 4,* 539–548.

Stanton, M.D. (1981). *Strategic approaches to family therapy.* New York: Brunner/Mazel.

Stanton, M.D. (1984). Fusion, compression, diversion, and the workings of paradox: A theory of therapeutic/systemic change. *Family Process, 23*, 135–167.

Stefanowski-Harding, S. (1990). Suicide and the school counselor. *The School Counselor, 37*, 5.

Stockton, R., & Morran, D. (1982). Review and perspectives of critical dimensions in therapeutic small group research. In G.M. Gazda (Ed.), *Basic approaches to group psychotherapy and group counseling* (3rd ed.) (pp. 47–68). Springfield, IL: Thomas.

Striegel-Moore, R., Silberstein, L.R., & Rodin, J. (1986). Toward an understanding of risk factors for bulimia. *American Psychologist, 41*, 246–263.

Strupp, H.H. (1981). Clinical research, practice and the crisis of confidence. *Journal of Consulting and Clinical Psychology, 49*, 216–219.

Strupp, H.H., & Bergin, A.E. (1969). Some empirical and conceptual bases for coordinated research in psychotherapy. *International Journal of Psychiatry, 7*, 68.

Szmukler, G.I., Eisler, I., Gillies, C., & Hayward, M.E. (1985). The implications of anorexia nervosa in a ballet school. *Journal of Psychiatric Research, 19*, 177–181.

Talmon, M. (1990). *Single session therapy.* San Francisco, CA: Jossey-Bass.

Taub, D.E., & McLorg, P.A. (1989). Anorexia nervosa and bulimia. In H. Tierney (Ed.), *Women's studies encyclopedia: Vol. I., View from the sciences* (pp. 101–121). Westport, CT: Greenwood.

Taylor, J.W. (1984). Structured conjoint therapy for spouse abuse cases. *Social Casework, 65*, 11–18.

Teusch, R. (1988). Level of ego development and bulimics' conceptualizations of their disorder. *Internal Journal of Eating Disorders, 7*, 607–615.

Thiessen, I. (1983). Using fairy tales during hypnotherapy in bulimerexia and other psychological problems. *Medical Hypnoanalysis, 4*, 139–144.

Thompson, R.A. (1990, February). Strategies for crisis manangement in the schools. National Association of Secondary School Principals. *Bulletin*, 54–58.

Thompson, R.A. (1993). Post-traumatic stress and post-traumatic loss debriefing: Brief strategic intervention for survivors of sudden loss. *The School Counselor, 34*, 133–138.

Towers, D., Wollum, S., Dow, E., Senese, R., Ames, G., Berg, J. & McDonald, T. (1987). *Metaphor as a tool for counselors.* Paper presented at the Annual Convention of the American Association for Counseling and Development, New Orleans (ERIC Document Reproduction Service No. ED 285096).

Truax, C.B., & Carkhuff, R.R. (1967). *Towards effective counseling and psycho-ltherapy.* Chicago: Aldine.

Valentine, D.P. (1986). Psychological impact of infertility: Identifying issues and needs. *Social Work in Health Care, 11*, 4.

Vriend, J. (1985). *Counseling powers and passions: More counsling techniques that work.* Alexandria, VA: American Association of Counseling and Development.

Wachtel, P.L. (1977). *Psychoanalysis and behavior therapy: Toward an integration.* New York: Basic Books.

Wachtel, E.F. (1982). The family psyche over three generations: The genogram revisited. *Journal of Marriage & Family Therapy, 8*, 335–343.

Wachtel, P.L. (1987). *Action and insight.* New York: Guilford.

Waldo, M. (1985). A curative factor framework for conceptualizing group counseling. *Journal of Conseling and Development, 64*, 1.

Walen, S.R., DiGiuseppe, R., & Wessler, R.L. (1980). *A practitioner's guide to rational emotive therapy.* New York: Oxford Press.

Walsh, W.M. (1992). Twenty major issues in remarriage families. *Journal of Counseling and Development, 70*, 6.

Ward, D.E. (1983). The trend toward electicism and the development of comprehensive models to guide counseling and psychotherapy. *Personnel and Guidance Journal, 62*, 154–157.

Wassmer, A. (1978). *Making contact: A guide to overcoming shyness, making new relationships and keeping those you have.* New York: Dial Press.

Watzlawick, P., Beavin, J.H., & Jackson, D.D. (1967). *Pragmatics of human communication.* New York: W. W. Norton.

Watzlawick, P., Weakland, J., & Fisch, R. (1974). *Change: Principles of problem formation and problem resolution.* New York: W. W. Norton.

Weakland, J., Fisch, R., Watzlawick, P., & Bodin, A.M. (1974). Brief therapy: Focused problem resolution. *Family Process, 13,* 141–168.

Weeks, G.R., & L'Abate, L. (1982). *Paradoxical psychotherapy: Theory and practice with individuals, couples, and families.* New York: Brunner/Mazel.

Weight, L.M., & Noakes, T.D. (1987). Is running an analog of anorexia? A survey of the incidence of eating disorders in female distance runners. *Medicine and Science in Sports and Exercise, 19,* 213–217.

Weinhold, J. (1987). Altered states of consciousness. *Journal of Humanistic Psychology, 12,* 14–17.

Weinrach, S.G. (1991). Selecting a counseling theory while scratching your head: A rationale-emotive therapist's personal journey. *Journal of Mental Health Counseling, 13*(3) 367–378.

White, J., & Fadiman, J. (Eds.) (1976). *Relax: How you can feel better, reduce stress, and overcome tension.* USA: Dell-Confucian Press.

Wilde, G. (1992). *Rational counseling with school-aged populations: A practical guide.* Muncie, IN: Accelerated Development.

Wilde, G. (1996). *Treating anger, anxiety, and depression in children and adolescents: A cognitive-behavioral approach.* Muncie, IN: Taylor & Francis.

William T. Grant Commission on Work, Family & Citizenship. (1988). *The forgotten half: Pathways to success for America'a youth and young families.* New York: William T. Grant Foundation.

Williams, W.C., & Lair, G.S. (1991). Using a person-centered approach with children who have disabilities. *Elementary School Guidance and Counseling, 25*(3), 194–203.

Witmer, J.M., & Young, M.E. (1985). The silent partner: Uses of imagery in counseling. *Journal of Counseling and Development, 64,* 3.

Witmer, J.M., & Young, M.E. (1987). Imagery in counseling. *Elementary School Guidance and Counseling, 22*, 1.

Woodman, M. (1985). *The pregnant virgin: A process of psychological transformations*. Toronto, Canada: Inner City.

Wolpe, J. (1982). *The practice of behavior therapy* (3rd ed.). New York: Pergamon Press.

Wright, J., Coley, S., & Corey, G. (1989). Challenges facing human services education today. *Journal of Counseling and Human Service Professions, 3*(2), 3–11.

Yalom, I.D. (1985). *The theory and practice of group psychotherapy*. New York: Basic Books.

Yapko, M. (1986). Hypnotic and strategic interventions in the treatment of anorexia nervosa. *American Journal of Clinical Hypnosis, 28*, 224–232.

Ziegler, D.J. (1989). A critique of rational-emotive theory of personality. In M.E. Bernard & R. DiGiuseppe (Eds.), *Inside rational-emotive therapy: A critical appraisal of the theory and therapy of Albert Ellis* (pp. 27–45). Orlando, FL: Academic Press.

Zilbergeld B., & Lazarus, A. (1987). *Mind power*. Boston, MA: Little, Brown.

Zimbardo, P.G. (1977). *Shyness: What it is and what to do about it*. Menlo, Park, CA: Addison Wesley Publishing Company.

Zimstrad, S.W. (1989). Brief systemic therapy for families of the close head injured: Therapy with two hands. *Cognitive Rehabilitation, 7*(3), 26–28.

INDEX

ABOUT THE AUTHOR

Rosemary A. Thompson, Ed.D., NCC, LPC, is administrator for Gifted and Talented Education for Chesapeake Public Schools, Chesapeake, Virginia, and Adjunct Professor, Department of Educational Leadership and Counseling, Old Dominion University, Norfolk, Virginia. During her 24 years in the public school sector, she has been a teacher, school counselor, guidance director, and school administrator. She has published widely in national counseling and education journals on issues critical to counselors, educators, and practitioners.

Dr. Thompson is a National Board Certified Counselor and a Licensed Professional Counselor and maintains a private practice in educational consultation. She currently resides in Virginia Beach, Virginia, with her husband, Charles, and their children, Ryan and Jessica.